Wild Nights

by

Mary Ellen Courtney

PBC
PorterChanceBooks

Wild Nights

This novel is a work of fiction. Any references to real people, events, establishments, organizations, or locales are intended only to give the fiction a sense of reality and authenticity, and are used fictitiously. All other names, characters, and places, and all dialogue and incidents portrayed in this book are the product of the author's imagination.

First edition, 2013

Layout & publishing services by W. Bruce Conway

Printed in the U.S.A. on recycled paper

ISBN: 978-0-9889536-9-7

Porter Chance Books
Friday Harbor, WA
www.porterchancebooks.com

Wild *Nights*

by

Mary Ellen Courtney

For my husband Wayne Fitzgerald

One

A lit butt flew out of the car window in front of me and bounced red sparks before it disappeared with a last puff into the soft ash by the side of the road. Too late for that, numbskull. The foothills were already smoldering, already burned up. Traffic crawled and I was stuck crawling with it. I shouldn't have skipped breakfast; it looked like I was going to miss lunch too. I was so hungry the bitter cold smoke that blew in the air conditioner reminded me of butterscotch pudding, well, scorched pudding.

My phone rang. I hit speaker and Mom started right in.

"Where are you, Hannah?" she asked.

"Driving," I said. "Where are you?"

"We're at the Anchor, we're almost done with lunch."

Her voice was going soft around the edges of her tongue. More like a snack with wine. My sister Bettina, aka Binky, was the designated driver. What a joke. It might be safer if Mom drove.

"Take your time," I said. "I missed the exit. I'm heading back north now, stuck in fire slowdown. I'm not going anywhere fast."

A burnt out San Diego back road at 1:00 in the afternoon isn't green scenic; it's more over lit moonscape. The manzanita bushes, their smooth tangled limbs once a lush blood red, looked like ashen spirits with hot feet. They writhed across the charred hills. I imagined their voices as the ululations of distraught Moroccan women.

Fire fighters in day-glo yellow jackets dug at pockets of red-hot embers. They smothered the fire that native plants need to release the seeds that would repopulate the hillside.

Local Indians used to set fires. Their dusty feet moved quietly through the chaparral. No squawking walkie-talkies or whoop whoop warnings, just the sounds of dry rustling leaves and distant birdcalls. The manzanita only plays dead. They would try again when conditions were more favorable. Memory roots, hidden deep in the earth, will let fly tender new leaves. The leaves will attract game while the fresh cover shelters nesting birds that will take flight and scatter the messages in the seeds. The Indians knew that.

Except for the stray firebug, the new locals don't set fires intentionally; they fear them. Fire comes anyway and life presses on.

One life that had stopped pressing on was my grandmother's. She had died a few days before. I was headed to meet Mom, Binky, and Mom's sister Judith, aka Aunt Asp, at the funeral home to make arrangements for her viewing. Everyone in the family but me lived in San Diego. I had to drive down from the Hollywood Hills to participate in what my mother thought would be a bonding experience. Plus, she had some screwball idea that being a production designer meant I'd know how to set the scene for the viewing. Come on, Mom, I do a lot of research to develop the look of film projects. Except for an occasional winging it, I don't just make it up as I go along.

Anyway, we were burying someone we knew. Everyone was bound to show up with their own storyline about Grandma already running through their head. The only ones missing from the exercise would be my brother Eric and his wife Anna. They could have driven up from La Jolla, but they were too smart for that.

I hoped the day would come when I could say no. I had a hard time refusing my family. I'd had that conversation with a therapist, many times. I said I couldn't go home and visit friends without seeing my family; it would hurt their feelings. She said it was my hometown too. I'd said, "No I can't." She'd said, "Yes you can." We bounced that ball back and forth. Every once in a while she'd stick her tongue in her cheek and shake her head like she was thinking, *this poor person*.

At least today we were meeting in Vista, halfway. I doubted I'd see any old friends there. I'd already stopped at the rest home and picked up my grandmother's few belongings. I looked at the small wooden box on the passenger seat. The lid's design had been wood-burned then painted. It was a spring scene rendered without the burden of perspective. At first glance you'd think it was Chinese crap, but it was an old box, a handmade gift from my father's mother to my mother's mother. It sounded so civilized. My ex-husband's mother and my mother never exchanged gifts; they barely exchanged words.

The box held my grandmother's dead canary. It was wrapped in an orange silk bag with a red drawstring. I'd left behind an old nap blanket and a few worn nightgowns. Her dentures and wire-rimmed glasses, both of which totally creeped me out, were in the trunk with her burial dress.

The little bird had been an unwilling hero. Grandma said he'd sung quite a bit on his days off. I don't know why that thought made me so happy. He deserved to ride shotgun.

Grandma had had courage. As a young widow with small children she traveled from Minnesota to North Dakota and bought a coal mine. It was there that she met her second husband, my grandfather. They were still using canaries to warn about any buildup of mine gas. The birds either passed out or died when the gas got too dangerous. Grandma's bird died, but he saved my grandfather who skedaddled before the mine exploded. He grabbed the birdcage on the way out. Grandpa said we could all use a canary in our lives.

Grandpa always talked about the mine like it was a chancy but generous lover. He used to chuckle that the explosion had been *close, but no cigar,* like he'd just survived her latest temper tantrum. It was her last. He loved that mine, but she burned underground for a couple of years and, unlike a real lover, it was no use to wait her out. So they packed up and moved to the city.

To show her gratitude for his sacrifice, Grandma had the bird preserved by a taxidermist. She didn't want him brought back to life, so to speak, with tiny glass eyes and feet wired to a perch. He looked just like what he was, a dead bird. The eyes were squint shut and tiny translucent talons were curled at the ends of scaly legs tucked up close to the body. He felt even lighter than a feather with his life force gone. My grandfather said he got a kick out of the dead bird. He would. Thanks to the bird he was still around to get a kick out of Grandma, which produced two daughters.

The daughters thought preserving the bird was crazy. You'd think they would appreciate his life-giving sacrifice, maybe build an altar and burn some incense like the Vietnamese ladies in my local nail salon. But they took the stuffed bird as further evidence of their mother's weirdness. For some reason they never mentioned their father being weird.

There were exceptions. In Mother's world, all roads lead to Mother. When she was feeling especially slushy she said the bird died so she could be born. It wasn't a story she ran with when her sister was around. My grandmother's eyes lost focus when her daughter talked like that. Even mothers get sick of listening to their offspring's bullshit apparently. I thought the bird should be buried with Grandma. I had a vision of them reanimated in a new place, maybe hooking up with my grandfather.

I didn't know much about my other grandmother, my father's mother, the wood burner. She was already a widow when I was born and a bit severe. I'd had little contact with her even when my father was alive, almost none after he died. My mother said she never approved of their marriage. I've since learned from my cousins that she didn't approve of any of the spouses her children chose. It was so typical of my mother to leave out that part.

My father died twenty years ago. I remember his mother running out of the viewing room crying, saying that that was not her son in there. It was a shock to see her show emotion, but I could see her point. It didn't look anything like him. She died soon after my father. The grief hit her rigid back and knocked her down.

My attention snapped back to traffic; it was finally starting to speed up. My Prius was whirring behind the pack while it built up momentum. Sparky is an okay car, but she won't break any speed records. I listen to the radio on scan. A former boyfriend said I listen to the radio like I'm on speed. Drug runners know those things. He was a drug runner masquerading as an investment banker. He had a great sense of humor. Well the drug runner did; the investment banker could get a little condescending. Leave it to me to find someone for myself, and someone for my mother, in the same man. I ran into him right after I bought Sparky. He couldn't understand why someone like me, with what he referred to as a zero-to-sixty personality, would drive a Prius. I was reining in my tendency to go too fast.

Traffic slowed down again and Sparky started acting funny. When I braked she lurched forward until I stomped down hard with both feet. She stopped just inches from the fender in front of me. Shit! I inched along giving the guy ahead of me a little more room, but each stop was an adrenalin rush. I looked for a place to pull off. The only thing in any direction was a truck stop with a café and motel.

I turned into the crowded parking lot and parked on the perimeter where the asphalt died into the edge of a field, a soft place to land in case the brakes failed. The diner was a brown-and-orange fifties model with bad maintenance. I could see only slashes between the hulking semi-trucks that surrounded it like behemoths at a watering hole. They'd probably blown past me in their rush to get food poisoning at the place.

I called my mother. They were still at the Anchor, swilling I'm sure.

Binky grabbed the phone from Mom. "Did you get my blanket at Grandma's?"

"I didn't know you wanted it, Binky. I left it for one of the residents."

"I wanted to give it to Amber. Something to remember her great-grandmother by."

"Remember her by? She never even met her."

"She did too. I took her when she was a baby."

"Amber is ten, Binky."

"Time flies when you have kids, Hannie. They're a time suck. You'll see if you ever get around to having any."

"Ten years isn't just a suck, Binky, it's more like a full-blown warp. You only live thirty minutes away."

"Don't scold me, Hannie. I made her the blanket."

"Oh please, that blanket is ugly as sin, eight feet long, and barely wide enough to cover her body."

"She loved it. She always mentioned it to Mom."

What was jaw-lock annoying was that my grandmother never failed to say how nice it was that Bettina had made her a blanket.

"Well call the nursing home then," I said. "Go get it. You're right there."

"You were supposed to be taking care of everything, GG."

"Well I didn't take care of that, Bettina."

"Oooo Bettina. You getting all serious on me, Hannie?"

I couldn't say Bettina when I was little, so I called her *Binky*. Binky is too nice in a fight.

"I've gotta go," I said. "I need to figure this out."

"Oh don't get all stiff neck on me, Hannah," she hung up. Apparently my family had stopped saying good-bye.

I wondered what a spoiled brat like Amber would say about her great-grandmother's blanket. About her mother who made it for that matter. That gift could come back to bite Binky in the butt. As far as I could tell Amber didn't know much about anything. Unlike her brother and sister, she hadn't carved out a niche in either sports or academics. She was cute, she knew cute, except for her sneer. She could really sit on the sidelines and sneer. She'd sneer at that blanket. We had that in common. I needed to hear a friendly voice so called Steve, the man I was dating.

"I'm stuck in the boondocks with a broken car."

"Did you call triple A?"

"Not yet. I thought I'd explain it to you and see if you knew what could be wrong."

I told him how the car was acting. I don't know why. Steve was a film editor from New York. He didn't learn to drive until his late twenties when he was forced into it by taking a picture in Los Angeles. For negotiating subways in New York or Paris, he's your man, but even after ten years of practice, he drove like a beginner. He had no rhythm. It set my teeth on edge.

"I don't know anything about cars, you know that," he said. "I know about town cars and triple A. Are you somewhere safe?"

"I'm somewhere, safe remains to be seen."

"Well hang up and call, lock the doors, then call me back."

He must have thought boondocks meant the Bronx or South Central L.A. I got out and stretched while I assessed the safe factor. I could smell smoke in the air and in my hair. I sniffed my forearm. All of me smelled like smoke; and it wasn't that nice flaming marshmallow-on-a-stick campfire smell.

It was a definite Oh Shit situation. My parents didn't allow profanity when we were growing up, except when things went south. My father enjoyed reading us excerpts from a book of black box recordings. The last words uttered by pilots before hitting terra firma or taking the big plunge; good stuff, Dad. A tiny few said, "Oh Jesus." My mother always said they were praying, which always made my father laugh. Fewer still said adios to the spouse. Most threw out either "Oh Shit" or "Oh Fuck" to join the Gettysburg Address and "I have a dream" in the ether, for all time. Unlike Lincoln or King, I doubt it was one of their finest moments. We could say one of those when, for example, the car let us down in the middle of nowhere.

A big green truck with a leaping yellow stag was parked nearby. The cab was tilted up and a guy was so deep in the engine that his legs were hanging in the air over the side. A large German shepherd was guarding a tool chest on the ground. It was broad daylight and the legs guy looked like someone who might know a thing or two about cars. I wasn't sure about the dog. I took a few steps toward the truck. The dog watched. A few more steps, dog still cool with it. I got all the way to the truck and started to tap the guy's leg, but the dog stood up. Got it. I just called.

"Hello?" The dog lay back down.

"Yeah?" said a muffled voice at the end of the legs.

"Can I ask you a question?"

"I *can* hear you, so I suppose you *may*."

Oh brother, that was a smart ass at the end of the legs. I decided to go inside and ask around, but his muffled voice came back: "Fire away if you're still there."

I imagined firing away at his ass. In his surprise, he'd jerk his head up and gash it on the hood. Then he'd slide to the ground unconscious and bleeding. I'd want to help, but his dog would keep me at bay. Smartass would bleed to a slow gasping death. I'd say, "May I help you?" over his death rattle. An animal control officer would finally arrive and shoot a tranquilizer dart into the snapping beast, while the late-arriving EMTs waited helplessly on the sidelines. Too late, can't help ya. I've probably seen too many movies.

"Is there a car repair place near here?" I asked.

He was quiet under the hood. Then he slid out far enough to look down at me. I envied him his core strength; I'd be a heap on the ground if I tried that. He was a young guy, about my age, dressed in greasy overalls with a bandana covering his hair. The look in his vivid blue eyes said I'd dropped down from Mars. He slid out farther, hitting his head while he was at it. Yes!

"Fuck," he said as he slid to the ground rubbing his head with the relatively grease-free back of his hand.

"Sorry." I looked for spurting blood. Sometimes a little fantasy is better than nothing.

"What are you sorry about?" he asked.

"You hit your head," I said.

"You didn't hit it." He gave me the barest squint, but I hid my tiny riff of glee. He looked over my shoulder to Sparky. "That must be your car."

"Yes, it keeps lurching. It barely stops."

"There isn't anywhere around here that knows how to work on that. You need a dealer."

"Okay thanks." I headed back to my car. I looked back at him; he was watching me with a smirk. I don't know why I cared, but I wished I still had my old VW GTI instead of the wimp car. I grabbed my phone and searched for Toyota dealers. Shit. I really was in the middle of nowhere. I called triple A before I realized I didn't know where I was. The trucker was putting away tools so I yelled over to him.

"Excuse me," I said. "Can you tell me where the fuck I am?"

"Grub 'n Scrub. They'll know." He was smiling.

Triple A said at least an hour. I called my mother. I thought maybe they'd rescue me, or at least come and get Grandma's stuff. She talked it over with Bettina.

"We can't, Hannie. Bettina wants to stop by the rest home for the blanket, so Judith is driving me home and they have dinner plans."

"Mom, I'm stuck in the middle of nowhere. You're just going to leave me out here over that stupid blanket?"

"Oh, Hannah, don't be so dramatic. You're a big girl. You'll be able to find a place to stay while they fix the car."

"What if they can't fix it? Tomorrow's Sunday, I could get stuck here. I have plans. I have a job."

"Oh well, if you get stuck, rent a car and come stay with me."

I hung up and headed into the diner for god knows what to eat. A waitress in a brown-and-orange uniform led me to a booth right by the kitchen. They had a Thanksgiving dinner special, aka Ptomaine Special. I ordered split pea soup and coffee. She did an eyeball half-roll when I asked about espressos. I took in the room.

The cook looked like he had pancake batter glued to his beard with bacon grease. He wore a grimy apron and one of those little captain hats with the small brim. He glanced up, smiled, and winked as he ticked the brim in salute. He'd done it before; there were greasy tick marks all along the edge. He had a nice smile through the globs.

I took out my phone to fire up a solitaire game. My screen image was an old picture of the family camping under the wing of our plane in the Idaho backwoods before it filled up with suspicious survivalists. It was taken a still happy month before my father died. We sure hadn't seen that one coming, except I guess I sorta had.

Before my grandmother's dress and bird, the only other time I'd cleared out someone's things was for my father a month after he died. My mother said it was just too painful, so I did it.

I'd had a clear premonition of my father's death exactly one week before it happened. I was watching a sunset out my sister's bedroom window. My mind's eye didn't see the plane crash into a mountain of snow; it simply saw the end. So even while we waited for the call about his missing plane, I knew he was gone. It was a strangely calm place to sit and wait. Nobody in the family appreciated me saying that he was dead. The premonition, what felt like a psychic connection, made me wonder which one of us made the decision that I should stay behind that day; I always went with him.

I can barely remember the month between the phone call about the crash and clearing out his things. Except for a few film clips, it's all kaleidoscopic shards with what felt like cotton-stuffed ears. I've bored friends and lovers, and even the occasional therapist, to tears, recounting how disconnected it all felt. The only one who didn't mind my endless word circles was my ex-husband. I thought it meant he cared. It turned out they overlapped with his endless circles like the Olympic rings of a bad marriage.

I don't remember what my brother and sister were doing during that month; they are close in age, so maybe they were consoling each other. My mother went into full retreat. I don't know how she spent her time. It wasn't with me. Aunt Judith, who never had children, offered nothing but tight lips and arched eyebrows at what women wore when they came to visit the family. The men in the family talked a lot about money. They were worried, with good reason.

I remember swimming unseen through the sea of adults milling around our dining room table at the reception after the funeral. It was subdued. My father had been the life of the party. He had always moved fast. I overheard one friend say that if you were talking to him and you blinked, he might disappear. I knew about that. I had blinked and he had disappeared on me too. I was good at changing frequencies and spotting other planes. I'll always wonder about spotting that mountain; I might have saved his life. Not all of life's wonders are wonderful.

I loved flying lingo like "no joy" and "roger that." My father's name was Roger. He always smiled when I said, "Roger that Roger." After the tenth time I would have strangled me. I sometimes imagine that I would have still been saying it as a rebellious teenager and that he wouldn't have smiled. It's all in the delivery. I could imagine him saying, "Don't Roger me that, little girl," or whatever he would've called me. I wonder what he would have called me when I wasn't a little girl anymore. As it turned out, I was never a rebellious teenager; my mother just wasn't up to the challenge.

It's funny what we remember. People kept dropping off food. It was nice of them, but the strange tastes from other homes just added to the dissonance. I remember being sent to stash casseroles in neighbors' freezers when ours got full, and then going back to get them when we needed more food. It was strange to drop in and out of households where nothing had changed. People were already looking at me from a distance that I didn't understand. Life was already upside down without my father there.

I remember feeling tiny standing by his heavy mahogany casket in the huge church. I remember turning a corner at the funeral home and running into my uncle who looked so much like my father with his blue eyes, it scared me. I remember touching my father's dead hand.

My sister and brother were angst-filled teenagers more prone to my mother's melancholia than to my father's buoyancy. I was my father's child. My mother said he had picked me up the day I was born and had never put me down. In many ways I had stepped into his shoes after he died. I became the child my mother refers to as GG Spring. Good Girl Spring. I packed his things for the last time. I learned how to fix toasters. Before long I learned how to throw a blanket over my mother when she passed out on the floor. I was twelve years old.

Now I'm thirty-two and Grandma had made it to ninety-eight so clearing out her few possessions was a simple thing to do.

I tried not to breathe when I packed for my father. I tried not to breathe the smell of him. His citrus and bay rum aftershave drifted around his suits and rose up out of his drawers. It was still fresh and alive and having a good time with the smell of leather and with his hair in sweaty baseball caps. If our lives run like seasons, he had died in his summer.

Grandma had died in her winter, in her three hundred and ninety-second season. The season when things turn grey and odors are faint. When life feels more still, the resting season. Her smell had faded away to dust and old breath, and an unidentifiable perfume with only the bass notes still alive. But it wouldn't give up. The dusky smell clung to my skin under the veil of manzanita smoke. There were tenacious pockets hidden up my nose that burst like bubbles in unpleasant moments.

Her last dress smelled like that. I'd packed it in the trunk. It was tissue-thin cotton in a faded pattern of summery flowers. I could almost remember her in the dress, sitting in the old wicker chair by her bed, her substantial ankles crossed. She always had glasses and dentures in place. She was big on appearances. It was always a surprise when she rolled her dentures around. They made her lip stretch out like a Ubangi woman with a lip plate. They clacked. She used to slide them back and forth sideways like she was scratching her gums, then send them back to home base. Dentures must be annoying as hell. Mom and I had already argued about burying her with her dentures. I'd blown through a Black Friday sale to buy a pale lavender chiffon scarf; her daughters wanted it swirled around her neck like a cloud.

Once Grandma hit ninety it seemed like she'd live forever. Now I felt lonely for the years I'd missed talking to her while I was married. I couldn't believe I'd thrown her over to do time in a shitty apartment and bad marriage. Deep down, not even deep really, I didn't want to marry him in the first place, but I'd been living pretty wild and he was a man full of rules that I mistook for a grown-up. Once I married him I was determined to live up to my obligation. I knew the decision to end the marriage was right the day he moved out and took the teakettle he never used. He knew I loved it.

Grandma had no teakettle or anything else in the end. She'd been bed-bound the last five years. On the day she died she asked to get up and sit in the chair. I guess she'd enjoyed the view from her perch for about fifteen minutes, then got back into bed, went to sleep, and never woke up. It was Thanksgiving Day.

"Here ya go. You need cream?"

"No thanks," I said.

Thank god my lunch had arrived! I was really working

myself over with ruminations. Recrimination was about to enter stage left and start mud wrestling with my so-called buoyancy.

Surprise! The soup was made from scratch. It wasn't the safe slime from a can that I was expecting. Chunks of carrot, potato, celery and ham had been simmered with peas you could actually see were peas and then dressed with chopped parsley. I bet the ham was local; I was just south of Corona, a pig-raising capital. My nursing home nostrils were washed clean by the aroma of real food, warm spices, and a generous pig.

"This is delicious," I said to the cook.

"Thanks, it's my mother's recipe. I think the nutmeg makes it."

I could smell his mom's nutmeg. At some point everyone has a mother. That's easy to forget. I set my phone on the table and went back and forth between fragrant bites and solitaire moves, which makes for a Prius-paced game.

I was startled when the trucker slid into the booth with me. I didn't recognize him at first. His bandana was gone and his hair was black and wet from a shower. He was in jeans, a blue shirt, and a broken in leather jacket. I knew he wasn't particularly tall, and now I could see that he wasn't particularly handsome either, but he had a look about him, like maybe he knew more than the difference between *may* and *can*.

"We got off on the wrong foot," he said.

"It's fine. Help is on the way."

"I didn't mean to give you a hard time. I didn't expect you."

"Expect me?"

"A little car."

"I didn't expect a cranky grammar lesson, so we're even. How's your head doing?"

"You enjoyed that," he smiled.

"A little," I nodded. "Do you do that with everyone? It must wow the girls."

"Yeah, that was bad. I was doing battle with a stuck spark plug."

The waitress appeared and glared at the trucker. "You sitting here?" He looked at me. I hate eating alone. He looked like about a hundred film crew guys I knew. How dangerous could it get?

She looked at me, "You don't have to let him sit here."

"It's okay," I said.

"Well, don't buy his bullshit." She walked away.

"What was that all about?" I asked.

"She's my sister."

"Ah, yeah, I have one of those."

He went into the kitchen, helped himself to a bowl of soup and sat back down. "The cook's her husband. They bought the place from his folks."

We ate in silence. My phone rang. Steve. I'd completely forgotten to call him back.

"Sorry," I said to my tablemate.

I answered while I got up and headed outside to talk. "Sorry I didn't call you back."

"It's okay," he said. "I was tied up anyway. What's the situation?"

"It'll be a few hours at least. I'm waiting in a diner for the tow truck."

I promised to call him as soon as I knew what was happening. We were supposed to have dinner the next night with Margaret, a production designer with whom I'd done five projects. Margaret should have been my mother. She and her husband Ed had been filling in as parents for years.

I went back inside. My soup was cold. My companion took it in the kitchen and came back with a fresh bowl.

"My name's Hannah."

"Stroud." We shook. He'd cleaned his fingernails. His faintly citrus smell was getting all tangled up with the earthy soup. It was a whole new world.

"How'd you end up here?" he asked.

I told him the story.

We were done with lunch and just paying our bills when the tow truck showed up. He walked out with me and talked to the guy while the car got hooked up. I assumed I'd ride with the beard and one-earring truck driver and his two overwrought Yorkies. They were yapping and bouncing off windows covered with nose smudge. I dreaded the small dog smell. He wasn't insured for passengers. He gave me a card for a local taxi company. The dealership was in Escondido, not too bad, maybe twenty miles. I watched as my car whipped left on the end of a hook and headed back the way it came.

"That was shitty," said Stroud. "I'll give you a ride."

"That's okay, I can take a cab."

"No, you can't. No one's going to come out here. Especially not with the fire."

I looked at him trying to judge my chances of survival. Like I'm some kind of judge. "Are you a rapist or murderer?"

"Not so far," he said.

"That's not very reassuring."

He was smiling and shaking his head. I did sound pretty ungrateful, and he'd just gotten me a bowl of soup.

"Let's go." He whistled for the dog and headed for a blue Volvo station wagon parked over by the motel. He opened the door and the dog jumped in the back.

"That's Rex." The dog did a gentle survey of my neck and ear from the backseat.

"I know, Rex," I turned to the dog, "I smell like smoke."

Stroud glanced over at me and said, "He can smell a lot more than smoke."

Okay, call me insane, but that remark hit me like three cherries ping ping pinging in the slot machine two inches below my navel, maybe lower.

"Is that what your sister means by 'your bullshit'?"

"No idea. I tuned her out years ago."

"I haven't managed to tune out mine yet," I said.

We drove in quiet.

"It's like kindling out here," I said. "It's good they got the fire under control."

Despite the civilizing avocado groves, you can feel the grip of the dry desert's fingers as it pulls itself up and over the eastern hills, dragging itself inch-by-inch closer to the ocean. Imported water slapped at the desert fingers trying to loosen their grip. Everyone was lulled to sleep by the chuck-chucking of sprinklers. My father had torn out the lawn and planted succulents and sage in a bed of gravel.

"You smell like my father," I said.

Oh boy. I was reverting to strange small talk, one of my specialties, along with singing the wrong lyrics to songs.

"Is that good or bad?"

"Good as far as I know. He died when I was twelve. Have you always been a truck driver?"

"No. I taught high school biology until the budget cuts."

"Do you miss it?"

"I don't miss teenagers. They're a pain in the ass. Just the word *biology* sets them off."

"How do you get work?"

"I have a contract to haul bees during the almond growing season in the Central Valley. The rest of the year I take what comes my way, usually along the southern part of the country.

It's always different."

"What kind of name is Stroud?" I asked.

"A nickname."

A couple of canary breeders in the Central Valley had asked him to take their birds to customers along his route. The birds really sang and guys could hear it over the CB radio. There was a lot of chirping, by men not birds, over the airwaves. Some guy in the Bay Area started calling him Stroud, after the Birdman of Alcatraz, the prisoner who got into birds. The name had stuck. I showed him the old box and told him about my grandmother's canary in the coal mine who sang on his days off.

"What's your real name?" I asked.

"Alan."

"Alan what?"

"Watts."

"Seriously? Like the Zen guy?"

"Just like. They named us depending on what they were into at the time. My sister is Joyce, after James Joyce."

"They sound interesting."

"They had their moments."

"My mother said they named me Hannah because it's spelled the same way both directions, but my father always said it was because it means beauty and passion."

He glanced over at me, then back out the window.

"What?" I asked.

"I didn't say anything," he said.

"No, but you gave me a look."

"I was just thinking about what your father said."

There went those pinging cherries again; I could even hear them over my blabbering.

"I don't know what you mean," I said. I might have been gulping for air at that point.

"No?" he asked.

"No what?" I asked.

"Okay, here's the dealership." He turned in the driveway.

My car was already in the service bay with guys standing around scratching their heads. They didn't know what was wrong, which meant I could probably Google it and find out it was a chronic problem. The last time I had a car with a we-don't-know-what's-wrong problem it took a year of being stuck on the side of the road, untold aggravation, and the California Lemon Law to get them to fix it. They knew exactly what was wrong.

I related this to the boys in the band. They stopped looking so perplexed and put the car up on the lift. I avoid conflict in my personal life like I avoid babies with colds, but one thing you learn in my business is how to work union boys to get your job done.

We walked into the service office to see about rental cars.

"That was some ass kicking," said Stroud.

"I've seen that episode."

His phone rang. He glanced at the screen and walked off as he answered. I heard him say that he was just running someone who had broken down at the G&S in for service. I couldn't hear the rest of the conversation.

The dealership had a loaner, but they didn't want me to take it all the way back to Los Angeles and put on all those miles. They promised to have my car ready in the morning if I'd stay local. They'd even comp me a room within reason. I thanked Stroud and offered him money for gas. He said he'd rather I bought him dinner.

"I don't get down this way very often," I said. "Give me your number, I'll call you."

"I meant tonight. You have to stick around anyway."

"Do you have an idea of where you want to eat? I need to run to Vista. I could meet you somewhere."

He looked at me for a long moment. It didn't look like he was thinking about restaurants.

"Stroud?"

"I'm thinking."

He didn't want to run back and forth up the road so we decided to park the loaner on a side street and then he'd take me to Vista. We'd figure out food later.

We made it to the funeral home in half an hour. I called my mother while we were driving and filled her in. Then did the same with Steve.

"Your boyfriend?" asked Stroud.

"Yes, though I wouldn't call him a boy. Your girlfriend, the one who called?"

"Old friend, still a girl," he said.

The funeral home fell into the big yawn category. The building and arches were frosted with chunky dirt-catcher stucco in washed-out yellow. They were going for an Old Mission vibe. Skeleton bushes with tiny green leaves hugged the foundation, pruned hard so their struggle for life didn't make anyone uncomfortable. A stocky brown sign pounded low to the closely clipped lawn announced Vista View Mortuary and Crematorium in suggestively Goth lettering.

Old age and death are surrounded by one of two esthetics: Dead or Las Vegas. The buildings are bland or ridiculously overdone. The furniture is either a visual embalming or like some decorator lost their mind in a faux French showroom. Pile on the unfailingly tasteless food and it's no wonder people would rather do their fade to black in a ratty recliner, alone at home, eating off-brand hot dogs. My mother had called to let them know I was on the way.

A man in a brown suit met us at the door and ushered us with a hush into Slumber Room 3 where Grandma's casket sat empty. I bet he played a lot of tennis; there was a tan line from his cap. I could feel calluses on his right hand when we shook. The lady funeral director relieved me of Grandma's belongings and asked if I'd brought the book of poetry.

"Poetry?" I asked. "I don't know anything about a book."

"Your mother wants your grandmother's hands folded over a book open to her favorite Emily Dickinson poem."

"Hold on." I thought I was the production designer in the family.

I called my mother. Yes indeed. In her wine haze it had slipped her mind to ask me to pick up a book of Emily, what she referred to as her mother's obsession with that "old Victorian babe." Apparently my grandmother used to wave her arms and bellow, "Wild Nights, Wild Nights," when the brute North Dakota wind roared out of the Badlands. The funeral director told us about a nearby bookstore; we figured we just had time. I said I'd swing by in the morning to drop off the book. We got back in the car.

"I'm so sorry," I said.

"No problem." He was looking at the directions to the bookstore.

Kismet was the name of the bookstore. I thought kismet meant fate or destiny. The owners said it meant afterlife, which is what they were giving the books.

They remembered my grandmother. It felt odd to think of her in there. I could imagine her sliding her dentures back and forth while her fat feet in white leather shoes walked the aisles in search of a good read. They were sad to hear she had passed away. Passed away, what a dumb expression.

They didn't have any of my grandmother's old books, but they still kept their customer's accounts with ink on three-by-five cards. Her bunch was bound with a rubber band that snapped into brittle pieces when they pulled it.

They found me an old volume of Emily's poetry. It would make a great prop, the spine was tired and laid open flat; it was only a little musty. Oddly enough, my grandmother still had enough credit on her account to pay for it. My mother said she had lived right up to her last dime and died. Not true. She'd left enough for two books of poetry. She bought one for me, too.

I'd never read Emily so the owner found a student volume with some analysis. She also bundled up my grandmother's three-by-five cards with a new rubber band and put that on top. Account closed. Stroud had been listening in as he browsed.

"That's kismet," he said as we walked out.

"I didn't know it meant afterlife, did you?"

"No. Where next?" he asked.

"My treat, you pick."

He knew a Mexican restaurant in the old downtown area. I read some Emily while we drove. The first lines of each poem organized the contents page. I scanned the list for "Wild Nights" and several lines jumped out at me.

"Listen to some of these first lines." I read, "'The heart asks pleasure first', 'Hope is the thing with feathers'. That would work for her bird."

I turned to "Wild Nights."

"Okay, here's Grandma's poem." I read aloud.

> Wild nights! Wild nights!
> Were I with thee,
> Wild nights should be
> Our luxury!

Futile the winds
To a heart in port,
Done with the compass,
Done with the chart.

Rowing in Eden!
Ah! the sea!
Might I but moor
Tonight in thee!

I had expected the cautious voice of an old Victorian babe sniffing around in ruffled silk and velvet, with strings of pearls and a pince-nez draped around her neck. Archaic language or not, Emily didn't pussyfoot around. The text described it as "a poem of unrestrained sexual passion and rapture." Got it. Two epiphanies. My grandmother understood passion and rapture. And bellowing "Wild Nights," during storms required a sense of humor.

"Wow," I said.

"Sounds like Grandma understood passion," he said.

"Yeah, and was funny. All I knew was a little white-haired lady with fat ankles."

We found a place on the street right in front of the restaurant. The décor was subtle; they'd held back on the sombreros and striped rattles.

He smiled as he dipped a chip. "This has been an interesting day."

"You think? I can't imagine what my repair bill is going to be. It better be under warranty, I'm about out of a job."

He wanted to know about work. I was just finishing up a television show called Layla's Loft; the edgy adventures of a hip political-social single woman artist.

"We all think Layla's a mouthful, but the writer met Eric Clapton once so it was non-negotiable."

I told him Layla went to a brooding Gorky's café, like Cliff went to Cheers in the old TV show; she slept around with the other artists in her building. She was twenty-two and going through a nihilist phase. She had a misunderstood pit bull, which always caused complications. Somewhere along the line she sold enough paintings to get by, but we never saw an actual sale.

"You don't sound too excited about it," he said.

"Nobody was. We've been canceled."

He thought the business sounded interesting. I told him it was, but that a lot of time was spent standing around bullshitting with blockheads. He said that sounded like his job.

I told him the director had spent our hiatus in rehab. His coke habit blew up after the show was canceled. He had maniacally shot an hour of material for every half hour show. The editor was losing her hair, either from stress or her constant pulling. When the studio sent down the suits to rein him in, he screamed, "I will not be held captive by the laws of mathematics!" Off he went.

"The suits?" he asked.

"Ten year-old MBAs. They run things. In his case it was a good call."

"Should make it tough for him to get a new job."

"It'll be the excuse for not hiring him, but the real reason will be having a flop. It's a business of short term memory."

I told him I was deciding between a project in New Mexico and one in India. I didn't happen to mention that the one in New Mexico was with Steve.

Dinner came and we feasted. I had a margarita, then a Bohemia, my favorite Mexican beer. Probably ill advised. We split an order of flan for dessert.

"That was real Mexican food," I said. "Good suggestion. Do you come here often?"

"I haven't been here since my divorce," he said.

"Do you have children?"

"No."

"You want children?" I asked.

"I figured I would. You?"

"I guess, but I need to figure out how to have a relationship first," I said. Uh oh, the Bohemia was blabbing, but that didn't stop me.

"My marriage was a bad idea that I've followed up with more bad ideas." Sigh. Really, Hannah? You couldn't just stop at *I guess*?

"What about the guy now?" he asked.

"He's my first good idea."

"Ah."

I paid the bill and we started to leave. I wondered if he could hear the pinging slot machine over the live music that was blasting out the door of the restaurant's side bar. The band obviously had a following; the place was packed and people were dancing.

Stroud grabbed my hand, "Let's go."

He spun me out onto the dance floor. He was good. I wasn't bad. He taught me some version of what he called the Texas Two Step. The band, Nancarrow, played a country honky-tonk sound with a lot of rock riffs.

We only stayed for a few dances, but we did great. I missed dancing. Steve danced the same way he drove, except that he had some rubbing up against me thing he did. He thought it was sexy; I thought it was embarrassing.

I bought one of the Nancarrow CDs. I have a habit of buying CDs in the heat of the night. They're never as good the next day.

We headed back to Escondido.

"You're a good dancer," I said.

"That's cowboy shuffling. You caught on fast. The band was good."

"They were great, I don't usually like country. Do you know anything about places in Escondido? Nothing fancy."

"We can just head in, see what's close to the dealership."

There was an Econo Lodge only a few blocks from where I'd parked the car. The vacancy sign was lit.

He parked behind the loaner and killed the engine. We sat in the dark, the engine ticked; Rex dreamt a chase sequence in the back.

I turned to him, "Thanks for doing all this."

He leaned over and brushed my lips with his, then ran his thumb across them with a gentle stroke.

"I didn't know I'd find you under the hood of my rig."

I felt a hot flush and then an up-suck between my legs that felt like a wild animal. Heat surged to my belly button, then fanned out around my heart. My breasts stood up and my breath caught. I know Emily would put it in more delicate terms, though she might keep the wild animal part, but that's what it felt like.

He kissed me again, not just a brush stroke. I knew I shouldn't, but it was like an unstoppable force. I had never felt that with Steve. We were like teenagers trying to get at each other. Except that we knew what we were doing which made it better in form and worse for my carping conscience.

He pushed the seat back and I climbed up straddling his lap. He unbuttoned my blouse and unhooked my bra. I could feel him pressing up under me as he held a nipple gently in his teeth. If we didn't stop I was going to end up having sex, to put it mildly, in the front seat of a car on a side street in Escondido. If word somehow got back to my mother, she'd be relieved that at least it was a Volvo.

It was not the moral rehabilitation I had been working toward. I had a vision of him doing it with a woman at every truck stop. I had a vision of Steve's disappointed face.

"Oh my god," I said. "My god. I can't, I can't do this."

He rolled his tongue slowly around my nipple before letting it go and burying his face between my breasts. I held his head between my hands with my face in his hair.

"I'm sorry," I said. "I can't do this. I just can't."

He didn't say anything. Rex stuck his head over the seat and nuzzled my ear then went back to lie down.

"I'm sorry," I said.

"It's okay," he was looking up at me. "I don't want you to do something you don't want to do."

"I think you know that's not it. I just can't."

"We can work around things if that's what you're talking about," he said.

"It's not that."

"We're consenting adults, Hannah."

I couldn't bear to break away from him, but I knew I couldn't go forward.

"I know we are. But the other adults around us wouldn't consent."

"We're not married."

"No, I know. I just can't," I said.

I don't know how long we stayed like that. I couldn't get enough of his scent. The car started to get chilly but the contact between us was still burning. He slid his hands up and covered my breasts then re-hooked my bra. He started to button my blouse.

"Is this what you meant by taking whatever comes your way?" I asked.

He froze mid-button and looked at me. His expression was so dark the whites of his eyes flashed. I felt like I was rooted to him and at the same time I was trying to insult him away. He finished buttoning my blouse, "Yeah, that's what I meant, but I'm not you, I don't feel bad about it."

It took a lot of awkward effort to climb off him and sit back on the cold seat.

"I'm sorry," I said.

"You shouldn't apologize so much."

I put on the shoes I'd kicked off at some point and gathered my purse.

"Thanks for everything," I said.

He just nodded while he looked out the front window. I got into the loaner. His headlights hadn't come on by the time I turned the corner toward the motel.

I called Steve to let him know I was in for the night, and then I took a long hot shower and washed the smoke out of my hair and citrus off my skin. His saliva was slick on my nipple under the warm water. It seemed like I tossed all night.

Two

I must have finally dropped off to sleep because I awoke to the sound of my mother calling. The woman at the funeral home had stayed late and arranged Grandma's scarf. She'd emailed photos to Mom. Mom said it looked like grandma was wearing a necktie or ascot, not a cloud of lavender.

"I didn't even know you could do that with a scarf," she said.

"I'll take care of it, Mom."

"Thanks GG," she hung up.

The phone rang again. It was my best friend and current work partner, Karin.

"Hey," she said. "Where are you? We stopped by your house last night and went for a swim."

I've worked with Karin on two shows. Unlike me, she never second-guesses herself and she doesn't space out and miss exits either. It makes us a great team. She approaches her life the same way. She's from white money outside Chicago and has two kids with a stunt man named Oscar. He's a great guy and wonderful father; he's also black. Her parents were not amused by her choice, but they've come around. Their kids are the kind you can actually enjoy. Karin keeps saying they're going to get married and make the little milk chocolate bastards legal, her words not mine, but there doesn't seem to be any hurry.

I filled her in on events. She was disappointed that I had felt compelled to insult Stroud instead of enjoy him, but that now I understood Oscar heat. She thought I was deluding myself with the notion that Steve and I could develop chemistry. Especially since I still hadn't gotten around to showing him what I liked. I kept hoping he'd figure it out. It reminded her of a card she'd seen, something about how it takes a thousand words to fake an orgasm, but only three to say "here's my clit." I doubted it actually said that; she'd seen it at the car wash in West Hollywood. There wasn't a clit within a two-mile radius. She was right. All the faking was just making things worse. It wasn't like it was a total bust. Every once in a while the chemistry kicked in. Karin said it was just Mother Nature trying to get me knocked up.

Now I realized the main problem was that the wild animal wasn't reaching out to grab Steve like it had Stroud. I was determined to give Steve some help, buy him citrus aftershave. I hoped the wild animal would at least come out to shake hands.

I used the washcloth to clean my teeth, brushed my hair and turned my underpants inside out before putting them back on. I'm in the film business. I know better than to leave home without clean underwear. You never know what's going to happen on location, and I don't mean that in the Biblical sense.

I pulled on my long skirt and buttoned my smoky citrusy blouse like a hair shirt. The odor made me feel uneasy, like I was supposed to be taking care of something important, but I'd forgotten where I put it. I knew that if I'd stayed in that Volvo I'd feel ill with guilt; but not staying felt ill with longing.

I went downstairs to check out. The clerk handed me a brown paper bag some guy had dropped off early. *Hannah hannaH* was written in ballpoint pen. He said the guy hadn't known my last name.

It was Grandma's box; I'd left it in his car. I opened it to check on the bird. Stroud's business card was on top of the wrapped body. It was as unsettling as an impenetrable whisper. I could feel his hand putting it in there. I peeked under the card to see the bird's tiny beak and claws pushing in sharp little points against the orange silk skin, then I closed them in together again.

"Did he leave a note?" I asked.

The guy looked around on the desk and held up a piece of paper. "Just his name and number, said to call if we missed you."

I went next door and had oatmeal to settle my stomach, then reclaimed Sparky and drove to the funeral home.

The gray-flocked casket had a few sprays of flowers behind it. I hate the smell of dying flowers.

It was the first time I'd seen Grandma dead. Even propped up on the slumber pillow, she barely broke above the rim of her box. She looked especially gaunt. I had to trust it was she. I could see how people who were asked to identify their loved ones could, like my grandmother when she saw my father, deny it. You really have to search for traces of the person you knew. Grandma's skin looked like thin rubber film stretched over a gray leaden core. They'd added daubs of impossible pink to her cheeks. I knew if I touched her, as I will forever regret doing with my father, she would be hard and stone cold with embalming fluid just under the surface of her fragile skin.

Her dentures were in. I thought she'd hated them in life, so why inflict them on her in death, but I could see why my mother had been so adamant. Her mouth would have looked caved in without them. Her whole body looked caved in. Mom was right about the scarf too; it looked like something on a gay 70s gigolo.

I didn't have any choice but to take it off her and rearrange it. It was tricky; I'm not a scarf person. And I needed to avoid skin-to-skin contact. I tried to not think about what I was doing, then I pretended I was at work. Finally I just loved her and told her that I'd had a taste of wild nights and that I hoped she'd have more of her own. I wanted to ask her about it. I could ask her things that I couldn't ask my mother, but she could only listen.

The funeral director arranged the book, glasses and hands under my supervision. She sent a picture to my mother and aunt while I got out the bird. It reminded me of burying our sweet dog Wags when we were kids. We'd put some dog treats and his favorite stick in the hole to have in heaven. The funeral director lifted the bottom door of the casket. My grandmother's feet were bare and looked as delicate as a young woman's. Much better than jammed into tight shoes for all eternity.

It was a gut wrench to see that Bettina had not only retrieved the blanket, but that she'd stopped at the funeral home and folded it under Grandma's feet. Did she remember Wags? I wondered who knew she'd done it. I gently tucked the weightless bird wrapped in orange silk down in the folds of the blanket. Then I pulled out the bundle of 3x5 cards from the bookstore and tucked those in with the bird; they might help Grandma remember who she was. I closed the door. My work was finally done.

I headed back up the road, past the burned out hills and dairy cows knee-deep in muck. Warm November air, smelling of rancid farm crap and chemicals mixed with smoke and diesel fumes, blew in the open windows.

I wondered if Bettina had always planned on putting the blanket in with Grandma. Why couldn't she tell me? Was I really such a scold? It always hurt when I discovered their small secrets, the things they all seemed to know but I didn't. Small secrets don't feel small when you're searching for clues and holding your breath while you try to fill the hole under you enough to hold your weight. I wondered if she or Eric had saved something from my father.

Until yesterday, the memory of packing up my father's things had been buried so deep it might as well have been left to dry out and frost over like a casserole in the neighbor's freezer. He'd died young. Unlike Grandma, he hadn't spent years peeling away the unnecessary.

I had walked into the closet with all his suits still hanging in a row, deflated and empty shells. They would never again walk through the kitchen and steal a piece of bacon on the way out the door. They would never slide across my mother's ass with appreciation when he thought no one was looking. They would never go to a meeting with my teacher, or be hung on the back of his office door when he put on his white doctor's coat with the swirling blue embroidery, *Dr. Spring*. They would never again fix the toaster.

He'd used linen handkerchiefs; he said it was more environmental. There was a new box, monogrammed with the letter 'S', that I'd given to him. The gift tag was still stuck inside from Christmas morning.

I had used paper grocery bags for his socks and underwear; I didn't think about it. He had a favorite tee shirt that was full of holes; he loved to wear it when he raked patterns in the gravel around his desert plants. He said it was air-conditioned. It drove my mother crazy that he wore it in the front yard. She thought the neighbors would think we couldn't afford clothes. I had kept that.

I also kept a small cedar box where he kept his watch, loose change, and the random drawing tickets he always bought from the kids outside the grocery store. He never checked to see if he'd won. I hid the box under my bed until I left home. The inside was unlined. Except for a few scrapes and pen bleeds, it was raw like the day he'd made it in high school shop. His tiny black dress shirt studs and links were mixed in with my jewelry now.

His soft leather flight jacket with patches and pins had disappeared in the post crash confusion. Maybe it was bloody or torn. The plane hadn't burned or anything; it landed softly in deep snow on the side of a mountain. But he had been injured and had died before they could reach him. Maybe he froze to death. That's supposed to be painless. Details were unclear; there was no black box in our little Cessna.

He would have loved being buried in that jacket. He wouldn't have cared about a few holes, but by then my mother had full control over his wardrobe decisions. He was buried in a dark blue suit with a white shirt and nondescript striped tie. It didn't look anything like a tie he would wear; he was a Dead Head, he loved his collection of crazy ties.

I packed some of it in his suitcases, like he was just going on a trip. The rest I put in trash bags. I didn't know what else to use. I don't know what happened to any of it.

I slowed at the Grub 'n Scrub. Stroud was back in his overalls and bandana looking through his toolbox. I turned in, drove over, and parked. He watched me get out of my car and walk toward him. He glanced over my shoulder at the diner then back at me. I stopped eight feet away.

"I'm not going to embarrass you," I said.

"Embarrass me?"

"You don't even know my last name," I said.

"We didn't get that far."

"We got pretty far."

He didn't say anything.

"Thanks for leaving her bird," I said.

"Did your name matter last night?"

"Not then."

I was not going to add insult to insult by pretending for a

second time that I had been tricked into being there last night.

"The bird is with Grandma now," I said.

"Good place."

"My sister put a blanket in with her."

He just nodded, he had no idea what that meant.

"It's Spring," I said. "My last name."

"Okay, Spring."

"I should go."

"You have my number," he said.

"Do you ever get to Los Angeles?"

"Sometimes."

"I was scared," I said. "I don't want to go down those roads. I'm sorry I insulted you."

"Kinda left field."

"I'm sorry."

"Don't do that," he said. "So much apologizing."

Rex got up from the shadows. He yawned and stretched out in both directions. The tension must have been getting to him too. He came over and gave my hand a nudge. I stroked his ear. He went back and stood with Stroud. I got in the car and pulled away. I looked in the rear view mirror and could see them watching me go. A semi pulled in and blocked the view as it parked in front of the diner. When the picture was clear again Stroud was gone.

I stopped at a huge farm stand by the side of the road. It felt like step one of re-entry. Working the cash register was a strong looking woman in a thick sweater and bandana. She looked like she'd shucked a lot of corn. I bought a bag of tangerines. I love having a basket of tangerines on the table this time of year. They smell like a promise of warm citrusy days to come.

I turned up my narrow street and parked. I'd scored a dream rental, a small guesthouse on a private lot with a big pool. It had been part of an old movie star's ranch. The story was that the glamour boys used to ride their horses over, probably with someone else's wives, and party. It was marooned in the middle of a residential neighborhood, hidden behind an ivy covered grape stake fence that ran along the street. A non-descript gate led to a set of steep uneven brick stairs that hugged the hill down to the house and pool. The pool was large, a simple rectangle.

The house looked bigger than it was. The big 1950s prow-shaped roof looked more South Seas than Los Angeles. It stretched out to form a deep overhang to the south creating a huge covered patio area. Karin and Oscar brought the kids over a lot during the summer. We spent long days cooking burgers and playing Marco Polo, or as her son Richard renamed it, Roger Wilco.

Inside was basically one big room, with a small kitchen retrofitted into what had been a fancy wet bar. The high copper-covered bar top and hanging glassware cabinets screened the view from the rest of the room. The south-facing side was a wall of huge glass doors that slid open to either side of a Swedish fire pit built from stones. The copper hood looked like the Tin Man's hat. I used it all the time. Finding firewood in Los Angeles was no picnic; I scrounged around every construction site I passed. The flagstone floor ran under the doors, across the patio, and over the edge of the pool. It was totally private. The hillside coming down from the street was planted with jacaranda that put on a mesmerizing display of color.

A luxurious party bathroom, with an oversized shower tiled in a checkerboard pattern of turquoise and cream, adjoined a dressing room. The dressing room could have been a dinky bedroom, but it felt claustrophobic. I'd hung a large Japanese paper ball lantern over the small dining table. I filled a flat basket on the table with the tangerines. It felt good to be back in my cocoon.

Steve was picking me up at seven for dinner. I jumped in the pool and swam laps to get the kinks out. I was getting dressed when the phone rang. Aunt Judith.

"Binky's upset about the blanket," she said.

"Still? She got it back. I had no idea she wanted it. I'm rushing, I have a date."

"A date? Anything with promise?"

"I've been dating him for a while. So I guess there's promise."

"That's nice. Is he coming for Christmas? What's his name?"

"Steve. I doubt it, he's Jewish."

"So you'll be doing Hanukkah now. Well don't wait too long, you only get three chances."

"What about Zsa Zsa Gabor?"

I could never resist throwing out Zsa Zsa.

"You're no Zsa Zsa Gabor," she said. "She knew what she was doing."

Two sisters, two rules chiseled in stone. Judith was on her third husband, so in her world you get three chances. Her current husband is nice, though he once told me, rather inappropriately I thought, that he's into tailbones. His finger had drifted down mine as he said it.

Apparently she hadn't talked to my mother. My mother said I'd marry a doctor, have three children, and be happy just like she was. We'd seen how great that worked out for Binky.

My parents went out three times in one weekend and he proposed. According to her it was a match made in heaven. She wouldn't approve of Stroud, but she might relate to the lightning strike aspect.

"You should have gotten the blanket for your sister," said Aunt Judith. She hung up. Incivility was sweeping the family.

I hated the kernels of truth buried in the nasty remarks they all made; but she was right about Zsa Zsa. I had no idea how women like her thought about men. I had missed the memo about how *a smart woman can control any man*, one of Judith's many mantras. Except for the strange side road when I implied a woman in every truck stop with Stroud, I thought of myself as having an uncomplicated approach to men. Judith would say clueless.

The phone rang almost instantly, my brother Eric.

"What did I do to deserve this family, Eric?"

"You're asking me? The burial is on for Saturday at noon, you good with that?"

"That's fine. You need me to do anything?"

"No, we're set. Thanks for handling the poetry and glasses bullshit at the mortuary."

"No problem. Binky put the blanket in too."

"And you put in the bird and some paperwork, I heard. It's a good thing she'd shrunk and left some room."

"Did you put in something?"

"I didn't have anything to add. I bought the headstone."

"Did you keep anything of Dad's?"

"His watch and logbooks. You still have the box and tee shirt?"

"You know about that?"

"Binky went through your room."

"Christ, this family. What happened to his jacket?"

"They had to cut it off him."

"I didn't know that. What about Binky, did she keep anything?"

"You'll have to ask her. Anna says hi. We can have lunch

when we're done."

"Okay," I said. "Bye."

"Bye," he said. "Thanks again."

Etiquette breakthrough. Eric, Anna and I were the only ones attending the burial. No one wanted to drive all the way to Altadena to see Grandma stashed in the old family plot. Eric had arranged the burial; he wanted to be sure it was done right. I had to rush to get dressed by seven.

Steve let himself in and called hello while I rooted around looking for a pair of shoes. I dropped them by the front door and gave him a welcome kiss.

"Why don't you pour us a glass of wine while we wait for my mother to call and tell me I'm a childless old maid?"

Steve knew that every foray behind the Orange Curtain, what we called the area south of Los Angeles where my family was holed up, triggered a flurry of phone calls and emails.

"I don't know why you put up with that shit." The emphasis was on shit while he pulled the cork.

"Oy, and this from a man with a Jewish mother. Weren't you supposed to be the doctor I'm supposed to marry?"

"I'm not supposed to marry a Presbyterian, no matter what I do."

"Ex-Presbyterian and we have a fallen Jew hidden a few generations away. Let's sleep at your house tonight, your mother will never know."

Steve was wrapping post-production on a picture on the Warner Brothers lot just down the hill from me. The driving logistics worked out great, a huge consideration in all matters Los Angeles. Relationships, like home values, can hinge on location location location. People can actually be considered geographically undesirable, GUD for short.

Diving into Steve world seemed like a good antidote to

Stroud world. They couldn't be more different. My mind tripped over to drug runner/investment banker. Truck driver/film editor? I smiled; it was worth a shot.

"What are you smiling about?" asked Steve.

"I have no idea. It hasn't been a forty-eight hours to smile about. Sparky is two months out of warranty."

I filled him in on all the details except, obviously, anything that involved hiking up my skirt and grinding in the blue jeaned lap of a guy in the boondocks. I got a jolt just thinking about that, but I took the fact that I was starting to make light of it as a good sign that it might not get added to my black box of shame.

We met Margaret and Ed at our favorite Chinese place on Beverly Blvd. I retold the dentures, dead bird, and 70s gigolo story. Ed and Steve were learning to play golf; they spoke their foreign language. Margaret pressed me to go to India with her. We did effortless work together. We communicated with minimum words, quick sketches, and rudimentary hand waving. The producer was a woman and first-rate, as was the director, who was Indian. It would be a long shoot; they expected to be in India for nine months. Steve's shoot would only be four months in New Mexico; almost like not leaving home. Maintaining relationships in our business is a problem. Steve wanted me in New Mexico; it had been an ongoing discussion.

We got home to Steve's hillside lair. The film business is divided into above-the-line and below-the-line people. In shorthand, the above-the-line people live in better neighborhoods, generally west of Laurel Canyon. Steve is above-the-line, so while I parked on the street, he had a garage. His house was hidden on a winding one-lane street. Thick courtyard walls were covered with ivy like mine, but his rustic and faded-turquoise gate was obvious, with big hammered nail details and a pierced metal lantern hanging under the arch. It opened onto a quiet courtyard. His gardener kept the native plantings right on the edge of chaos. A jar fountain burbled just enough to mask the street noise. It was a compact hillside house, like a New York loft in a warm and fuzzy Mediterranean shell.

We went through our brushing and flossing rituals and slid into bed naked. I had some residual Stroud heat and decided it was now or never. I took Steve's face in my hands and kissed each eye, then guided his hand down between my legs while I watched his face. He was smiling with a mixture of surprise and curiosity. I showed his hand what I wanted. He didn't get it exactly right, but he was game. The problem was, every time I let go of his hand it wandered off the mark.

Having to do all the thinking and all the work meant no buzz for me. He didn't have a feel for it yet. I figured he needed to build a little body memory around it, but he had to stay put to do that. I didn't want to discourage his effort; so after half a dozen tries at showing him precisely where he should be, I gave up. As my grandfather would say, *close but no cigar*. But just the fact that I'd gotten that far was a glimmer of hope for both of us.

He was totally turned on by the whole project so decided to try what he hadn't nailed with his hand, with his tongue; a good idea in theory. It was like cruel shoes to discover that when his tongue hit the mark, the bridge of his nose hit another, very painful mark. I tried sliding up the bed while pushing down gently on the top of his head. He took it to mean bear down, which was exactly the wrong approach.

I humored him so things finished on a high note, at least for him. It's just that, let's face it, we all have a sweet spot. It might drift around a little depending on what our mind is playing around with, but at a certain point, things get real focused and want lots of attention. You have to be at the station and wait around to catch the train. That's where hot chemistry works like a mind-altering drug. It takes care of the first fifteen minutes and expands the target area to things as far afield as your big toe. I only mention that because the night before with Stroud, my big toe had moaned and I still had all my clothes on. Steve got up a happy man. I'm a generous person at heart so that much was nice. Time would tell if I'd made headway or created a monster.

He dropped me at home with a little extra on his good-bye kiss. I changed clothes and ran downtown to meet Karin for our Monday morning breakfast at Café Café. I told her the story. When I got to the part about pushing down on his head and trying to escape through the headboard, she started laughing so hard green tea shot through her nose all over her granola. Nice.

"It's not funny! I showed him where the clitoris is as instructed." I dropped my voice for that last part.

She couldn't stop, so I looked out the window and drank coffee to wait her out. She finally came around.

"Okay," she said. "Baby steps."

"Baby steps, my ass. It was like being impaled," I said.

"Is that the first time he's gone down on you?"

"Of course not. And he's always been in the neighborhood so it's been nice. It's just the first time he's been at the right house and now we discover his tongue and nose don't fit in the overhead compartment."

"I think it can be fixed," she said.

"Oh really, by whom, that gyno-plastic surgeon on the Westside?"

"No. He's just got to make his approach from a different angle."

"I can't believe we're having this conversation. It sounds just like him when he's talking about golf."

"Well if you'd had it with him in the beginning you wouldn't be trying to break a bunch of bad habits. Maybe a golf analogy will make it easier."

I knew she was right. I wasn't exactly a novice at the whole thing, or maybe I was. But I'd never run into anything like that. There'd been plenty of bores, but they were like driving a Prius, a matter of patient endurance, low fuel consumption, and ultimately regret.

My husband and I tried to generate something past boredom. We watched strange people on DVDs. All the women had French manicured claws; is that supposed to be hot? We never could make a connection. The fact that we hated each other probably didn't help. I could mark my calendar at six-month intervals when he invariably said he wanted a divorce. I spent years getting shot through with that adrenalin, not taking jobs, not making a plan. I didn't call his bluff until the end. Steve and I like each other. And I was impressed with his willingness to learn.

"This isn't an old habit. I'm afraid it's one of those quickly learned new ones," I said. "I should have just said ouch."

"Yeah, ouch comes in handy."

We spent the day getting the sets up and running so the lighting guys could rig and run tests. Location shoots are a hassle. They had to keep cops at either end of the block to keep out the real drunks and homeless dogs, so they could run actor drunks and actor homeless dogs through the scenes. We ate lunch with the crew under a tent in the middle of a peed on downtown street. Film crews are like families; everyone talked about what they'd done on their hiatus. They thought dressing my dead grandmother sounded like a horror film. I said it was more Bergman meets Fellini.

"Who's that?" asked the twenty-year-old assistant to the assistant of somebody or other. Oh Jesus.

"A couple of ancient directors," I said.

Needless to say I didn't give up the trucker story. Unlike a real family, they're a non-judgmental bunch. They would have loved the Thelma and Louise visuals, if they knew who that was. But still. Karin and I wound down with cups of tea.

"So when are we going to meet Stroud?" she asked.

"I think that's better left down there."

"Have you heard from him?" she asked.

"Crickets, he doesn't have my number."

She thought I should call him. I said I was just getting around to acting like an adult with Steve. She didn't think there should be so much thinking involved with good sex. And so the conversation went. Karin voting for playing with fire because life's short, me hoping my fire playing days were behind me.

She couldn't understand why I would turn my back on the wild animal; it might wander off and not come back. I reminded her that that particular wild animal wandered for a living. Besides, the logistics were difficult. Steve and I floated back and forth between each other's houses; we both had keys and he frequently showed up to swim. No decision was made by the end of the day.

I swung by Nordstrom's on the way home and sniffed through men's aftershaves until I hit a bingo. I went home and swam laps. Steve had left a message saying he was going to New York on Friday to do more work with the sound guys. He wasn't satisfied. I should have known that was coming. Nobody was that good without being a tad obsessive. He planned to spend the weekend with his family and come back Tuesday or Wednesday, depending on how much work they got done. He was on his way over with food.

My mother called and started right in.

"I'd just like to see you get married again. I'm afraid you're going to miss out on having children."

"I don't want to have children with just anybody," I said. "I'm not sure I want children. I never even liked dolls."

"Every woman wants children. I wish you'd had them in your first marriage, then it would be done."

"Done with a crazy person. I'd be tied to that whipping post for life."

"He wasn't that bad, Hannah."

"Then you marry him. You didn't even like him."

"He grew on me."

"Mom, stop. He just wore you down."

"I never understood where he got all his rules is all."

"Thin air. And they didn't apply to him."

She'd been to her mall-walking group, Silver Sneakers, and had met a man who invited her to an AA meeting; he'd been going for twelve years. She said he didn't seem like the kind of person who would go to AA.

Half my friends go to AA or Alanon. I didn't see any particular pattern, except that they might be more interesting. They were definitely faster on the uptake when it came to jokes, that is if they'd quit drinking before every cell was fried. I decided to not get into it with her.

"Anyway, I told him you think I drink too much," she said. "And he invited me to go with him."

"You told him you drink too much in the first hour?"

"Oh, Hannah, I told him you think I drink too much. I was just trying to find some common ground."

"Are you going?"

"We have a date to go tomorrow. It's his birthday."

I kept my reaction down to a low roar. I didn't want to

sound too excited and scare her off. Years living with a knock down, and frequently drag out, alcoholic had been hard on all of us. Binky's even worse; she'll try to put a stop to it for sure. Mom was really going because she felt like there was some chemistry between them.

"I thought you just met him today, Mom."

"I'm a good judge of these things, Hannie."

"Well I think it's great. Call me tomorrow night and let me know how it went."

"Okay, sweetie. Well, I better get to bed. I want to run out in the morning and get him a birthday present."

I told her to skip the birthday present until she knew him a little better. I figured she'd see what I really meant once she got there. I had a picture of her introducing herself: "Hi, my name is Jackie and one of my daughters thinks I drink too much." They had their work cut out for them.

Steve came in with take-out. He jumped in the pool and I got out the new aftershave. I took it into the bathroom as he was getting out of the shower.

"I bought you a present."

"You don't like mine?"

"It's great, but I smelled this on one of the guys and thought I'd like to smell it on you. Variety is good."

He looked at me with the same curious smile from the night before. I told him I was going to fix dinner, meaning transfer from cartons to pottery.

He came in the kitchen and put his neck near my nose. "What do you think?"

I sniffed. "Yum, I think I love it."

I lit candles, dimmed the lights, and added a log to the fire. We talked about his trip to New York and our last run before wrapping the show for good.

We decided to spend our first Christmas/Hanukkah in Hawaii, religiously neutral territory, not that either of us cared about religion. He always went some place sunny when he finished a project. He needed sunlight to purge the gray pallor that developed after sitting in the dark for six or more months editing a picture. I loved Hawaii period; it was my favorite place. We'd make plans when he got back. We did dishes and got ready for bed.

We were lying looking at each other. We started out very slowly, taking it right from the top. We roamed around each other while things heated up.

He slid his hand between my legs and looked at me. "You need to keep showing me. I can't be completely responsible for both of us."

"I know." I showed him again, he stayed put twice as long.

We talked in low voices. I almost started laughing when I considered making a chip shot analogy, not that I'd even know how to do that. Instead I rushed him when it felt like his nose was going to revisit. It still involved a lot of academics, but we were improving, if you call avoidance an improvement. Baby steps. He's a nice man. I squelched the thought that maybe he wasn't a slow learner at all, just stingy.

Steve decided to stay behind and do some laps when I went to work.

Karin was already on the set talking to Jim the gaffer and his assistant David. I loved Jim; I detested David. His frequent sexual observations were always creepy.

"Is Vampire Chick going to meet someone before this is over?" asked David. "Or is she going to end the show just rubbing them out herself?"

David always referred to one of the saddest characters in the show as Vampire Chick. She's an uninspired young artist who really belonged at home with her parents in Palos Verdes. Instead, she sewed shirts and baked cookies for ungrateful deodorant deficient poseurs, and secretly masturbated to vampire shows on her computer. The masturbating part was off screen.

"They're not mutually exclusive, David." He snorted, either at the idea that we could take care of ourselves thank you very much, or because I was using my snotty voice.

Karin and I went back to Café Café for lunch so I could give her a progress report in private. I told her that we'd had a definite jump up in skill level, but that I didn't want to overwhelm him with the bad news about the overall fit.

"A little talking goes a long way," she said.

"Did you and Oscar talk?"

"Not technicalities. What we said isn't appropriate for the lunch crowd. We talk now."

"That's what I mean, I don't want a bunch of talk. The whole Stroud thing felt like it had a mind of its own. Steve says he can't be responsible for both of us. What part of him is he responsible for?"

She started cracking up. "Steve? A heart beat is my guess."

"He's okay."

"You've got some magic glasses, girl."

I told her he was headed to New York. She said I should call Stroud. I told her she needed to let it go.

"Just call him and see if he's coming this way. Keep it simple."

The rest of the day was uneventful. The Director sets the tone and ours was much calmer since rehab.

Steve and I talked early in the evening; he was going to bed and catching a ridiculously early flight to allow time for a meeting at the other end. I said I'd start researching beach houses but he already had a deposit on one and he'd send me the link.

I let out my breath. I'd been trying to stuff the memory of Stroud, how that had felt, but now, with space and time opening in front of me, it rushed back in with a vengeance. I slid the Nancarrow CD in. It sounded almost as good at home as it had dancing in a dark bar. The lead singer had been a hottie. I got out Grandma's box and found Stroud's card. I wandered around the house turning it over and over in my fingers. My bare feet rippled over every bump and cleft in the stone floors. I poured a glass of wine and ate a banana. I felt so guilty. I called.

"Hi Alan Watts, it's Hannah Spring. Or should I call you Stroud."

"Whatever makes you happy."

We were quiet. Part of me was embarrassed that I'd called; but the wild animal part had opened her lazy eyelids and pricked her ears when she heard his voice. She smiled.

"I wondered if you'd call," he said.

"I thought I'd give you my number in case you're coming this way."

"K. Now I have it. Car still okay?"

"It's fine."

We fell quiet again.

"Do you have plans to come this way?" I asked.

"No. Maybe Bakersfield on Sunday, quick flip-flop though."

"We're burying Grandma in Altadena on Saturday."

"Be good to get that done."

"Well I just thought I'd call."

"I heard that. Your not a boy boyfriend?"

"He's going to New York for a week."

We said good-bye and I kicked myself around the house for a good hour. What was I doing? I knew exactly what I was doing, or at least I thought I did.

Three

"I feel possessed," I said. "Like I've lost my mind."

"There's nothing rational about it," Karin was back at the granola. "I don't know why you're beating yourself up over this."

"Because it's not fair to Steve. Can you imagine his reaction if he knew I was even fantasizing about a truck driver from the boondocks, much less calling him?"

"He wouldn't be happy no matter who it was."

"Well, he didn't say he's coming."

"He'll come."

We put in another day making sure that Layla's slobbiness was in all the right places, that Vampire Chick had fresh looking cookies to offer some asshole who was taking advantage of her, and that the old lady landlord had her doilies and chipped cookie jar in order. Bruce, our director, sent his assistant to see us after lunch.

"They've written in a sex scene with a living person for the vampire girl," she said.

"Really?" we said in unison.

"Yeah. Her agent has been hammering the writer. He doesn't want her left hanging like that, too hard to shake the image. They're going to do some heavy petting; then cut to train in tunnel stuff. She's still a nice girl."

She handed us the new script pages and rushed off.

"Why can't she have on-camera sex and still be a nice girl?" I asked.

"She's from a good family," said Karin. "And we're not on cable."

I drove home in mostly stopped traffic. It would be nice to work in the wide-open Southwest. I had no idea what India was all about; Margaret said we'd have drivers. That alone could seal the deal. Both projects were starting up at the end of January. I needed to make a decision.

I called Steve when I got home. He was heading out for dinner with friends. I envied him a trip to New York while I was pinned down in the last gasps of a bad show.

The phone rang. Eric. "There's been a hang up. Mom went to an AA meeting today. I guess you knew about that. She came home, called Binky, and read her the riot act about being an alcoholic."

I thought my brain would explode. "Mom is blaming Binky because she's an alcoholic?"

"No, Mom is blaming Binky for Binky being an alcoholic," he said.

"Perfect. I think maybe Mom missed the message," I said.

"No maybe. World war three has broken out down here."

They'd been screaming and crying for hours. Mom was insisting that everybody attend the burial. After going to the meeting she had decided to see her mother buried, I didn't get the connection. She was also hoping that Binky and I would make up. I didn't see that connection either.

"We need to get Grandma buried before we leave for New York on Monday," said Eric.

"You're going to New York?"

"Business trip. Binky has agreed to be there, but it has to be

Sunday."

"I can't do it Sunday. I have plans," I said. "Can't we just go back to Plan A? Let them all stay home?"

"Mom's coming and now she won't do it without Binky," he said. "She says it will be good for her."

"This is nuts."

"It gets better. The nice man is coming."

"What? She just met him. Well she can't be drinking then."

"Who knows? As you like to say, he's a man. Anyway, what do you say, Sunday okay? We plan to get there by 11:00 and do the internment at noon."

"Mom has a call into me. She probably wants to tell me all about it."

"Or to tell you you're an alcoholic."

"Well if she does, I won't be there."

"Relax, I'm kidding. Ted said that during one tirade Mom told Binky she's a selfish alcoholic bitch, unlike you. You should bring Steve, round things out."

"He's in New York."

"Lucky bastard."

"What's Ted think about all this?" I asked. "He must know she's an alcoholic."

"He says what he always says. She's just tired."

We both said good-bye like the polite people we are. I went straight to the kitchen and poured a glass of merlot. The irony was not lost on me.

The phone rang, no way mom. If she had quit drinking that morning, it meant she had just set the world speed record for obnoxious self-righteous converts. She even beat out Bettina who, when she became a Catholic, after she'd converted to Judaism, after being a fallen Presbyterian, spent six months carrying around some catechism book with her name embossed in gold. I could see Mom getting just *Jackie*, embossed on an AA big book. Nope, not ready for that phone call.

I swam laps until my inner voice went hoarse nattering about Mom, then went to bed.

I was having breakfast the next morning when Mom called.

"Hi, how'd your date go?" I asked.

"The date went fine. His name's Arthur. You probably heard I had a little disagreement with Binky."

She was using her breathy little hiding out voice, like I might hurt her.

"I did. Have things calmed down?"

"Yes. Though she hasn't admitted that she's powerless over alcohol."

"Did you mention to anyone at the meeting that you were going to confront your daughter?"

"No. Why would I? Everyone was talking about their own problems."

"That's my point, Mom. AA is for the people who're there, not for people to get armed and take the fight to their children."

"That's what Arthur said; I don't see what difference it makes. Your sister's an alcoholic and she should get help."

"She has to want help. It's totally different."

"Well I talked to Ted last night. He said she might drink too much. He knows."

"You know Ted, Mom, he probably just said it to get the situation calmed down."

"Oh well, Hannah, I don't know why you know so much about this."

"Because I've gone to Alanon."

"What for?"

"Never mind."

"Is Steve coming on Sunday?"

"He's in New York."

"Well I hope it works out. Men like kittens, you're almost a cat."

"I have to go to work." I hung up without being polite.

Waiting to talk had given the situation a chance to mellow. I was spared the blow-by-blow; I was not spared being called a cat. How do they do that? They roll in the Trojan horse of family concern and out pops the fucking cat.

The buzzer at the gate announced a flower delivery guy with a huge vase of anthuriums, possibly the most overtly sexual flower on the planet. Talk about a clitoris, no man could miss those.

One of the experienced guys I'd known briefly in my wild young days said he'd known a few hookers who looked like that. It's amazing, really, how freely the men who don't love you tell you things in bed. I'd heard a little too much honesty from men. I'd like to say it was fun, but in the recesses of my heart it hurt. It got stored away, unexamined, in the shame box. Maybe getting paid to listen made it okay. Hookers must get an earful on top of everything else.

The note said, "Aloha—Steve." I put them under the white paper lantern where they'd be lit up. They look like wax and have no scent, but the visual can't be ignored. They murmured under the light like an oversexed Greek chorus. Steve may be in New York, but he was imposing his vision on the film playing in Los Angeles.

We got Vampire Chick all set up for her big breakthrough, then watched as the action unfolded. She chewed-up the scenery. Like the rest of us, she did not want to go out a pathetic rubber-outer. Unlike the rest of us, she had an agent to make sure that didn't happen. We were getting ready to take down the sets for good. The landlady was scheduled to die the next day; then we'd pack up her doilies and send her to storage.

I got home and called Steve. He planned to take Anna and Eric to dinner. I read scripts by the fire. Steve's was set along the border with Mexico and revolved around drugs, money, and humans dodging rattlers, cactus, and rubbing bad aftershave against cheap perfume.

Margaret's took place in 16th century India as the Mughal Empire was in ascendance. It would be a lush period piece that spun around an arranged marriage and palace intrigue. The wife ended up dying for cheating on her husband.

One sounded depressing as hell and involved a lot of gun-toting sadistic assholes with metal-tipped boots, half of them wearing badges; and one conjured silk and incense swirling around people who were depressed as hell with their partner assignment, hapless hoards, and one depreciated woman dying at the hands of sword-toting sadistic assholes. At least the swords were jeweled. I was in a foul mood.

I jumped naked in the dark pool and put in some half-hearted laps before getting in bed with Steve's script and my laptop. I would be working as an assistant to their guy. I didn't know him, so overall feel was all I cared about at that point. I was really drawn to working in India with Margaret; she'd never treated me like a peon, even when I was one. But the New Mexico project meant being with Steve, which meant keeping our relationship, which I still hoped meant getting rubbed out one way or another before too long. I was deep into the so-called war on drugs when the phone rang, A. Watts.

"Hello Stroud."

"Hello Spring."

It was quiet. There was a charge, even in the silence pinging off three satellites in the cold black space of night.

"I'm coming your way," he said.

"When?"

"I can pick up my load early Sunday. Drive up."

"We're burying Grandma on Sunday now. But we could have dinner after."

"Is there a place to park my rig?"

"I guess you could park it down on Mulholland. That's what movers do."

I gave him directions and told him where the key was hidden under the Buddha head by the front door. So obvious I figured a burglar would forget to look. So he was coming. The wild animal licked her chops.

Four

Karin called early the next day to say she wouldn't be in. Both kids were puking their brains out. It was no problem. All we had to do was kill off the old lady and we were wrapped. I told her about Stroud, but said there would be no meeting. I didn't want Steve to hear about him from one of her loquacious kids.

I got home to a link from Steve for the place in Hawaii; it was very high-end. I called him and told him I'd decided on New Mexico.

"Good," he said. "It will be good to work on a project together, before puking kids complicate the picture."

"Kids? We haven't talked about kids."

"Don't you want kids?"

"I don't know. There's so much pressure from my mother, I haven't really had the space to think."

"I know what you mean."

"It would be complicated with a fallen Presbyterian. Do they even know we're dating?"

"They will when the time comes."

"Do we have to decide now?"

"No," he said. "Hawaii will be good for us."

We said good night. I looked past the fire and the hot red flowers to the turquoise pool. We'd never talked about getting married and he was leapfrogging to kids. Apparently before breaking the news to his family that he was seeing a somewhat Presbyterian. We needed to figure out what we were doing before things went much further.

I spent Saturday cleaning house, washing sheets, shaving my legs, and food shopping. I checked in with Karin, now Oscar had it, and she was queasy.

Burial day and I overslept. I grabbed Emily and rushed out the door. I'd decided to read "Wild Nights" as a send off. The sun was shining, the air was clean and the mountains were out; it was a beautiful day to be buried, even in Altadena.

Eric and Anna were in front of the cemetery office talking to the funeral director. I could tell from fifty paces that my brother was uptight.

"The hearse broke down," he said. "Grandma is stranded on the 15."

"Wow," I said. "Did you call Mom and Binky?"

"Not yet. We're going to Plan C. We have to get this done today, even if it's the middle of the night."

"I have to be somewhere. I can't spend all day with this."

"I know, I'm sorry. These guys are going to send one of their cars down to pick her up. We should still be able to get her in the ground by dark."

I could see Stroud and Rex roaming around the Hollywood Hills; he might want to skip the whole thing. I called him.

"Hey," he said. "What's up?"

"Things have changed."

"Ah, I wondered."

"Not that. Grandma's ride broke down on the 15. She's stranded. They're sending a hearse from here, but it's going to add hours to this process."

"I'll drive right by her."

"Well pick her up and bring her with you!"

Eric looked at me with laser vision. I shook my head. I was kidding!

"Who's that?" asked Eric.

"It's a friend, Eric. He's coming up for dinner. He just mentioned that he'll be driving by Grandma."

"What's he driving?"

"A truck."

My brother does hired gun computer problem solving for the highest bidder. I could swear his earlobes lit up and flashed in synchronicity with his snapping synapses. "How big?"

The funeral director caught the drift and protested. "Not just anyone can transport a body. We have a hearse."

Eric spun on him wild-eyed, "Is it illegal?"

"Well no," said the funeral director, "but it's not dignified."

"I don't think she's worried about being dignified anymore," said Eric. "I know I'm not."

Eric turned to me and stuck out his arm, "Let me talk to him."

"My brother wants to talk to you," I said to Stroud. "His name's Eric."

Eric walked off toward the mausoleum of eternal slumber. He talked to Stroud, he looked at his watch; he walked back toward us, nodding his head and saying, "Thanks. I'll call you in a few minutes."

He hit end. "Okay, Plan D. He's bringing Grandma."

Eric pulled out his phone and started programming in Stroud's number.

"What's his name?"

"Stroud, like the birdman."

"It says here A. Watts."

"His real name is Alan Watts."

He looked at me for a second. "Two names?"

I shrugged.

"Alan Watts?" he asked. "What's that, an enlightened alias?"

"He said it's his name. His parents were into Zen for a while. They had their moments."

"So did ours, but they didn't name me Ringo Spring." He was shaking his head as he punched in the last of the information and walked into the office with the funeral director.

"That was lucky," said Anna.

"Yeah. Ringo Spring is seriously schlocky. But Mom was in love with George Harrison. George Spring isn't too bad. Dad would have named him Jerry Garcia Spring."

"I wouldn't have married someone named Ringo. I'm not sure about Jerry either," said Anna. "But I meant the truck is lucky."

"I guess. Now I'm worried that bad car karma has run amuck, and Grandma's been shanghaied by an enlightened criminal who does a mean Texas Two Step."

"We'll know soon enough," said Anna. "At least she loved to dance."

"There is that. What's the deal with this Arthur? Has Mom really stopped drinking?"

"For now. It's only been a few days."

A late model BMW in silver gray pulled in. Mom waved through the windshield. Mom and Arthur walked our way. Mom, normally the picture of propriety, was wearing the tightest jeans I had ever seen on just about anyone, ever. She must have had to lie on the floor to zip them up. She had on a sweater set in pale green; the shell was so Marilyn Monroe tight, I could see jiggling mounds of breast escaping the top of a new push-up bra. Interesting, she was always a stickler for not having obvious underwear. To finish it off she was wearing what can only be described as *fuck me* pumps. The only familiar notes were her trademark pearls and what Karin calls her rich bitch bob. She looked great.

"Whoa," said Anna.

"Whoosh," I said.

"Hi girls!" Mom jiggled our way.

Arthur was central casting handsome. He was tall, trim, had silver hair to match his car and a golf course tan that really set off his straight white teeth. His sweater was cashmere, his shoes good leather, his fingernails buffed. Huh. Maybe she would stay sober. I know at least half of me would.

"Why are you standing outside?" asked Mom.

"Eric is making some arrangements," said Anna. "So we're enjoying the sun."

"It's a gorgeous day," said Mom. She remembered her manners and introduced us.

"Great to meet you both," said Arthur. "Jackie has told me a lot about you."

Eric came out of the office with the funeral director quick stepping behind. He introduced himself to Arthur and took in Mother's new look with nary a blink.

"We're running a little late," he said. "Grandmother's hearse broke down so we've arranged a truck to pick her up. We'll only be about an hour late."

"A truck?" asked Mom. "Like a delivery van?"

My mother was no dumb bunny and the jeans weren't squeezing that part of her brain. She knew dissembling when she heard it.

"No," Eric said. "A truck truck as far as I know. Hannah, you want to jump in here?"

"It's a John Deere," I said. My mother blinked. "It's green with a leaping yellow stag."

"Oh, that's a great truck," said Arthur. "A classic American company."

Mother looked at him like he was speaking in tongues.

"A friend is bringing her," I said. "His name is Stroud, or Alan."

"He has two names?" asked Mom.

Eric put his arm around her shoulder, "Come inside, Mom, I want you to see the headstone."

A white Mercedes pulled in with Ted at the wheel. It was a duplicate of Binky's car, total lack of imagination. Besides Amber they have two Sams, Samuel and Samantha. We call them both Sam; like a bad TV show. Binky was dressed far more appropriately than Mom, in a trim suit, pearls, and low fat heels. Ted, like Eric, was in a coat, tie and man loafers. Binky was cool while Ted made the introductions. She was beginning to remind me of Aunt Asp, always a bit turned sideways, always a little closed. She used to dance around like Debbie Gibson and sing "Shake Your Love."

Arthur said to Binky, "Your mother's inside."

She gave him a look that said she thought he was worming his way into the family a little too quickly. Wait until she got a load of Mom. She went into the office. We had started to tell Ted about the snafu when Binky stuck her head out the door and called him in a shrill indignant voice. He hopped to.

"So, Arthur, what do you do?" I asked.

"I'm retired now. But I was an aeronautical engineer."

"Interesting. Did my mother tell you our father died in a plane crash?"

"She did. I'm sorry. It sounds like it was equipment failure."

"Yes. He slammed into a mountain in the dark."

Wow, I was really laying it on. I didn't even have any charge left on the topic, but apparently I was going to give Arthur a hard time.

"That's what your mother said, that the altimeter failed," he said. "That's an unusual instrument to have fail. It must have been very hard for all of you."

"It was. Do you fly?"

"No. I was always too busy designing planes to fly them."

I managed to bite my tongue before launching into the idea of designing something bigger than a bug-jammed pinhole to run an altimeter.

Binky and Ted came out of the office.

She snubbed Arthur and said, "What's Mom got on? She's dressed like Samantha."

Arthur excused himself.

"Nice, Binky," I said as we watched Arthur walk away.

"What? She looks like a tart."

"Samantha's kinda young to be a tart."

"Oh you know what I mean," she snapped.

My phone rang. A. Watts. "How's it going?" I asked, as I walked toward the glen of everlasting life, or never-ending family, depending on your mood.

"Fine. I picked up Grandma, no problem. I'm almost to Grub 'n Scrub."

"You're not going to stop are you? I'm dying here."

"Nah. Grandma's behind schedule. What's going on?"

"My mother showed up dressed like a hot middle-aged hooker with her new man. My sister called her a tart. I'm trying to think of an excuse to go for a drive. Will you call me when you're half an hour away?"

"Will do."

We hung up. I walked back to the family unit plus one.

"It's very nice of your friend to bring your grandmother," said Mom. "I hope it's not too big an imposition."

"It's fine, Mom. He was coming this way anyway."

"You have a friend with a truck?" asked Binky. "How many men do you have, Hannah?"

"Four or five," I said. "I'm going to run a few errands while we wait."

Binky said she needed lunch, so they took off too. I made it back to the freeway, neutral territory in L.A. I went a few exits to Sierra Madre, pulled over and called Karin.

"Where are you guys?" I asked.

"Football game. I thought you were burying Ella Minerva and all her treasures today."

"We will eventually, but right now I'm hiding out on a side street in Sierra Madre."

She was howling with laughter at the story. I could hear Oscar in the background asking, "What? What!"

"Take pictures," she said. "Are they *fuck me* shoes, or *fuck me fast*?"

"Just *fuck me*. They have backs, but a lot of toe cleavage. I don't think pictures of this day are a good idea."

"So she's hot for Arthur. Are we?" she asked.

"We don't know yet. I have a feeling today will be a test of his character."

"And his sobriety," she said. "I better go; the good parents around me are giving me the evil eye."

We hung up. The phone rang. Stroud.

"You close?" I asked.

"Yeah, be there in half."

Binky and Ted weren't back from lunch. The funeral director had arranged for sandwiches and drinks. Everyone sat in the sun at a stone table and bench encircled by boxwoods trimmed in graduating sizes that swept around them like green arms. A fountain, with a peeing cherub, was the focal point. I thought of the homeless people downtown that pee and bathe in the fountains.

"Stroud just called; he's only a few minutes away," I said.

"What should we call him," asked Eric. "Stroud or Alan?"

"Whatever makes you happy," I smiled.

Mom turned to Arthur, "Hannah had a man friend; he had two names, but we didn't know it at the time. He was a criminal."

"Mom, really," I said. Anna and Eric zeroed in on her; this could get good.

"It's okay, Hannah," she said. "Arthur goes to AA. He hears lots of stories."

"I'm sure he does," was all I could think to say. Arthur gave me an understanding look.

I went in the bathroom and brushed my hair, wiped off some creeping mascara, and was putting on fresh lip-gloss when I heard the sound of air brakes. Stroud.

I went outside as he jumped down from the cab. Rex jumped out and disappeared. The funeral director frowned. He probably wondered where he'd find dog shit.

Stroud was in his uniform of jeans and blue long-sleeved shirt with the sleeves rolled up. His black hair looked longer than I remembered. He could not be described as tall, dark, handsome, or polished. He was shy of six feet tall, stocky, and smelled good. The wild animal purred like a big fat cat. I mean it, it felt like an actual paw flexing and purring cat.

He scanned the small gathering. He took a beat longer on my mom, then sought out my face with an amused smile. Rex came back and flipped my hand with his nose for a rub.

The funeral director ushered out a guy pushing a chrome gurney. Stroud went around to the back of the truck and opened the big door with Eric and me in curious pursuit. Arthur put his arm around Mom and led her back to the stone table.

Grandma was wrapped securely in quilted blankets and sandwiched between cartons of IV tubing and nitrile gloves. There were flower sprays and small arrangements tucked in here and there. They moved boxes and slid her around until they'd maneuvered her onto the gurney, which they wheeled quickly in the side door.

"I appreciate you doing this," said Eric.

"No problem," said Stroud. "I was coming this way."

I gave him a hug, the blue shirt made his eyes even richer. I think my nipples reached out and stroked his chest. "Thanks. It's nice to see you."

He glanced down at my breasts and the corners of his mouth turned up, then he met my eyes, "You too."

The funeral director was back and they discussed escape routes.

"You're leaving?" I asked.

"Yeah," he said. "I'll meet you there."

He whistled for Rex. They climbed in the cab, did some impressive maneuvering, and drove away.

"He seems nice," said Eric. "Do you realize your cheeks look like red apples?"

"That obvious? He taught biology."

"College?" he asked.

"High school," I said.

"Huh. Well next thing will be sprayed on jeans with pumps," he said.

"You noticed her get up?"

"I'd have to be blind. Let's get this over with. Where's Binky?"

Binky wasn't back yet. Eric punched in Ted's number while I got Emily out of the car and wandered back to the table. We could hear Binky's voice before she was out of the car. Her walk looked a little drifty.

Eric went into the office to marshal the troops. The funeral director solemnly led us to the family plot. I hadn't been there in years. Grandma would be buried with familiar names.

I don't know when they'd done it, but Grandma was waiting for us. Her casket, adorned with a large floral spray, sat on a low platform with what looked like a poufy bed skirt. There were no chairs set up. We hadn't planned on a crowd, which is where we hit snag number two. In all the hubbub about the guest list and who's an alcoholic, no one had planned an actual service. Binky's current Catholicism notwithstanding, we're not a religious family. No one knew any good prayers off the top of their head. I had Emily, but it seemed like someone needed to kick things off. Enter Arthur.

"I didn't know Minerva," he began. "But in the little time I've known her daughter, I know she must have been a strong and loving person. I'm happy you included me today."

Well done, Arthur. I glanced at Mother to see if she'd missed the Ella. I figured she'd feel touchy about him getting her mother's name wrong, even if they had only known each other for a few days. I was. Ella is my middle name. I liked it, even though I thought it sounded odd with Hannah; it made a clip clop sound. No one had asked me. Mom was starting to cry; probably because her heels had sunk in and taken root in the grass. She was firmly planted, with a slight backward tilt. Her hand gripped Arthur's arm like a claw. Nice manicure, Mom. He undoubtedly thought she was feeling loving and just trying to be strong.

I looked at Eric and raised my eyebrows. He shot the funeral director his this–is-what-you're-paid-for look. The funeral director caught it.

"Why don't we say the Lord's Prayer," he said.

We bowed our heads and he began, "Our father who art in heaven…."

Oh boy. It's the prayer they say at the end of every Alanon and AA meeting; too preachy for my tastes. Arthur was delivering in a sonorous voice while the rest of us mumbled along. I looked at Mom and Binky when it got to the trespasses part, but neither was listening. Both had their heads down, Mom so she could sneak peeks at her sunken heels, and Binky so she could flick bugs off her suit. Ted had his arm around Binky's shoulders, probably to keep her upright. Eric and Anna had their heads bowed and were holding hands.

"Would anyone like to say a few words about Minerva?" asked the director.

Now he was calling her Minerva. I wondered what the headstone said.

"I'd like to read one of Ella Minerva's favorite poems." I read "Wild Nights."

"That was lovely, Hannah," said Mom through her sniffles.

Binky rolled her eyes. We stood reverentially, waiting for someone to break from the pack. Mom's back must have been feeling the awkward angle. While Arthur steadied her, she stepped out of her shoes revealing a bright red pedicure, then weeded her shoes out of the lawn, tiptoed to the walkway, swiped grass off her feet and put them back on. The rest of us wandered slowly, heads bowed slightly, resisting the urge to run. Ted and Binky made a quick escape. Mom and Arthur were waiting to say good-bye.

"Thank Stroud again," said Eric.

"You guys did a great job," I said. "I'm going to Hawaii with Steve for the holidays so won't see you. He's going to call you in New York, take you to dinner if it works out."

I was about to get in my car when Mom came over to me.

"You know what they say, Hannah."

"Who they?"

"They they. They say a man has an affair for variety, but a woman has an affair to make up her mind."

"I'm not having an affair."

"Well." She smiled gently, gave me a hug and went back to Arthur.

That was a new one. I'd put it in my life's lessons book under *'A' for affair*, right next to *A smart woman can control any man.* I was building quite a playbook from those sisters. To her credit, Mom had never trotted out the controlling men rule. I kept waiting for the day when she started combining. She could tell me what *they cats* had to say about my life choices, such as they were.

Unfortunately I'd spent enough time in the self-help section to understand that I needed to *own* my choices, which can really be a bummer when you have such a great mother to blame.

The scenic artist on our show had some woo-woo thing going. She swore we pick our mothers and fathers at some pre-womb point in time and space. I had started giving that a little thought but hadn't gotten very far with it. I wasn't quite ready for the edge of that wedge. Every time I tried to think about it *I felt a cleaving in my mind,* as Emily would say. It might be empowering to think we have that much control; on the other hand, it's a heavy load. I was trying to stop controlling everything, not rope in what my previous self and my parents were doing before his little tadpole crashed Mom's party. And just when she thought she was free, free at last with her two kids squirreled away in school all day.

And what did the scenic artist know? She was paid a paltry sum to produce paintings for a pretending artist who was really a rather vacuous actor, who sold them, off-camera, to people who found meaning in them, despite the fact that her character ranted around in a nihilist haze about how nothing means nothing. And the paintings were damn good. The scenic artist should have picked parents who sent her to the Rhode Island School of Design instead of some two-year trade school out in the valley. La dee dah. Mom always made me feel so good about things, even though I knew she couldn't *make me feel* anything.

I called Stroud.

"Hey," he said. "I just got here, nice place. Rex thinks the pool is his water bowl."

"That should be safe. Light a fire if the house is cold, it gets chilly. There's wine there."

The road was wide open and it was only 4:30 p.m. Things had worked out great thanks to Stroud. I thought about him in my house, wandering around with Rex. I pulled up to the grape stake fence in forty minutes flat.

I opened the gate and looked down on the scene below. It was almost dark. He'd figured out how to turn on the pool lights, steam was smoking off the surface of the water. He had his shoes off and was reading in the chair by the fire.

"Hi," I said. "You look so comfortable."

"Good spot. I took Rex for a walk. The coyotes were out for dinner."

"They'll be howling like banshees in a few minutes. Lots of people find just their cat's collar in the morning."

"A lot of pressure on their environment," he said. "So how'd it go?"

"It was fine. I read her poem."

I went into the closet and changed. I took off my pearls and grabbed my all-purpose jacket.

"Well. You saw my mother."

"Sure did. She didn't look like your average hooker."

"You should have seen her pedicure. And those shoes will have her on ice tonight. What's an average hooker look like?"

"Not like your mother. If the tall tan guy is her new man, I doubt she'll be on ice."

My phone rang. Steve. I let it go to voicemail. I glanced at the screen; he'd left a message.

I offered to make breakfast for dinner unless Stroud really wanted to go back out. I scrambled eggs and made toast while I confessed about how awful I'd been to Arthur. We sat down by the fire to eat.

"Your father was a pilot?"

"Yeah. He learned as a young man. We had great times."

"Did your mother fly with him?"

"Sure. Her name's Jackie. We all did."

"And he slammed into a mountain?"

"Well, not slammed, I said that for dramatic effect." I told him the story.

"Sorry."

"We should go swimming and look at the stars," I said.

"You can see stars here?"

"Uh huh. Three, sometimes even four, manage to pierce the ambient light when there's no moon like tonight."

"Out in the flat desert it's like being under a huge bowl of stars. They arc from horizon to horizon," he said.

"Hmm, I'd like to see a bowl of stars. Let's swim, then I'll fix some tea."

We turned off all but a few lights. I opened the damper and added some wood to the fire.

"I don't have trunks," he said.

"You don't need trunks, nobody can see us. There are towels in the bathroom cupboard."

He went in to undress while I stripped down in the closet. I wrapped in a towel and grabbed the bottle of wine and glasses.

I don't care how warm it is; those first few feet getting in the water are a doozy. The air was colder than the water so it felt wonderful to hold a beat too long in the cold air, and then slip into the water. The water felt like warm skin sliding up my legs and torso. I rolled over and slowly breast-stroked down to the other end of the pool. It was darker at that end and my eyes began to adjust to the night sky. Stroud dropped his towel and stepped into the pool, taking his time with the first few steps; then dove in with a small splash. He swam half the length of the pool underwater then surfaced.

"Hey," he said in a low voice.

"Hey. Nice, huh?"

"Yeah." He glided my direction and turned his back to the wall so we were both looking up at the sky. Our legs brushed against each other as they gently held us in place below the surface. I put my hands over my shoulders and held onto the edge of the pool to keep from slipping under. I had to arch my back to keep from floating to the surface.

He looked over at me, then came closer and faced me, with his hands on the edge of the pool next to mine.

"Nice," his face was just a few inches from mine.

We kissed. His warm tongue made a slow exploratory circle around the smooth skin just inside my lips, then brushed my tongue. Electricity raced down my core and arched my back; I floated up to meet him. The water pressed me up against his body and legs so that he was lying on top of me, suspended in the warm water. Our cells seemed to be buzzing some language back and forth through his soft but purposeful tongue, through his strength, the hair on his legs, the breath from his nose on my lip. My nipples brushed against his chest in rhythm with the gentle tidal wave our body motion created.

I was completely lost, so when my fingers slid off the edge of the pool and I slipped under water, my mouth was still open. I felt his arm wrap around my waist and fish me out, back almost to where I had started. Our legs were in a state of confusion now that our delicate equilibrium had been lost. He managed to hold me and hold the edge of the pool. I coughed.

"Are you alright?" He looked very amused.

"I think so."

It was at that moment that his steely grip on the pool gave way and we both went under with him on top, of course.

We pushed away from each other in a mad play for survival and surfaced a few feet apart. We looked at each other and laughed; then we just looked at each other. Despite the floundering finale, we both sensed the wild animal on the loose.

"Would you like a glass of wine?" I asked. "I brought the bottle out."

"Sure. Do you swim laps in here?"

"Yes."

"Naked?"

"At night, yes. Why?"

"I just wanted the picture for the future."

"We also play a lot of Marco Polo. We call it Roger Wilco."

I took off swimming and made it to the wine in a matter of seconds. Stroud swam right behind; he's a good swimmer.

"Nice ass."

"Thanks," I said. We sat on the bottom step with the warm water up to our shoulders, sipped wine and gazed at the starless sky.

"I'm getting cold," I said. "You ready to get out?"

"Yeah."

I rose from the water as nymph-like as possible, then jumped in the shower to heat up fast. I hung up a guest robe for Stroud.

He was standing by the fire wrapped in a towel, looking thoughtful.

"I left you a robe if you want to rinse off. I'm going to start some hot water."

He came up behind me in the kitchen and pressed into my back and kissed the side of my neck. He slid his hand inside the fold of my robe, took the weight of my breast in his hand and brushed the nipple like he was gently stroking a cat's ear. I turned around to face him.

"Can you stay?" I asked.

"Unless you've changed your mind again."

"I haven't."

He took a shower while I fixed tea and added a log to the fire. I curled my bare feet under me as I sat in a chair close to the fire.

He came out of the bathroom wrapped in a robe I'd seen Oscar wear many times. It fit about the same way; they both had broad shoulders. He poured tea, took a cookie, and sat in the chair opposite me.

"Nice fire," he said.

We drank tea and watched the fire. When he looked up the warm light danced across his face like living camouflage. I thought of early man sitting by a fire under a bowl of stars.

"Okay then," he said.

We turned off the lights. He flipped the pool lights back on. The soft light undulated on the ceiling and stretched the room out, past the warm round fire, into the soft blue glow of the water. I pulled the covers back. He turned me around; he was already naked. He undid the belt on my robe, slid his arms around my waist and pulled me close to him. We kissed. My robe slid off my shoulders to the floor. There was a barely contained fierceness to it all. Hot waves, set loose, were washing up and down deep inside my body. He lowered me onto the bed and lay down next to me with one of his legs hooked over one of mine. He was propped up on one elbow, exploring me with his eyes.

He dropped his head and gently took a nipple in his teeth, circling it slowly with his tongue. I ran my fingers through his thick waves of hair. He did the same with the other nipple, leaving them cold and wet and wanting more. He looked at me, then kissed me again. Our tongues found endless places to explore in endless ways. His hand slid down and smothered my pubic hair in the palm, a finger slid between my lips. The wild animal threw open the door and pulled him in. I slid my hand down and explored him. There were so many more things I wanted to do with him. But spasms of urgency burned under his hand. I tried to guide him into me. He covered my hand, his voice a low husky sound, and said, "Wait."

He reached over the side of the bed and got a condom. He tore it open with his teeth, the ghost of a swashbuckler, and then held out the package for me to take it out. We both watched as I slipped it on and smoothed it. He grunted with pleasure. I looked at him while I licked my hand and then continued stroking and smoothing, playing my fingers over the ridges and cords. Next time I'd do it with my mouth. He pushed the pillows up against the wall and sat up, he lifted me up and I lowered down on him. I shifted forward going deeper and deeper. He took my breast in his mouth as I rocked back and forth.

I'd never felt anything like it before. I was tethered to my sweet spot. I put my hands on his shoulders and my back arched as I erupted into wave after wave squeezing him in a way beyond my control. I was making sounds like a wild animal. I rode the sensations from guttural to keening to guttural. He was matching my sounds with groans. He got a far away look as he grabbed my hips and pulled me down hard. His muscles turned to focused tension as he looked into my eyes and I could feel him bucking deep inside me. He grunted, "Oh Jesus." My body answered with more spasms. The rocking slowed and I collapsed onto his shoulder; our hearts were pounding. He held my head and stroked my hair. One more wave shuddered through before my body started to settle down. He lifted my face with both hands to look into my eyes and saw tears. He smiled and brushed them away with his thumbs.

"That was a little intense," I said.

"More than that," he said.

I put my head back down on his shoulder as he ran his hands over my hips. I was pretty sure I was going to have a sore throat. I lifted my head and smiled at him.

"I want to do that again," I said.

"Okay," he smiled. "But you're going to have to get your nice ass off me for a minute."

I gave him one last rock of the hips to show him who was boss; he smiled and winced. He held the ring of the condom to keep it from slipping off and I lifted myself off of him. I sat next to him and pulled the covers up to my breasts. He took my hand and compared the length of our fingers; I could feel every inch of skin on his hands.

"I hope your neighbors don't complain about noise," he said.

"Was I too noisy? I've never done that before."

"I shouldn't have said noise. That was a wild display."

"Was it distracting?"

"Hardly." There was still some residual grunt in his voice.

"Maybe they thought it was coyotes."

He turned to me and said in low voice, "No creature on the planet would mistake that for coyotes."

"Do you think my mother and Arthur are doing the same thing tonight?"

"I think Mom packs a coochie and knows how to use it. But I don't know if Arthur's heart would hold up to what just happened here."

I realized I didn't want to inject images of my mother and Arthur into this night. But really.

"Coochie? Do guys call it a coochie?"

"Sure, you hear it on the CB all the time."

"Seriously?"

"Sometimes."

He was smiling. He was having fun. And I realized I like the word.

"I wouldn't refer to my mother's coochie around my brother."

"I won't." His eyes got soft and he slid his hand under the blanket and down my belly. Coochie called out and he went right for her.

It was slower the second time. My mouth had a long time to explore. The second time, I made him wait.

We fell asleep for an hour after that. I woke up to him pressing against me from behind. I offered him a lazy welcome. He slipped in, then reached over me and covered me with the palm of his hand again. We fell asleep that way.

I woke up at 6:00, alone. He came out of the bathroom buttoning his shirt. I sat up and watched him.

"Hey," he said.

"Morning," I said. "Are you leaving?"

"I'm going to let Rex out. Get a clean shirt."

"Would you like coffee? I have granola and yogurt."

"Sounds good."

He sat on the edge of the bed and brushed my lips with his thumb. Then he kissed one nipple. I reached down, unzipped his jeans and stuck my hand inside. There was no talking. We were lying facing each other an hour later.

"My fire's not out," I said.

"I can tell. I'll be back."

He went out the door and I buried my head in the pillows and breathed in his scent. I pulled myself away, started coffee and turned on my phone. There were calls from Steve, Mom, and Karin. I called Karin and left a message that I wouldn't be in. Steve had left a message that he was hung up and would call later.

I fixed breakfast while he took a shower. He came out of the bathroom barefoot, but dressed for work. We had breakfast and took the bowls to the sink. He opened my robe and pulled me close while he slid his hands down over my ass. His belt buckle was cold on my skin.

"I have to go. I'll call you."

He tied my robe, then put on his shoes and walked out the door. He said, "Let's go," to Rex in a low voice.

I stayed at the sink until I heard the gate latch. I didn't know what to do with myself for the rest of the day. I called Karin.

"How you doing?" she asked.

"I don't know. The whole I'll call you thing. I feel like I've regressed about ten years."

"Do you regret it?"

"Not yet. I can't believe how that felt. It's just so reckless."

"You want to come down for dinner tonight?"

"No thanks. I'm going to wash the sheets and do some India research."

"You taking India?"

"Looks that way."

"You're not going to confess are you?"

"No, but I know."

I started a load of laundry while I swam laps. Then I took a shower and put on fresh clothes and made up the bed with the clean sheets. I now knew about Stroud sex. That genie would never go back in the bottle.

Steve called; he thought he might be even longer back there. He was headed out to dinner with Eric and Anna. It was probably my guilty imagination, but he sounded a little distant. I wondered if there was any way he could know what had happened.

I lit a fire and started trolling for information about India. Stroud called. I considered not answering.

"Hey," he said. "You want to swim?"

"I already did."

My stomach was clutching in the quiet between us, wild animals everywhere stood stock still as they listened in.

"That it?" he asked.

"No."

"Which no?" he asked.

"That's not it."

All the animals breathed a sigh of relief and went back to their wild ways.

"Okay," he hung up.

I slid the Nancarrow CD in. He walked in an hour later with a bag in each hand and a smaller one under his arm. He dropped the bags in the kitchen and threw the other on the table by the flowers.

"With the truck, I could only find a Mexican place." He took out containers and opened drawers until he found spoons to dish up. I peered in the bag on the table; it was a box of condoms. He looked up from his work in the kitchen, the corners of his mouth turned up again.

"We ran out," he said.

"Jesus."

"You hungry? There's Mexican beer here. Not your Bohemia, it's what they had."

"I'm starving." I moved the flowers to the side. I imagined them looking on in dismay and saying, "Hey! Hey! Hey!" as they were shoved off-stage. He brought out bowls of food, while I got plates and forks and opened a couple of beers.

"That was a good band," he said.

"Yeah, the CD is still good. That doesn't happen often. How was Bakersfield?"

"It's a garden capital. What did you do today?"

"I stayed home."

"You okay?" he asked.

"I'm fine. We haven't talked."

"What do you want to talk about?"

"I don't know. Things."

"Things?" he asked.

"Who is your friend?"

He looked at me over his beer. "Old friend. Known her all my life. Got to know her again after the divorce."

"You sleep with her?"

"Why are you asking me that?"

"Well, you know I sleep with my boyfriend."

"I have. Does it matter?"

"I don't know. Does it matter that I sleep with my boyfriend?"

"Neither of us would be here if it was like this with them."

"My mother says men have affairs for variety."

"Your mother calls you a cat."

I laughed; I'd forgotten I'd told him that.

"Come on," he said picking up our empty plates. "Let's not waste any more time on this. I need a shower, want to join me?"

We cleared the dishes and I turned off the lights over the

flowers. It was a relief to put them to sleep. He put some loose condoms on the nightstand. We got in the shower and experimented with all the ways you can turn on a person with soap and water. We barely made it back to bed. At some point we tried the chair by the fireplace and agreed it was more comfortable than a Volvo, though definitely not as stable. We were back in bed. He was holding my back close up against his stomach, idly stroking my belly. His face was in the back of my neck.

"Where do you live?" I asked.

"I've got a place down there. Small house."

"May I see it some time?"

"You sure may."

He slid his hand down my belly and we started in again. If anyone had told me that two people could have that much sex in that short a period of time, I would have said they were nuts. But except for catnaps and glasses of water, we didn't stop until we finally fell asleep at three a.m.; even then we woke up for a little something before work. He got dressed.

"You taking off?" I asked.

"I'm going to get a clean shirt. You making coffee?"

I took a shower while coffee started. He still wasn't back by the time I got dressed. I'd picked up glasses, washed dishes, and made the bed before I saw Rex coming down the stairs.

They came in. Stroud didn't have a clean shirt. The skin around his mouth and eyes was stretched tight.

"Are you all right? You look like someone hit your truck."

"Truck's fine." He was standing with his back to me looking out at the pool.

"What's going on?"

He didn't say anything. I got a cup of coffee for each of us. I added cream to mine to soften the blow to my churning stomach. He took his cup, "Thanks." He kept looking out at the pool.

"Did I do something?"

"No, Hannah, this has nothing to do with you. I can't imagine why you'd even ask that."

Assuming it was me was an old habit I'd fallen back on, in this room, with all the oxygen sucked out of it. I waited. Rex wandered over and rested his chin on my knee, his head a worry stone. Stroud finally turned around and sat down in the chair we'd been in last night.

"What is it?" I asked.

He was leaning forward with his head down over the cup of coffee between his knees. He looked up at me.

"It happened months ago," he began.

"Okay."

"You know my friend."

"Your old friend."

He smiled a sad ironic smile and nodded his head a little. "Her name is Leeann."

"Leeann," I said trying out her name. "Has she been hurt?"

"She's pregnant."

"Is it yours?"

"She says so. I have no reason to doubt her."

"What are you going to do?"

"I don't know. We'll talk it over when I get home."

"No abortion?"

"It's too late, if it's when I think it was. She's been keeping it to herself. She wants to have it."

"Didn't you use anything?"

He looked at me and said in a quiet voice, "Hannah."

"What? You've been so careful with me."

"I've been careful with both of us."

"You're right. I'm a slut and she's the hometown girl. This has nothing to do with me."

"I don't know why you talk like that. We just met. I don't know what your boyfriend is doing. You don't know where I've been either."

"Are you going to marry her?"

"I don't want to have this conversation between us."

"The only thing we have between us is this conversation."

"I can't have her raising my child on her own. She can't do it alone, she's not like you."

"She made the decision on her own."

"I was part of the decision when I slept with her."

"How noble. Do you love her?"

He looked out the window for a full minute. "It doesn't matter."

"And she's willing to have a baby with a man who doesn't love her? That's crazy."

"Half the world lives like that."

"And you're willing to be in that half?"

"I just heard. I don't know what I'm willing to do."

"What do you mean she's not like me?"

"You could have a child on your own. I wouldn't worry about you."

"You have no idea how wrong you are."

We sat in silence. On top of everything else, I was shocked that anyone would think I could raise a child on my own. I barely kept my own life together. That I was sitting there seemed evidence enough.

"Okay, well. I need to get going," I said.

I took my mug to the kitchen. I started crying, the blurred vision a comfort. He put his hands on my shoulders.

"I'm sorry," he said.

"Don't apologize. It's just as well."

I didn't turn around. He took his hands away and left behind cold handprints. I could still smell us and feel our lovemaking. The universe was mocking.

"I'll call you," he said.

"No. Please don't say that."

Rex's toenails clicked on the stone floor, the door opened and closed. Just like that. Given and taken. In an instant, a faulty altitude reading, a mountain in the darkness. I stood frozen at the sink until I heard the gate latch.

FIVE

"I should have known from the second I met him," I said. "A truck driver, what was I thinking?"

Karin had come right away.

"Does it matter what he does?" she asked.

"It feels like it now."

"It sounds like he's a good guy, he's stepping up," she said.

"I know, I know. I get it. It's all very noble."

"What's the alternative? We can't have it both ways."

"I can't have it any way."

"That sounds a little crazy. You have Steve."

"Steve and I don't have that. He said he doesn't have it with her either."

"Would you really want children with him?"

"It's the first time it felt like the right idea. I've never felt that before. It was like, I don't know, that's all some part of me wanted."

"I know, but would you be okay taking a truck driver to parties?"

"He taught biology, he's not just a truck driver."

"He is now, that's what people would see. Your mother sure wouldn't like it."

"It's not my mother's life, " I said.

"I'm just being realistic. You're the one who brought up his job."

"Do you ever wonder what would have happened if you hadn't gotten pregnant with Oscar?"

"I don't know what would have happened to us. But my parents would like their own lives better."

"They love your kids."

"They'd love them more if their father was a white guy from the country club."

We were quiet again.

"He said he wouldn't worry if it was me who was pregnant," I said.

"Because? It would still be just as much his. It's not just about the kids. It's a lot of work."

"I don't know. He says she's still a girl."

"There's no way to even begin to make sense of that. Sometimes I think it's the girls who have it easy; that's all they want."

"I can't imagine having a child on my own. I can barely imagine it with someone. Steve's been talking about having children."

"Steve? He's never struck me as the father-type."

"What does Oscar think of all this?"

"He wants you to have it, that energy. But he told me that if I ever considered taking the kids, he'd lock me in a closet until they're grown. He understands about raising your own kids. It would make him nuts to think another man was raising his kids, even a little bit."

"He's a good guy. Let's go, it helps to work. I don't want to sit at home."

We locked up and headed downtown. My phone rang, A. Watts. I didn't want a message from him. I hit answer and end with two quick jabs. I did not want to talk. My ex-husband used to talk until I wanted to cry with confusion and frustration. I did not want tenderness, or pointless silences. We didn't need talk then, and we don't need it now. I glanced at the screen and realized I hadn't heard from Steve after his dinner with Eric and Anna.

Shooting was over; everyone was laid, dead or got a cookie. We started the tedious process of packing up and labeling everything to be sent to prop storage on the lot. Over the next week we would clean up our files of photos and notes to be buried somewhere with all the other dead television shows. If someone two thousand years down the road could figure out how to read our flashdrives, they could recreate Layla's world, not to be confused with the real world, or maybe it is. I was beginning to feel like Vampire Chick. I'd been snotty with creepy David, but I didn't want to spend my life rubbing them out alone either. I needed an agent to jump down the throat of who ever was writing my sex life.

Steve left me a message that he'd caught a flight home a day early and was headed over to my place to swim some laps; he'd pick up dinner. He'd had a great time with Eric and Anna. Eric had left a message that they approved of Steve, even after he'd taken them to Chinatown for cooked chicken feet, not something you see every day in La Jolla.

I was looking forward to seeing Steve, happy that he was back so I could stop thinking about what had happened, and rededicate myself to getting on with my life and his education. I walked in the front door to him sitting in the chair Stroud and I had rocked the night before, drinking a Mexican beer.

"Welcome home," I said. "Did you swim yet?"

I went over to give him a kiss but he held his arm out to keep me away.

"You drink bad Mexican beer now?" he asked.

"A friend stopped by, he brought it."

"A friend?"

"Well, not a friend really."

I started the story of Grandma's hearse, but he cut me off.

"Eric and Anna told me about it."

I shrugged, "So you know. He came into town and I took him to dinner. I felt like I owed him that much."

"What else did you owe him?"

"What do you mean?"

Cold guilt was making my lungs contract. I could hardly breathe. I couldn't imagine Eric and Anna being anything but polite and discrete.

"You just couldn't wait could you?"

"Wait for what?"

"Until we figured things out."

He got up and put his empty bottle on the counter next to a take-out bag. He didn't look at me again.

"You should take out your trash." He walked out the door.

I watched him walk up the steps and out the gate. Take out the trash? I didn't know what he was talking about. I looked in the kitchen trash. There was nothing but take out containers and a few empty beer bottles. I went in the bathroom. The trashcan had a half dozen empty and crinkled up condom wrappers and the empty box folded flat. I saw a flash of Stroud doing that after he had emptied the rest of them in the top drawer of the night-stand. I sat down on the toilet seat and stared at the image. I tried to imagine how Steve had felt. I don't know what I would have done were it me. Thrown it at him maybe, but probably not. Presbyterians don't throw things. I felt sick to have done that to him.

There was no way to undo it. I couldn't think of one thing I could say to him that could put a dent in the picture he was carrying around. I got my phone to call Karin and sat down in the chair. I couldn't punch in her number; I couldn't talk. I was barely breathing. My throat felt swollen shut. My skin itched like I was breaking out in hives.

I searched under the bed where I found two more wrappers. There was one under the chair. I wondered if he'd noticed that. I emptied all the trashcans, and carried the bags outside to the big can.

I swam laps, breathing on both sides; it's like a meditation. I pushed myself harder every time thoughts of Stroud, and of Steve holding that vision, tried to insinuate themselves into my brain. I stopped, my heart slammed. Despite the cool air, my face felt on fire like a shameful blush. My core systems were beating their drums while my brain went off to war with itself. I floated under the starless sky, my mind trapped in circles of thought that led nowhere. It was engaged in feints and skirmishes to avoid feeling hollow shame and futility. I'd felt this when I was married. One of the only things that got me through those days and nights was telling myself that it wouldn't always be like this. At the moment, all these years out, all I could hear was that it would. It would always be like this.

I went to bed. I hadn't changed the sheets; they were steeped in the dense odor of us. The bed pulsed with lust and fresh humiliation. My stomach was in a knot. I stripped it down and put on clean sheets. I had to get up a second time and throw the pile outside. Even across the room, I could smell us. I finally stopped trying to sleep at 5:00 a.m. and booted up my computer. Eric had sent pictures that someone had taken of them all eating in New York. There was one of the three of them in the back of a cab; the driver had taken it from a crazy angle. They all looked happy, and grown up, and like they knew what they were doing.

I made coffee and ate a banana so I could take a painkiller. I had terrible cramps. My mother said having a baby had put an end to those for her. I'd always been plagued by stomach clutching, couch writhing cramps. Not the best reason to have a baby, but on these days, it hit the top of the chart.

It was hours before I needed to be at work, so I went to the car wash. I paged through a soggy year-old *People* about people who make a living airing out their tawdry shit in public. I over-tipped the man with the silver-capped teeth who dried my car. I got to the set so early the catering people were just setting up. I started in dismantling Vampire Chick's set; I felt a special tenderness for her. Karin arrived on time and found me working.

She looked at my face. "It will pass. When does Steve come home?"

"Steve's back. He came home a day early."

She sat down on the couch and looked off into space while I told her the story.

"I feel like I got you into this," she said.

"Don't be ridiculous, I got myself into this."

"But I kept going on about calling him and hot sex."

"I'd love to blame you, believe me. But as my last therapist said, if I blame you then you're in control of my life."

"She was talking about your mother."

"Okay fine. It's your fault."

"What a clusterfuck," she said.

"That pretty much covers both bases."

She glanced at me over that remark. I wasn't completely gone.

"Are you going to call Steve?"

"And say what? Why'd you come home early and look in my trash? I can't imagine how that must have felt."

"I can. He wouldn't take your call anyway."

We spent a subdued afternoon working. I was pounding down painkillers.

I spent the evening cleaning house. I washed the sheets again, scrubbed the bathroom, and vacuumed and mopped up every trace of dog hair and ash. I opened the windows and burned sage. I cleaned out the fireplace and even the refrigerator. I drank beer and listened to Vivaldi traverse the four seasons in endless cycles. It sounded neutral, even though Steve and I had heard a chamber quartet perform it under the blue vaulted and gold starred ceiling of the Chapel of St. Chappell in Paris. The stone floors had been cold but I'd insisted on wearing a skirt with new curvy-heeled silk shoes. I knew he liked the look. I had caught a cold. I took a shower and opened a second beer; it helped pry loose the fingers dug in and squeezing my belly.

I got on-line and deleted all the jokes, inspirational angel crap and cute puppies. I dumped the it's-a-beautiful-world slideshow with Japanese subtitles, bad dissolves and sappy music. Out went my most ardent suitor, a guy in Nigeria who still wanted to give me sic million dolars US$ if I'd just send him a few bucks. I was left with nothing but pictures of smiling, well-adjusted grown-ups eating chicken feet.

I recognized the shrill place I was sliding toward. I'd been there after my divorce. Even a bad relationship leaves the yawning void. I could end up like a bird that accidentally flies into the house and, frantic to get away, keeps banging against the window, injuring itself on the promise of freedom. It's the place where you cut off your hair, exhaust your friends with second-guessing, and try to force the passage of time by taking up short-lived hobbies, drinking too much at parties, and no joy fucking random, ideally unavailable, men. I would call Margaret first thing in the morning and get busy with work and India. Maybe I could short circuit the impulse to take up wood burning.

Our work would be finished in a week and I couldn't afford

to spend time unemployed. I had rent to pay and a staggering repair bill for a car I hated. The last thing I wanted now was to lose my home base. Despite the Stroud debacle, home still felt safe. I'd sublet so I wouldn't have to give it up.

Everyone had talked at lunch about where they were headed for their winter break. I still wanted to go to Hawaii. Might as well pull the scab off my Visa bill along with the rest of my life. I did a quick search on the off chance I could find something; nope, not at that late date.

The next day we jammed all morning. I called Margaret over lunch to tell her my decision about India.

"How's Steve taking it?" she asked.

"Steve and I broke up."

"We didn't think he'd take it well."

"We didn't break up over India. I strayed off the path."

"We wondered about that too."

"You wondered if I was straying? I only took a few steps. I barely knew it."

"We wondered if it was enough. We'll have plenty of time to talk about it. I'm so happy you'll be with us. What an adventure."

Ed was going with us. He'd started going with Margaret after he retired from production at one of the networks. He found a hobby in every location. He cooked for us. He entertained visiting family and friends who never understood we really were working. He kept the home fires burning, so to speak. Margaret was in her mid-70s; it would probably be her last big foreign country work. They were going to New York for the holidays and then we would put in a month working in L.A. before heading to Delhi. I needed to contact the production office to set up the logistics.

"I'm still thinking about going to Hawaii," I said. "Might as well make my pauper status official."

"Good for you," she said. "It will all work out."

"Do men only like kittens?"

Margaret chuckled her experienced broad sound.

"Your mother. Men like any feline that shows up and acts interested. That's never been your problem. It's your choice of tomcats that gets you into trouble. Someone will come, maybe a nice Indian man; that could be interesting. Which reminds me; don't worry about packing a lot. We should buy clothes when we get there if we want to look like we know what we're doing. Ed plans to live in their man pajamas. Go have fun in Hawaii."

An Indian man? Talk about geographically undesirable. Steve had left a voice message to call him. I didn't want a work-day fight; my ex-husband loved those. He'd even call me at work at the six-month mark to ask for a divorce. He was, if nothing else, consistently full of shit.

I ignored Steve and went back to putting the last stuff in boxes. A few hours later he texted: "call me Hannah." I figured I'd call when I got home, but at 4:00 there was another text: "stop fucking around & call me." Okay okay.

"Where are you?" he asked.

"I work."

"We need to talk about this."

"I'm sorry. I don't know what else there is to say. It happened."

"Meet me for a drink later."

"I don't want to drag this out."

"Me either, just meet me."

We agreed to meet at Musso and Franks after work. I told Karin and she just shook her head.

"Nothing good can come of this," she said.

"You sound like Shakespeare or somebody. We're having a drink at Musso's so he can tell me what a deceitful bitch I am. I owe him that."

She rolled her eyes just like Binky.

"Your guilt. Are you sure you're not Jewish? Has he ever been rough with you?"

"Don't be ridiculous," I said.

I found Steve at the bar. I ordered a martini straight up. We sipped in quiet, looking at each other in the mirror behind the bar. It struck me that I looked much younger than Steve, even though he was only a few years older. His face was taking on angles that would soon be called craggy. A producer and his wife whom he knew came by; they said hello before going to their table. He didn't introduce me. I felt tired like a person does when they've been boing boinging around in different dimensions. I finished my drink and Steve indicated two more to the bartender.

"I'm not going to just sit here and get drunk," I said. "I'm sorry."

He turned on his stool and looked at me. It was a strange look, like he was seeing me for the first time, and not seeing me at all. The bartender put drinks in front of us.

"I'm so pissed about this," he said. "I can't think about anything else."

I don't know what sadistic punishment is hidden in the cheerful sounding words 'face the music', probably suffering through a full bugle rendition of taps before being delivered by gun fire. I hoped the second martini would dull the bullets about to thud into my body.

"I know we never said we're exclusive. I met someone in New York, a lawyer. Our parents are friends."

"But you had dinner with my brother."

"I like your brother and Anna. That's why I came back early."

"They liked you too, even with the chicken feet."

We were back looking past bottles and glasses at each other's reflection in the bar mirror. People were happy in the background.

"So it worked out anyway," I said.

"A truck driver?"

"Would a lawyer make it okay?"

"Nothing happened with her."

"Me either," I said.

"Yeah, right."

"I should go," I said.

"You can't drive."

"I'll call a cab."

"Stay, we'll have dinner, it'll be okay." He indicated that we were moving to a table where a red-coated waiter resettled our drinks and left menus.

"Tomorrow is our last day," I said.

"Then what? Visit San Diego?"

"I'm going to Kauai. Then India."

We ate in silence; it was so tense I had trouble swallowing. The couple stopped by to say goodnight; they looked at me. Steve ignored an introduction. We had coffee to wait out the full-blast of the martinis, and then walked out to the parking lot in back. He gave the valet both our tickets and tipped him when the cars appeared idling behind us.

"You can have the Maui place. My plans changed, we're going to Baja."

"No thanks, I like Kauai better anyway."

I made it home.

Karin came in for coffee the next morning. She was glad it hadn't turned into the gruesome showdown she had envisioned. He wouldn't do that in public anyway. We ran down to the studio and did our final mop up and check out on the project. It's nice when it ends, but it's also like getting a divorce. It leaves a hole.

Karin dropped me back home and I swam laps. I got out of the shower to a message from Mom. She wanted to talk about a dress for a New Year gala. I could remember her dressing for parties. My father always sat in one of their bedroom chairs, sipping a cocktail and watching her while they kidded back and forth. I reminded her to get some comfortable shoes so she could actually dance.

"Arthur will never replace your father."

"Do you feel guilty about seeing Arthur? It's been a long time."

"He had an affair."

"Arthur? I don't think you can really consider it an affair so soon, Mom."

"Your father. We had settled it between us a week before he crashed. I hadn't really forgiven him though. And now I don't know if I ever will."

"It doesn't matter to him."

"It matters to me. I've been mad at him all these years."

"That's a heavy burden, Mom."

"What if he was distracted about her?"

"Are you jealous that he might have been thinking about her when he crashed?"

"He felt he needed to get home, it was still so raw. I was still accusing him of seeing her, even though he said it was over. He was going to wait for daylight, but I told him I needed him to come home that night. He tried. He wanted to reassure me."

"There's no way you will ever know."

"You don't understand, Hannah."

"I understand you can't possibly know what he was thinking when he hit that mountain."

"Except, Oh Jesus."

"Atta girl, Mom. You should just enjoy Arthur. He's standing right in front of you."

"I didn't expect love advice from my daughter."

"It's not love advice. I wouldn't take love advice from me if I were you. Send pictures."

What a reversal. I remember my mother as the towering woman, at least when she was sober, issuing edicts from atop her high heels, the force of her mother's coal mine stories at her back. I was incredibly proud of myself for not stoking her fire with questions about my father's affair. What the fuck? I speed dialed my brother.

"We had a great time with Steve."

"I heard. We had dinner last night. When he wasn't with you, he was doing, quote nothing, with a Jewish lawyer his parents fixed him up with."

"Oh."

"Did you know daddy had an affair?"

"Who told you?"

"Mom."

"Was she slurring or had she hit maudlin?"

"She sounded cold sober. Why didn't you tell me?"

"It didn't matter. I didn't want to make him look bad."

"It did matter, Eric. I've spent twenty years thinking he was a saint."

"What difference does it make? He was a decent man."

"It makes a big difference. I needed to know that."

"I was seventeen."

"You haven't been seventeen for twenty years. Mom's been mad at him for twenty years. She thinks he was distracted thinking about the other woman when he crashed."

"Maybe he was. I didn't know she was using that."

"Well it's really sad," I said. "He was supposed to come home the next day, in daylight."

"You knew that. She's probably said it a million times."

"But I didn't know why. She blames herself."

"She would have found something to drink about," he said. "She was already drinking when he crashed. That may have been part of their problem."

"Why do you say that?"

"Years later I ran into a bartender who knew him. He said Dad used to stop in for a drink. He told him he had a beautiful wife at home, but that he was lonely."

"And you believe some bartender?" I asked.

"Yeah, I do, it was completely unsolicited. She was good at hiding it."

"Does Binky know about the affair?"

"Christ no. If Binky knew, you'd know. She'd drive Ted insane."

"He's already insane, he lives with her."

"It's easier for him right now."

"Anything else you're holding out?"

"Not off the top of my head," he said. "What happened with Stroud?"

"Oh fuck," I told him the basics. I left out details like frequency and thong handcuffs; you never know how it's going to blow with a brother.

"Sorry, Hannah, men are dicks."

"One woman's dick is another woman's almost husband."

"Yeah well, I'm your brother and he's a dick. You need to knock off the men with two names."

"At least neither one of them had a rap sheet. He said Mom packs a coochie and knows how to use it."

He was quiet for a second. Uh oh. Then he burst out laughing. That's what I mean about never knowing which way it's going to blow.

"You're such a man."

He laughed harder and choked out, "Oh Jesus, I love that. I gotta go."

I was smiling when I hung up. It's always fun when he laughs; he sounds a lot like our father. I fixed toast and peanut butter, drank the last beer, and went to bed.

My heart hurt for my lonely father with his eyes locked on the deep space of his interior life, instead of scanning in ten second intervals like a careful pilot. He should have been looking for the future that was slipstreaming toward him over the nose of the plane.

I understood how he could have been lost in thought, perhaps longing, perhaps guilt, perhaps in despair, when the mountain came out of the darkness; a permanent solution to a temporary problem. Maybe if I'd been in the plane, chattering away as usual, he'd have seen it. He was always extra careful when I was in the plane with him. Maybe my mother wouldn't have been worried about him being away overnight if I'd been with him. The things we can't know.

Saturday night was our wrap party. I arrived late. Karin and Oscar were there, listening to the director regale everyone with character sketches from rehab, only in L.A. There were a few non-pros, significant others who were not in the business. Unless they had a spectacular job like rocket scientist or star hot yoga instructor, they were simply pitied. A truck driver would be pitied. Steve would have been bored silly. A half hour television flop isn't his world. The evening was dragged down with false cheer. I left before dinner and was home by eight.

I was heating up soup when Steve called. "Where were you? I stopped by."

"You need to call first."

"I wanted to see you."

"I was at the wrap funeral."

"You free?"

"No. I need to go to bed, I'm completely worn out."

"Trucker there?"

"He's getting married."

"I really don't give a shit what he's doing."

"Have fun in Baja," I hung up.

I hated that I had devolved into talking like a teenager. I'd never talked like that even when I was sixteen. Not that I'd had a chance. I always figured no one asked me out because my father was dead and my mother was drunk. Hesitant young boys don't have experience with prisoners of war. It's not a practice step you should skip. I'd run into plenty of old boys since then. They didn't hesitate. I'd been unprepared.

As pissed as I was at Steve, I wasn't feeling Swiss neutral about him in Baja drinking margaritas and dirty dancing to some funky gray beard ex-pat band playing "Hotel California." Or about the image of tequila charged blowjobs on the outer fringe of bar light on the beach. That had been our scene when we were first getting to know each other. It's where we met. Message delivered.

I decided to check again for a place on Kauai. Kismet. There was a small cottage on the beach in a residential neighborhood. It was a little pricey. The owner had just reposted it after the first people backed out. I gave her my credit card information. Then

I booked a flight and reserved a car. My credit card whimpered. It's hard to be a flailing bird in Hawaii. If nothing else, I'd just stay outside, avoid windows altogether.

I took the next morning to Christmas shop in Santa Monica. I was dead in debt, might as well be buried. I came home with bags, lit a fire, and turned on slack key Christmas music. I spent hours carefully wrapping gifts for Karin's and my family. I love shopping for her kids. I got her sweet brainiac Richard the expanded Jurassic Era science kit. I used a sprig of dinosaur plant as his bow. He'd get it. He'd been studying an era a year; he was on Jurassic, a real crowd pleaser. Their daughter Callie was a total jock who wore nothing but pink. I bought her a pink mitt and a shirt from some over-priced sports designer that all the girls wanted but Karin wouldn't buy.

I bought myself a black tee shirt with angel wings silk-screened in glittery silver ink on the back. It didn't look like anything I'd wear.

I called Karin and invited her to our annual Christmas lunch, then kicked back for a few minutes and took in the view across my pool. I was going to miss waking up there, but I could feel myself detaching and moving toward India. I'm a chameleon when I travel, nine months could transform me into an Indian.

Steve called and broke my reverie.

"I'm done," I said. "Todos completo."

"That's lousy Spanish."

"It's better than your Puerto Rican gibberish."

"Let's have dinner," he said. "I don't want to end in some bullshit fight. We were too good for that."

He was going to Santa Fe for a few days so we made a plan for Friday night.

I had a haircut appointment with my favorite guy. They had an opening with a new nail person, and so I bought in for the whole ride. He cut my hair quite a bit shorter and chopped it up to give it some edge, then added chunky highlights. It would be easy in Hawaii; it looked like I'd just gotten caught in an especially rough wave. I could probably cut it that way myself in India.

I thought of my moaning toe with Stroud as the new pedicure person worked. I bet she heard about as much as a bartender or hooker. I asked her what she'd heard on the subject of men knowing how to find the sweet spot. I fully expected her to give me a blank look so I was shocked by her response. She pushed back on her rolling chair, spread her legs, and pointed a pink cuticle stick at her crotch.

"I could take this stick and point right at it," she said. "And they'd miss it, on purpose. I made a list once when I was twenty. I'd slept with so many guys I had to make columns. I can tell you they are a lazy bunch. They either don't know how or just plain won't give you what you want. The guy I'm with now knows where to find it, but he's complete asshole otherwise."

"Is that worth it?" I asked.

"I'm kicking him out tomorrow," she said. "He doesn't know it yet."

"She doesn't know it yet either," said the other nail person. "She says that every other day."

"This is the week," said my woman.

She spent an entire pedicure on male sexual incompetence while her work friend nodded along, and the woman next to me asked for her boyfriend's number. Apparently it's a rare man who has the patience or interest to spend the required amount of time at the site of love, war, or as one of her clients put it, the call button, of the female anatomy. Stroud said it was like tangling with a hot otherworldly force. Maybe you have to teach biology to hang with that.

I dragged the discouraging sex news to Christmas lunch with Karin. I'd worn black jeans and boots, and my new winged tee shirt. In honor of the holiday I'd wound a red scarf shot through with silver thread around my neck. I thought it was festive. Karin thought I looked like a trashy biker chick fresh from shock treatments.

She was glad I hadn't gone all out and shaved my head over Stroud. I told her I wouldn't give him the satisfaction. She doubted he was getting satisfaction. I fought back a sweep of longing sadness. It would be a while before that fire was out.

I told her about the pink-stick-pointing pedicurist living with the asshole Don Juan. She understood about the magnetic force of a man who's great in bed, and Oscar wasn't an asshole. Even with them, there'd been a definite transition period between the time she went off just looking at Oscar, and the time after two kids and exhaustion had set in. It was one of the reasons she hadn't married him for she thought it left some tension between them. They had worked it out; they knew how to take care of each other.

She wondered what I was doing with Steve, why the dinner. I told her we were going to finally finish it without the drama.

She looked at me. "Are you sure you're finished? It sounds like you're jealous about the lawyer."

"I'm not. I know it's not right with Steve. It will be good for me to end it like a grown up for a change."

"Huh. It sounds like it's the lawyer. Would you feel the same way if it hadn't been a truck driver?"

"What difference does that make?"

"I didn't say it did, you did."

"I don't want to talk about it anymore. I hate the whole going over men thing."

We exchanged gifts to open on Skype Christmas morning. We talked about work and about our great woman Senator who we both thought should be president. Proof positive we weren't stuck on my problems with men.

I spent the rest of the week doing research. I went down to the Indian district in town and let my senses roam free. My nose explored spices and incense. My skin studied silks and soft cottons. My eyes searched the surfaces of brass and pierced wood. It was an impressionistic journey that sidestepped the detail and list-making gatekeeper.

I took home chai and burned incense while I built a notebook for each location. I sketched ideas. I'd tossed the weary Greek chorus and spread my work out on the dining room table. Then I opened a folding table for more space. I could have moved into our office on the lot, but Margaret was gone and it felt good to work at home while I could.

Friday arrived and Steve wanted to try a new place in Beverly Hills. I'd heard it was funky casual so I reprised my angel shirt and red scarf over a long black skirt. He arrived looking handsome and smelling of his own aftershave. He glanced at my hair, but didn't say anything. He traced the angel wings with his finger while I poured wine.

"This is a different look," he said. "I like it."

"The new me. I surprised myself. Karin says between the shirt and the hair I look like a trashy biker chick slash mental patient."

"Or hooker."

I turned to look at him over that stray bullet, but he was

already walking away.

"Did you just call me a hooker?"

"I was kidding. You look great."

We sat by the fire and caught up. New Mexico had been cold; he'd found editing rooms and a little house. I told him my plan to sublet my house in case he heard of anyone.

We kept our dinner conversation light and focused on work.

"When are you leaving?" he asked.

"The 18th. I'm coming back right after the New Year. How about you?"

"We're staying less than a week. She needs to get back."

"Sounds like it's moving fast. Your mother must be happy."

"I don't want this," he said.

"Sorry, I didn't mean that like it sounded."

"That's not what I meant," he said.

The waiter came and we split a lemon tart for dessert before heading back up the dark canyon to my house. He walked me down to the door. When I turned to say good night he took my head in his hands and kissed me. The kiss didn't match the dinner conversation. It had a tinge of aggression. It was strangely comforting on top of the brooding sense of loss.

"Would you like some port?" I asked.

"Yeah."

I got the fire started up again while he poured into the tulip-shaped glasses we'd bought when we had gone through a port phase a few months before. I took off my boots and sat in the chair across from him.

"I heard the strangest thing this week. My father had an affair right before he died. And all this time I thought he was a saint."

I'd said it before I realized what an incredibly awkward thing it was to say under the circumstances. Guilty people leak all over the place.

"Did they work it out?" he asked.

"They didn't have time."

We sat sipping and looking at the fire. The lit pool water cast overlapping and undulating scales of reflection across the ceiling like a blue snake in one of the many hands of a Hindu goddess.

"I should go," he said. "I'm glad we did this."

"Me too."

I followed him to the door; I was surprised by how much it felt like tearing away to know he was leaving for another woman.

"I'm sorry we didn't have time," I said.

He slid his arm around my waist and pulled me in tight. "We have time."

"But?"

"It was nothing," he said. "I told you that."

He was looking at me as he backed me across the room to the bed and pushed down on my shoulders to sit on the edge. He stood over me looking down. I unzipped his jeans and he pushed me in by the back of my head. He wanted an apology. He told me to turn over. He pushed my skirt over my hips then wrapped an arm around my waist and lifted me to my knees with my face buried in the covers.

He tore aside my underpants and pushed into me while he shoved my hand between my legs and said, "Do yourself." I did.

There is immense power in penance mixed with sex. My face was buried in the bed but he could still hear me in ways he'd never heard before. I'd never heard any of his sounds either. Like frightened animals in call and response. Remorse tried to calm hurt, his fury heard placating, fear washed back and forth between us like echoes until it was over. He lay down on my back while our heart rates slowed. I could feel the outline of heavy inked angel wings crushed between us.

He put his mouth to my ear. "Don't ever, ever, do that again."

He rolled off of me, turned me over, and held me close. He kissed my temple. We were still dressed, though my skirt was twisted up around my hips.

We were quiet in our own thoughts. I was trying to make sense of it. It felt like he had just reclaimed me somehow, like I should go to New Mexico, stop running away from hard things. Part of me, my gut, was frightened by what had just happened. Not afraid that he would hurt me physically, but that there was a trap in it all. I wanted to run.

He got up and pulled down my skirt. He tucked in his shirt, zipped his pants and buckled his belt. Confused frames of emotion flickered like a silent movie across his face. My absolution had been brief.

Someone once told me it's always better to be the one asking for forgiveness. Watching his face, I knew it wasn't that simple. I thought about my mother, left holding the whole thing. I wondered if we really had the time. He put on his jacket and walked out the door, engaging the lock as he closed me in.

I didn't hear from him all weekend. I felt relief mixed with unease. I wasn't ready for that again, and I was. We needed to get some connections behind us to get back on track. Was there a track?

Six

Anna called on Monday morning. She said all was good with the kids. Their oldest, Adam, was getting ready to go to the prom. Eric and Anna had gone to the prom together; they'd seemed so grown up. It was right after our father died; as Eric said, he was only seventeen. They'd married out of college and never looked back.

"I assume Eric told you about Mom's coochie," I said.

"He couldn't stop laughing. He even broke up in church. Mom and Arthur were with us, which only made it worse. Every time Mom asked if he was okay, he'd start in again. It was a relief when they went home."

"I plan to come down before Christmas, drop off presents."

"Sounds great. Is Steve coming?"

"I don't know what's going on with us. He found out about the truck driver."

"I'm so sorry, Hannah."

"Did Eric tell you he met someone in New York?"

"Yes, it sounds like it's gotten pretty confused. He said at dinner that you two had started talking about having kids."

"He did. It was out of the blue. I can't see that happening. I don't even know if I want children."

"I can understand that, we're living with two accidents. For a while there we were worried that I'd gotten pregnant in New York."

"Would you have a caboose?"

"No no no. We talked about it for days, neither one of us wanted to start all over. We've replaced ourselves. I'm going back to law school. Your brother says he has too much gray hair already. He says having two teenagers now is hard enough. Knowing there was another coming when he's old and feeble would mean years of listening to that whine bombs make right before they hit you."

"I think it's the ones you don't hear that get you, but I get it," I said. "Was he actually going to go with you to the doctor?"

"No, we were going to ask you," she said. "He said he'd be fine going, but we both knew he'd just be trying to man up; he doesn't have any control over his squeamishness."

My brother may have a high-powered brain, but when he was in the delivery room while Anna was having their first child, the minute the full parade came into view and he saw firsthand the gush of water, the blotchy wax covered alien with the strangely blinking eyes, and the after-birth, coupled with the dirty looks she was giving him, he'd ricocheted out of the room, and keeled over in a planter. It took five stitches to close the gash in his forehead. He still had a scar.

"I'm leaving in a week," I said, "so I'll be down in the next few days."

I was packing gifts in bags for each family when Steve walked in the next afternoon. Having him walk in unannounced was disconcerting in that place between then and an unclear now. His face was more composed than the last time I'd seen him. He kissed me like the last weeks had never happened.

"I'm sorry," he said. "I think we should start over."

"Me too," I said. "I'm going to San Diego to drop gifts. Want to go? Meet the family? See Eric and Anna?"

"Let me think about it," he said. "I'm kind of in the middle of things."

We swam laps and went out to dinner. He got in bed to read while I worked. I was so engrossed I didn't notice he'd dropped off to sleep. I got undressed and stood looking down at him. He slept. He didn't lift the blankets to invite me in.

I had a memory of my parents doing that when I was a little girl with a nightmare. No words. They just lifted the blanket to invite me into the safety of their nest. I'd had lots of nightmares after my father died. There was a mirror over my bed. When I woke up in the night I could see my father's face in the mirror; it was a distorted and frightening mask. I used to scream and scream until my mother came into my room. Her only comfort was to say, "You're just upset." Like 'just upset' screaming isn't somehow really, seriously, fucking upset. I slid in with my back next to Steve.

We woke up and had lazy front to back sex. What Karin calls general maintenance.

"What do you think?" I asked. "You want to go?"

"Yeah, time to meet your family."

We packed his car with gifts and then dropped by his house for fresh clothes. I sat down at his desk to call my family. There was an envelope postmarked in New York on the desk with photos on top. They were pictures of him with the woman in New York. She was lovely and looked happy. They both did. His arm rested casually around her waist. It might have been a family affair; some kid was hamming it up by sticking his head in frame and making the peace sign. There was another of just her in Central Park; Steve must have taken it. The wind was blowing her dark, even hair. The card was signed with just a lipstick kiss and XXX. I felt like I'd been kicked in the stomach. I know chemistry doesn't care about bank accounts, but I could hear his words. She was no truck driver. He was standing in the door watching me; we held each other's eyes.

"I'm going down alone," I said.

"Come on, Hannah, our families were around."

"Your arm is around her waist."

"That's the only place it was. I don't think we should start comparing notes and going backwards here."

He swept up the card and photos and dropped them in the trashcan, then took my hand and pulled me from the chair.

"I can't control what she does," he said.

We traveled in depressed quiet. I spent most of the drive looking out the window. Steve kept reaching over and holding my hand.

We got to my mother's at 12:00. She and Arthur were thrilled to see us. I put their gifts under the tree while Mom and Arthur made small talk with Steve. I felt like I was floating on the periphery; a place with only a wispy thread connected to their grounded society. Steve kept glancing at me while they chatted; so much was unsettled between us.

We were on the road again at 2:00. Mom gave Steve a hug and told him how nice it was to finally meet him. Arthur was hail and hearty. He and Steve looked like they bought their clothes in the same places. I'm sure my mother approved of Steve. They wished us a happy holiday in Hawaii. I didn't bother to tell her that I had no idea whether or not we were going together.

We had a quick lunch in Del Mar then headed to Binky's. Ted was home. His hospital hours seemed random; you never knew when he was going to be around. I'm sure they knew his schedule; but to me he seemed almost ethereal in his wandering. Binky offered us a glass of wine. Steve accepted before I could catch his eye. She'd obviously had plenty already. I went in the kitchen to give her a hand. She yelled across their great room to Steve.

"So which one of Hannie's men are you, Steve?"

"Come on Binky," said Ted. "Don't start in with that." He came into the kitchen to see what he could do to shut her down.

"What? Hannah said she has four or five men."

"I was joking," I said.

The first approach was to play it straight, though I'd never known it to work with her.

"What happened to the trucker guy," she was using a stage whisper. "You two looked pretty hot and heavy. Ted, what was his name?"

"Alan I think, Binky," said Ted.

"Yeah, Alan," she said. "Mom said he had two names."

"Stroud," I said.

"We know, Binky," said Ted.

"Oh, Ted, shut up," said Binky.

"Mom saw him at Target with his wife," she said.

"That's nice," I said.

"Did you know he was married?" she asked.

"I knew he was getting married," I said.

"I thought you were his girlfriend," whispered Binky. She had spittle on her sweaty lips; lipstick was smeared on her teeth. Her breath was hot and sour. She used to be beautiful.

"You two looked pretty hot and heavy at the memorial." A drunk repeating herself, how I hate that.

"He brought Grandma, Binky," I said.

"Oh Hannah," she spewed, "Do you think I'm stupid?"

Steve walked into the kitchen, set down his full glass, and

said we better get on the road. It was artless, but we managed to escape in a matter of minutes.

We were quiet in the car as he put Eric and Anna's address in his GPS, as if I couldn't tell him how to get there. He stopped at the next corner and looked at me.

"Does the whole family know?" he asked.

"No one knows anything. He just brought Grandma. He was there maybe ten minutes. She's crazy."

We rode in silence.

"What difference does it make anyway?" I asked. "If I ever meet your family they'll all know about your woman, except that your family will hate me."

"My family will know about the lawyer daughter of a friend. They don't know anything anyway." Now he was looking out the window. "My family won't hate you."

"Oh please," I said.

We drove a few more miles in silence.

"Is there a lot to know?" I asked.

"I already told you."

We got to Eric and Anna's. The four of us walked along Prospect Street and ate dinner at a small place.

We said goodnight and checked into The Colonial Inn. Then we walked down to the park and sat in one of the small cliff huts in the dark and listened to the waves below until it got too chilly. We stopped in the hotel bar for a nightcap. It felt like we were stalling.

I got right in the shower and was just rinsing my hair when Steve got in. He soaped me all over and I did the same to him. He washed his hair and I buried my face in his chest hair to keep from getting soapy water in my eyes while he rinsed out shampoo. I dried my hair. I kept being surprised when I saw myself in the mirror. I had cut my hair after all. Karin was right about the shock treatment look; all the chopping away had released the natural curl. My smooth hair of the last few years was shooting off in wild directions. Lightning bolts of light pierced it like jittery brush strokes.

We made love like normal people. Or like we used to when we were normal people. Before all the drama, before I knew the difference between great sex and so-so sex. Before he knew the woman in New York with the dark blowing hair. At one point he was on top of me trying to smooth down my hair.

"I'm not sure about this haircut," he said.

"He got a little carried away."

We were laying on our backs in the dark; I had my leg stuck up in the air trying to catch the streetlight on my pedicure polish.

"What did you mean you can't be responsible for both of us," I asked.

"When?"

"In bed. You said you couldn't be responsible for both of us. I wonder what I'm not doing for you that you have to take care of. I don't want you to feel that way."

He was quiet.

"My husband used to call me frigid. Do you think I'm frigid?"

"What a thing to say."

"For him or for me?"

"For you. Why would you even ask that? My comment was a long time ago."

"I guess because you implied that I wasn't holding up my end of things. That you can't be responsible for both of us."

"I didn't mean you. I'm totally happy with you," he said.

"Then what did you mean?" I asked.

"I think the real question is how happy are you?" he asked.

"You weren't happy with me the other night," I said.

"I apologized. I was pissed. I'm trying to get past what you did. I'm still not there. I need us to have some normal days when we're not talking about this stuff."

We were quiet.

"You didn't answer my question," he said.

"I think we have some things to work on," I said. "But I'm happy."

"It's the things we need to work on that I was talking about."

"What would you do if I got pregnant?"

"We'll work it through. I'm not a big believer in abortion. I know that sounds Neanderthal."

"We'll both decide."

"I know," he said. "You asked."

We planned to head home the next morning but Aunt Judith called and invited us to lunch. I wanted to say no but Steve thought he had better meet all the players. They only lived a ten-minute walk from the hotel, at the other end of Prospect Street, in an old Spanish-style house that hung out over the cliff.

It's hard to tell now, but the street runs along the top of a cliff overlooking The Cove beach. Originally the waterside of the street had been lined with beach cottages. It was called the Green Dragon Colony and populated by artists and early beach bohemians. Over the years young people and couples moved in and then, one-by-one, the cottages were either torn down or dragged to new lots, and replaced by small commercial buildings. The funky and sagging green and red cottages, with their Asian rooflines, green lawns, and watercolor supplies piled on the porches, were replaced with shops full of metallic leather patchwork purses, and mid-range bronze reproductions of Remington-like cowboys and buffaloes, with a few eateries thrown in. I'd never seen a buffalo in La Jolla. I'd long ago stopped looking in the shops, they were a blur. They had nothing to do with my memory of La Jolla. The only memory that remained was the smell of eucalyptus resin underfoot mixed with salt air.

When they were first married, my parents lived in one of the original cottages, down the street from Judith and her first husband. My parents moved to the foothills when children started coming, but we always spent our summers at either The Cove or The Children's Pool. The Children's Pool was closed now, reclaimed by seals. And The Cove cliffs had developed such an intense bird stink it almost made your eyes water on hot days.

I remembered endless sunny days jumping off the cliffs behind the seawall. You had to time the waves just right. We were always on the look out for the dreaded eels that hid in the rocks. I'd only seen one friend with an eel locked on his foot. It's not something you forget. We dodged seagulls trying to get our peanut butter and jelly sandwiches while they crapped on our heads. We got sunburns so mind-boggling we couldn't bend our knees. The end of the day meant dragging towels up the hill to Judith's, sandy callused feet on heat-soaked sidewalks.

About once a week we'd pound abalone that Judith's second husband brought home from a dive off The Cove. You had to hit the tough muscle just so to make it something less than tire rubber. My mother had a great beer batter recipe for it. Everyone had abalone shells. They used them for ashtrays and soap dishes, and to line the tops of their adobe walls. Abalone is going extinct.

Our teen years were spent at the Shores and then Windansea or Sea Lane. Beach gangs out of range of our parents. In my case, I was never completely out of range of someone who knew Binky or Eric. It was a small town. I still knew my friends.

I'd had a boyfriend a few years before. He was from Los Angeles, but met me down at The Cove one summer afternoon.

He said he looked down on me reading down on the beach in a straw hat and big white shirt and thought he could take the woman out of La Jolla, but he couldn't take La Jolla out of the woman. For some reason, at the time, that sounded like there was something wrong with me. We didn't last long. Despite distance and changed landscape, the air still felt like home. If only Judith would move.

Judith had hung onto her house through two marriages and into her third. It was hidden behind a tangle of thorny Bougainvillea and mounds of Bird of Paradise. They kept the secret of its magic to themselves. You'd never know their funky front door, only a few feet from the street, opened onto a spectacular view up the coastline to Scripps Pier and beyond, disappearing into the seaspray haze. The house was small and impeccably kept up. Steve and I set out on foot to see them.

"It's strange to me that my grandmother was so courageous, buying a coal mine and all," I said. "Her daughters seem so soft."

"You think your mother's soft?"

"Don't you?"

"I wouldn't call her soft. She may be an alcoholic, but it took some guts to go back to school and start a career after your father died."

"It was that or starve."

"She could have moved in with her sister or mother. One of my aunts did that. Moved home to her mother with all her kids."

"I can see living with my grandmother. Judith would have been a nightmare."

"My aunt never had a life again."

"It still might have been better for me."

"I doubt it."

"She was always drunk, Steve, I don't know why you're defending her."

"Being drunk must have made it harder for her. There are worse things."

"Like what? She could have beaten me too? You don't know what you're talking about."

"I just think it could have been worse. You always talk like your father was your only parent. My cousins were raised by a bitter childlike woman; your mother is still alive."

"You're catching her sober. You have no idea. It was like I was her parent, not the other way around."

We walked in silence for a few minutes.

"You've never talked about your family before," I said.

"There's not much to talk about."

"What'd you think of Binky?"

"Binky could be a problem."

"Binky is mentally ill. She was a wonderful sister when we were little. How do you think our families would do meeting each other?"

"I don't know, he said. "My mother can be prickly."

"Wait until you meet Aunt Asp."

Aunt Judith was a few years older than my mother, tall, dark and calculating. She always criticized my mother. She had a biting tongue and a knack for stomping on my mother when her blonde openness dared to get too breezy. She never missed a chance to put down Binky or me. Eric's a man; he skates by untouched. Eric and I decided years ago that it's jealousy, pure and simple. Judith couldn't have the children her husband wanted. She always said her husband would have made a terrible father. We doubted she ever wanted children.

I don't know what having children had done to Bettina. It seemed she was always drunk now. She'd up the stakes from Mom who only drank after 5:00 p.m. Steve was right about that. Before 5:00 p.m. Mom was a successful and funny woman. After

5:00 p.m. she was a crying blackout drunk who blamed herself for my father's death, every single solitary night. It got very old. It was infuriating and impossible to stop. And until hearing about the affair and its aftermath, it was a total mystery to me why she thought she had any part in it.

I wondered which was worse: a mother you could count on being drunk all day, or my mother who disappeared in an alcohol blink every night. One is no hope you can count on; one is perpetually dashed hope you can count on. The latter is hard on an optimist. After the last few weeks with a sober mother, I thought a little sober time was better than nothing.

Aunt Judith opened her front door. Her stick thin body was dressed impeccably in trim slacks and a silk boat neck sweater. She was barefoot. She rarely wore shoes in the house. She took in Steve with an appraising look that said he passed the first hurdle, good clothes. She took me in.

"That haircut is unfortunate," she said.

"I didn't realize how carried away he was getting."

I made the introductions. Judith's husband came shuffling up behind her and got everyone past the front door and settled in the living room. He was the same age as Judith, but not aging well under her rule.

He offered coffee and passed figs stuffed with a very subtle cheese. Everything offered at their house is subtle and perfect. They spend exhausting amounts of time shopping for individual items at separate stores. Anna said no one with children would be so special about everything unless they were completely insane or didn't need sleep.

"So the burial ended up working out," said Judith. "I'm sorry we couldn't be there. We didn't expect everyone to go."

"It was very nice," I said. "Eric and Anna did a great job."

"Eric always does a great job."

Judith addressed Steve, "We had a trip planned. We decided to go ahead with that."

"Understandable," said Steve. "It sounds like things changed at the last minute."

I could see he was tense, waiting for the next big reveal about the trucker. Judith looked at me. It was the same look she got when she was judging the value of leather, or linen, or a piece of jewelry. She was deciding.

"It doesn't take much to change things in this family," she said. "I heard having the hearse break down made it an eventful day for everyone."

"It worked out," I grabbed another fig. "Have you met Arthur?"

"Apparently it did," she was holding on my eyes. "They were down for dinner last week with Bettina and Ted. He's very tall, not fun like your father."

"He is tall. Mom seems happy."

"Her new wardrobe is a little tacky. Your sister's a mess."

"Yes. I hope she gets sober too."

"Well, we'll see how long it lasts with your mother," she said. "Eric and Anna came by last week. I'm not sure what Eric sees in her, she has such English skin."

English skin? I felt like screaming. I love my sister-in-law. She is one of the nicest people I've ever known. My brother loves her to the bottom of his feet. Her English skin is beautiful and young, unlike Aunt Judith's. I hated that she talked about her like that. I felt hurt for her, even though she didn't know she was being trashed. I'm sure Judith never said anything to her face; it would infuriate Eric. She wouldn't risk that.

"They've been in love since they were sixteen," I said.

"Yes, well. She never let him out of her sight long enough for him to see what else was out there."

"They went to college on different coasts. He had a chance."

They served us a light lunch. It was pleasant enough, if you consider waiting for the axe to fall pleasant. Judith's husband is curious about everything. He had done some research on editing equipment so was prepared for a little tech talk with Steve.

"So you're Jewish, Steve," said Judith.

"I know," said Steve.

Something in his voice had shifted; he wasn't on the defensive anymore.

"My grandmother was Jewish, no one talks about it though," she said. "She quit her religion when she married my grandfather. He was Catholic."

"Did she convert to Catholicism?" asked Steve.

"No," she said. "He quit the church."

"Interesting solution," he said.

"What do you expect Hannah to do?" she asked.

"Why do you ask, Judith?" he asked.

"Well I assume you two are talking about marriage," she said.

"We aren't," I said.

"I see," she smiled.

"We've only talked about having children so far," said Steve.

"It would be like Hannah to do that," she said. "Have children without getting married."

"Hannah won't have my children without being married," he said. "What she decides about religion is up to her."

"That's good," she said. "She won't be left with a stray cat to raise like her mother."

"What are you talking about?" I asked. "Stray cat."

"That's what your grandmother called you," she said. "Your mother could have probably found a new husband, but you weren't a cute kitten anymore, you were a gangly cat. Men don't sign on for that."

"Grandma never said that," I said.

"You didn't really know her," she said.

"We'll keep you posted," said Steve. He looked at me. "We should head back and get on the road before it gets any later."

We were halfway back to the hotel before either of us spoke. I was still reeling from the idea that my grandmother had referred to me as a gangly cat. That I had been the reason my mother never found a new partner. I knew people had stopped inviting her to parties as soon as my father died. She was the young widow of a lively man, a threat in their world of couples. I wouldn't put it past Judith to say it just to take my grandmother away from me.

"You think Judith's soft?" he asked.

"I think she's weak under all that," I said. "Now you know why Eric and I call her Aunt Asp. I hate that she talks about me like I'm not sitting there. I wasn't thrilled that you were doing it either."

He smiled. "It was knee jerk. Her grandmother may have quit her religion, but she passed on everything else to Judith. My mother will love her. You could have waded in any time. You're going to need to learn to fight on your feet if you're going to survive in my family."

"I don't like the sound of that," I said.

I hate fighting. I'm no good at it. I just simmer then explode. We had a quiet drive home. He dropped me in front and I pulled out my overnight bag.

"Thanks for going," I said.

"It was interesting," he said. "We'll talk tomorrow."

Karin and I met for our weekly breakfast the next morning. I hadn't talked to her since the wrap party. They were hot into holiday preparations; the tree was up, the cookies were baked; her parents were arriving in a few days. She pushed her coffee aside and leaned in so she was close enough to talk without whispering.

"What part of this am I not getting? Steve goes to New York and bangs some lawyer just to make his mother happy. Then he comes back here, calls you a hooker and basically rapes you; and you feel like things are getting back to normal?"

"Don't be ridiculous. He didn't rape me, and it was only once. He said the woman in New York means nothing. I was doing the same thing here."

"First of all, you have no idea what it means to him, except he's getting laid at both ends. And not safely I might add. What the hell was that all about? And right after being with her. Totally shitty. Second, you were having the best sex of your life with an honest man who, unless you didn't tell me the truth, only played rape. He took care of you."

"He's upset that it was a truck driver," I said.

"Yeah, well, I hate lawyers."

"Steve is the right partner for me. We speak the same language. We'll be fine."

"Hannah, that is such pure bullshit. You're completely forgetting what it was like before all this. The impaling. You weren't speaking any language. I would hardly call you partners. A week ago you said you knew it wasn't right. That's why you ended up with Stroud in the first place."

"Did I tell you my father had an affair, right before he died. I just found out."

She was looking at me. "What's that have to do with anything?"

"I always thought he was a saint."

"So now you know he wasn't. Like everyone else on the

planet except Mother Teresa."

"Steve's been good to me."

"Not lately."

"We were okay. We've done a lot together."

"Then why are you hurting each other with other people?"

"It feels like this has caused a break through. I don't want to go backwards either."

"I'm not going to argue with you about it. I hope you're right," she said. "Let's have dessert, something that doesn't have red and green sprinkles."

We didn't talk about it anymore. Karin can be pretty hard-core when it comes to relationships. She always said she'd kick Oscar to the curb if he stepped out of line. But our situation was not as clear-cut as that; we'd both stepped out of line.

I went home, pulled out my suitcase and started packing for Hawaii. It doesn't require much. I was looking forward to sleep-read-float. Steve hadn't said anything more about Baja so, despite telling Karin that things were better, I really didn't know what he planned. He called and asked if he could come over.

I had a fire going while I listened to slack key and made piles for the trip. He swam and then took a shower. He came out of the bathroom in a robe, poured a glass of port and watched me pack.

"I'm going to Maui," he said. "Come with me."

"I've already committed to the place. I don't want to lose my money."

"I'll cover it. It's no big deal."

"It's a big deal to me, it's half a month's pay. Why don't you come to Kauai? The place isn't as big, but it looks funky and fun. It's right on the beach."

"I like Maui, there's more going on. I thought you'd like the pool."

"If there's ocean I don't care about a pool. What about Baja?"

"She was going anyway, she has friends there. I thought we put that behind us."

"Are you staying tonight?"

"I plan to."

We got in bed to just the firelight.

"I wish you'd come to Kauai," I said.

"Just come to Maui. Let's get back to some kind of normal before we both leave."

"Okay," I said.

We started out slowly; it had a lot more heat than the last few nights. There was that out-of-the-blue chemical buzz that comes around, Mother Nature's trick.

"Can I be on top?" I asked.

"Be my guest."

I was relieved to find the sweet spot with Steve. I had a wonderful time there. He didn't complain. On the contrary, he enjoyed the ride. It was fun and felt totally uncomplicated. When it was over I buried my head in his neck.

"That was nice," I said. "You want to do that again?"

He didn't say anything. I pulled away and was smiling when I looked at his face. He was looking at me like I was a stranger he knew. It was the same look he'd given me that night in Musso's. I rolled off him and lay on my back. I looked at the ceiling and wondered how long it would be, what it would take, to exorcise the ghosts. I wasn't the only one who had been out there. I felt humiliated to be there and apparently coming up short. My wild hair felt crazy on my head.

"This is stupid. You should go to Baja, that's what you really want."

"This has nothing to do with her."

"What then?"

"Maybe you're like your father except he died."

I was so shocked I didn't react at first.

"What did you say?"

He rolled over on top of me and held my arms. "Maybe it was just the first time."

I shoved him off me like he was an assailant. I had to kick at him to get him far enough away. He tried to fend me off, catch my legs, while he said my name over and over, like I was just upset, but I got away.

I went in the closet and got dressed, then threw open the front door. He was laying with his arm under his head looking at me.

"You need to leave."

"Come on, Hannah, I'm sorry. I shouldn't have said that."

"No. It's perfect. It's clear. It's so clear. You need to get out of here. I want to kill you."

"Oh, don't be so dramatic."

"Do not dramatic me. This isn't a movie. I don't know where you think you are, but you're not here. You keep saying you want to start over then you go backwards on me."

I stood at the door waiting; he took his time getting dressed. Cold air rushed in. The flames of the fire retreated into hot blue ridges to conserve energy for their unfinished work. The temperature in the room dropped thirty degrees. I waited; it was my house. I stood aside while he walked out the door.

He turned back. "Call me when you come to your senses."

"I just came to them. You're okay as long as I'm not."

I slammed the door in his face, threw the lock and pressed my back into it. My heart was pounding so hard I could feel it banging through my feet on the stone floor. I could see my mother hugging him and smiling as she invited him back. I could see handsome Arthur shaking his hand, man-to-man niceness. I could see Eric and Anna, candlelit faces laughing with him over the memory of their chicken feet dinner and volatile Russian cab driver. I could see my father, bent over his workbench whistling and glancing down at me with a smile, as he fixed the broken wing on my Chinese bird kite.

I'd only brushed up against that once, when I was throwing my husband out. I shouldn't have married him. But I was sick of having the earth pulled out from under me every six months. I wasn't half as angry then as I was now and he had dropped to his knees in the face of it.

Steve would never drop to his knees. He had never needed it the way my husband had. I could not remember ever being in touch with this place. My indignation was so fierce it jack hammered through the stone floors and bored into the earth's crust, deeper than any manzanita root could ever dream of going.

Seven

The airport shuttle came at 7:00 a.m. I kicked my bag ahead of me through security, surrounded by festive families headed for a Hawaiian Christmas. They'd all come home with crushed and browning leis. But at least they wouldn't be wearing those stupid fringed sombreros people wear coming out of Mexico. Well, Steve never would.

My eyes were light sensitive after twenty-four hours of crying with fury and self-loathing over my willingness to keep taking not enough just to have something.

Therapy might give you the words to put to your shit. Beyond that, I don't know what good it does. My last therapist said I was done: cooked, stick a fork in me. To just call if I needed a reminder of who I was. I never called; I had no idea what she was talking about. She must have mistaken me for a burned up manzanita bush. She'd joked that I'd have to buy my own subscription to *People*. Screw that. I had hoped for a brain transplant. I wanted to walk out her door whole, not some confused combo of half-understood ideas and addicted to a magazine that made me feel either superior or hopelessly behind, depending on my state of mind. I know, I know, a magazine *can't make me feel* anything. That one still had the power.

I boarded through first class, past men with scripts and their wives in resort wear wafting Beverly Hills perfume and reading *Town & Country* or *Marie Claire*. My last minute planning had landed me in the middle seat, in the last row of coach. It wouldn't even go back a few inches.

I was sandwiched between other ticket lottery losers. On the aisle was a young mother with an extra-fat crying baby. She was laid out on the tray table and needed a clean diaper.

Slouched in the window seat I coveted was a surly kid who looked like he'd been buckshot then plugged with rings and studs, and then covered with tattoos for good measure. What a mess. People who are going to decorate themselves should hire a good designer. Enough of the winging it people; make a plan. Hell, you can find out how to trick-up your pick-up on half a dozen cable channels. Isn't your body just as important? It's supposed to be our temple.

I wasn't opposed to tattoos; I'd even considered getting one. Karin had a tramp stamp on her tailbone that I thought looked kinda hot. But so far I hadn't been drunk enough to submit to the buzzing needle on the same day I thought it was a good idea. Never mind deciding on a design for all time.

Maybe I'd pitch a new show when I got back. *Trick-up Your Temple. Embellish Your Belly,* though that restricted the canvas. Maybe, *Design Your Shrine*. I could design personal tattoos. Whole families could get them, like micro-chipping their dog. I could call them *Clan Brands*. Even the dog could get one. We'd zap everybody at the same time. It would be a wholesome family show. I could take back the cowboy code that had been co-opted by gangbanger do-rags and taggers; families could "ride for the brand" again. Lovers may come and lovers may go, but families seem to stick like honey on your elbow. Obviously there were some things that needed to be worked out; like the divorce rate, and our obsession with *the individual*.

The kid who needed my show ignored the request to turn off all electronic devices. He blurped and grunted an alien dialect into his cell phone until the flight attendant threatened to take it away from him. He was wearing a nose clobbering after-shave, with not even fuzz in sight. Even with the dirty diaper and his whatever, I could already smell the phone booth sized bathroom. What a medley, and we'd barely left the ground. We would spend the flight with people standing next to our seats, smiling idly. I chose to ignore the fact that I'd gotten the worst of the worst seats and focused instead on having a superior *People* flight. In my defense, I'd spent enough time in Alanon to know I'd pay for being a snob before I died, probably before the day was out.

The plane left behind the brown and green foothills smelling of chemicals, cow shit and burned bacon. Stroud and Leeann were married and making plans for the baby. Steve would be getting his passport out of the bottom drawer of his desk and packing for Mexico and for a woman who fit his picture. I got out of my seat and stood in the galley bent over looking out the window.

We crossed the margin of the continent with its lines of white water eroding the shoreline. The solid rock would resist as long as possible, but would eventually give itself over to become pebbles, then grains of sand, then dust. I'd listened to a scientist on NPR during the shuttle ride to the airport. He claimed that if all the space between all the atoms making up all the people on earth were squeezed out, the entire population of the planet would compress down to something smaller than a cube of sugar. I saw millions of joyful little Matisse people dancing in a conga line on every grain of sand. The plane swept over dark water, farther out to sea.

I climbed back in my seat, which was a big production for the young mother. By way of apology, I bounced her Mama Cass on my hip while she used the toilet, then fetched her a coke. I picked at a box lunch of non-food items and talked to the baby in a normal voice while she gummed Cheerios. I'm not sure her mother appreciated me recounting the escapades of Vampire Chick. I gave her the PG version. I figured the sooner she knew to keep her sex life off camera, the better. She took a swig of cold water from a sippy cup, turned slightly blue, and then coughed a cold slime Cheerio ball into my face and hair. Fortunately my mouth was closed. The kid next to me snarked; I accidentally elbowed him. I held the coke and steadied the baby while the mother dug out wipes for everyone. I guess that falls under the heading *no good deed goes unpunished.*

I pulled the hood of my sweatshirt up around my face, bunched up my jacket and put my head down on the tray table. I was so tired I managed to fall asleep that way, even with the baby giving me little kicks to the head. We bounced our approach. The kid fired up and blurped, and the baby screamed with unpopped ears. I was never so glad to get off a plane.

Hawaii feels like home, the dense air wrapped like a hundred warm arms. I drove through a Waimea stuck in the 1960s, and followed the directions to a small cottage down a dirt residential road. It was remote, not good if you planned to slosh back mai tais, then drive. It was on the beach, but set back in a shady grove. It was a Hawaiian version of my place in L.A. A big bed was covered in a Hawaiian quilt with a romantic mosquito net on a ring overhead. Two rattan chairs with thick cushions shared an ottoman, table, and good light. An old bookcase held a worn copy of *Hawaii* and a tired checkers set with a red replacement piece made from a pizza box. Someone had carefully cut around a picture of a slice of pepperoni; it worked great. I love it when people leave a hit of their personality behind. There were two hurricane lamps and a big box of wooden matches.

The tiny lean-to bathroom light was a bare bulb in a socket with a metal bead chain. A hand-lettered sign with little lightning bolts warned me to be sure my feet were dry before pulling the chain. I realized I was alone. I could be electro-dead for a week next to the toilet and no one would know.

The kitchenette was a strip along the wall. A small drop-leaf table and two rattan chairs rounded things out. They sat in front of a window overlooking the back porch and beach beyond. I tried out the view from the porch; it was shallow enough to sit in a chair and use the railing for my feet. There was a classic round wooden hot tub for two. Steve would hate it. It was perfect.

I dumped my bag and drove back to Kapa for groceries. Then I opened shutters and doors and took pictures to send to Karin. I included a picture of the pepperoni checkers piece.

I called her. "Aloha. I just sent you pictures."

"Got them. Wish I were there, it's a zoo around here."

"How are your parents?"

"Fine."

"You don't sound so fine."

"At the moment I suspect the perky thing doing the chick stunts on Oscar's film is doing Oscar too."

"You're kidding!"

"Only sorta."

"You can't do that. You guys are my touchstone."

"If he is, we won't break up unless he gets stupid. I'm not raising these kids alone. I can't do a thing until after my parents leave."

"I'm sorry. Here I've been whining around. You always said you'd kick him out."

"I say all kinds of things, you know that. If we do break up, it would spare me growing old with a philandering and farting old man with shaggy eyebrows who misses the toilet."

"Whoa, where'd that come from?"

"My father. We're all dodging his drips."

"Has he been philandering?"

"I don't know, don't they all?"

"I was hoping not."

I told her about the last night with Steve.

"What a putz," she said. "I never liked him. And now that I've told you that, you can never get back together with him."

"Or I have to dump you."

"Don't even joke about it, Hannah. It's outrageous that he'd say that to you."

"My family is going to be so disappointed. He only has one name."

"I like hearing you again. I better run. I can't afford to get more than a half hour behind here."

"Okay. Hey, if you don't hear from me in a week, I'm electrocuted in the bathroom."

"We talking tenement?"

"Yeah, but on a nice beach."

"K. Keep calling. Love you," she said. "And hey back, we need to remember that pizza piece. That's a good one." She hung up.

I couldn't believe Oscar would do that. He seemed so dedicated to their whole thing. I hoped she was imagining things.

I put on my bathing suit and walked out past the grove to the sunny sand. The tree line ran away in both directions concealing the houses tucked behind. It was deserted except for a single paddleboard fifty yards to the left. I was tired and lonely. I decided to skip the swim and take a nap. I could barely make out my cottage; it was hidden so deep in the dark green bush. Two guys and a woman came out of an opening by the paddleboard.

I had just about made it to my tunnel when one of the guys called out. "Hey hi, you the new neighbor?"

They walked over.

"Not really, I'm only here a few weeks."

"Mike," he said holding out his hand. "I'm just visiting too. This is Jon and Kaia."

Mike was about 6'2". Jon was probably 5'5", 5'6" something like that; it's hard for me to say. But I'm only 5'3" and I didn't have to tilt my head all the way back to look at him like I did Mike. Jon was lanky and sun-bleached blonde, and looked like dozens of guys I'd known growing up on the beach. All sunburn, chapped lips, and a dusting of salt. His hair looked like mine, like he'd just rolled out of bed. He probably had. His girlfriend was a spectacularly exotic woman, with shining black hair to her waist.

Mike was dark with that kinda crazy handsomeness few guys have. He was hard to take in. He was made even more handsome by the fact that he didn't seem to know it. I wondered if I still had Cheerio goop in my hair. They headed off with the paddleboard.

I scratched the nap and dove in. I worked my way out past the breakers and then commenced one of my favorite activities in life, floating on my back supported by warm salt water. Swells passed benignly under me. The sky was clear with an occasional bird.

Two young boys were old school bodysurfing, no boogie boards. I played with them a while; then dragged out a chair and read. The boys came knocking around. They wanted to know if I'd worked on any of the pirate movies. They were on vacation with their grandmother next door for a few more days before heading back to California. They scampered off.

The grandmother came over a while later to invite me for

a cookout on the beach. She said the boys couldn't stop talking about what a good body surfer I was. Her name was Candace. She didn't look like someone's grandmother.

"That's nice of you. Can I bring anything?"

"No. Just come down the tree line to the right, the boys will have the entrance lit."

I packed up and put on warmer clothes. Tiki torches lined the tunnel into the belly of a bonfire at the center of their camp. The boys' voices were off in the trees.

Candace was lit up in the kitchen window where I joined her, "This looks great. Very mysterious approach with the torches."

"They're into the pirate movies. I'm sure they grilled you. They've named you Calypso. It's all very magical when the sun goes down. They're sleeping in a hut they built."

She'd brought the boys over for a week to give their parents a break. We dished up plates of salad and fish and sat by the fire to eat. She wanted to know all about the movie business. She was in the house getting a plate of mango slices for dessert when Mike and Jon walked down the torch lit trail. The boys bounded out of the bushes and swarmed them.

"Hey guys," said Jon.

Candace came out. She gave Jon a look that was more than a casual welcome. Aunt Judith would approve. I couldn't have pulled off that look if my life depended on it.

"This is Calypso," said Candace. "Your new neighbor."

"We met Hannah," said Mike.

Jon sat down with a slice of mango and nodded at me.

"How was the restaurant tonight?" asked Candace.

"Packed," said Jon. "It's a good week for us."

"Jon owns Luna's in town," said Candace. "There's one on

Maui and one in Honolulu too. Great food. Mike owns a microbrewery in Portland."

"Luna's is where the action is," said Mike.

"A brewery sounds like action," I said.

"He makes great beer," said Jon. "I haul it over here for the restaurants. They're trying to work up a label for us."

"We're using liliko'i," said Mike. "We haven't quite hit it yet."

"And you never will," said Jon.

"Oh we'll make it work, even if we just stick the flower on the label," said Mike. "We like the name too much. Liliko'i Luna, something like that. The beer crew plans to come for the launch."

"Liliko'i?" I asked.

"It's passion fruit," said Jon. "We make a margarita with it, and a pie. So far the beer is undrinkable."

"We'll get there," said Mike.

"And I'll buy it when you do," said Jon.

Jon had been teaching the boys to surf.

"Fun," I said. "I never learned, but I spent a lot of time watching boys surf. I decided I would never waste time watching boys surf again. I needed to live my own life."

Jon looked amused by that. "Watching other people live their life is overrated. Where'd you watch boys surf?"

"La Jolla," I said. "That's my home town."

"I went to college in La Jolla, worked at Scripps," said Jon.

"Jon comes for dessert every night he doesn't have to close the restaurant," said Candace. "I'd be eating their liliko'i pie every night if it was up to me."

"You really wouldn't," said Jon.

"Yeah she would," said Mike. He smiled at me. "It is passion fruit."

I felt tired and like there was some subtext that I wasn't

getting, and didn't care about. I thanked Candace for dinner and said my good-byes. I told the boys I'd be out first thing if they wanted to go another round, but she was taking them on a zipline adventure. I had a vision of my grandmother in a helmet, zipping across the jungle, hanging upside down on the line in her white leather shoes, dentures clacking with delight. I almost started laughing.

"Sounds great." I'm sure I was grinning way beyond a zipline trip. "Have fun."

It was a curious feeling to leave the intense heat of the fire and separate from the others. I felt lighter as my body cooled, like the heat had added to gravity. The sand was cool and squished underfoot. Small twigs and pebbles, unseen in the dark, gave my feet little stabs and pokes. I was almost to the opening in the tunnel when Mike caught up with me.

"I'll walk you home," he said.

"I'm okay."

"I don't doubt it," he said. "What are your plans while you're here?"

"Read, sleep, float. I'm resting between projects. I'm headed to India."

"Sounds interesting."

The moon was losing its grip on the night, but I had left a light on at my place to guide me home. Mike said good night at the porch and headed off through the jungle toward what I assumed was Jon's house.

I got in the hot tub. I had a flash of pith-helmeted white men boiling in a black pot surrounded by natives with bleached bones in their hair. A vivid imagination never goes on vacation. The walls of the hot tub were slick. I could smell the spongy wood melting cell-by-cellulose-cell into the hot water. Smoke from the bonfire drifted in slim threads through the grove. Jon's voice rumbled low through the undergrowth followed by Candace's laugh. Candace knew what she was doing. Jon did too apparently. I soaked for half an hour; it grew quiet across the way.

I got up early and headed out. It was warm and cloudless. The water was a sheet of glass between gurgling lines of baby bubbles. I went slowly, I hated to disturb the surface. I began my float. I tried it all different ways, arms and legs spread, just legs, just arms, then just like I was lying on a therapist's couch with my hands crossed on my belly. For some reason it's totally effortless. Half my body is usually out of the water. I don't know if it's body make-up, why some people float and some sink. I suspect the sinkers are fighting giving up control to Mother Nature. A shadow cast across my face. I looked up to the sight of a man standing on the water next to me. It took me a second to realize that it was Jon standing on a paddleboard.

"That's a weird visual," I said.

"You want to try it?"

"No thanks."

He sat down on his board and floated next to me. I floated on, breasts, belly, hipbones, kneecaps and toes out of the water. I asked him about the restaurant. He said it was right on the beach so caught a lot of bar hopping, which they liked. He'd grown up in Santa Barbara but had gone to UCSD; we knew the same beaches. He'd majored in math and had done an internship at Scripps Oceanography before moving to Hawaii to work at one of the marine labs. He asked if I knew anyone on the island.

"Not a soul. Why?"

"Women come here, get lonely and end up hooking up with one of the bar rats. You seem too nice for that."

"Good to know my disguise still works. I doubt I'm too nice

for anything. But thanks for the heads up. My hooking up days are over."

"That bad?"

"Worse."

"What was so funny about the zipline last night?" he asked.

"The zipline?"

"Yeah. You looked like you were going to burst out laughing."

"Oh. It was Grandma. I had an image of her ziplining."

"You don't think Candace can zipline?"

I turned my head as far as I could to look at him.

"Candace? Not Candace. I'm sure she can do it all."

I turned my head back and looked at the sky.

"I meant my own grandmother. I had a vision of her ziplining in her white leather shoes and clacking dentures," I said. "She died a few weeks ago."

"Sorry."

"It's okay. She was ninety-eight. She had a long wonderful life. My grandfather was fun; he loved the expression *close, but no cigar*. I can see her trying it at ninety."

He invited me to the restaurant for Christmas Eve. They had a tradition of family style eating with a group of people who came every year. He said it was a friendly bunch. I thanked him, but said I doubted I'd be there. We floated for a few minutes without talking and then he hopped up on his board and landed in perfect balance.

"Let me know if you want to try this," he said. He took a few strokes and glided away.

"I don't think I have the abs for it," I called.

"I think you do. Won't hurt to try."

I could see it hurting. Sore muscles and banged up legs to start. I'd entered a kayak from the water once. I had a pretty good idea of how a person looks when they try to hoist their ass onto a moving object that doesn't want company. He slid off down the coastline and I swam in and got dressed. I was starved so drove to town for a batch of poke.

I spent days like that, floating, reading, sleeping. The boys and I fell into a regular bodysurfing routine. Jon wandered over once a day to see if I'd changed my mind about paddling; I hadn't. He spent some time in the water with us. But he seemed to spend more time over at Candace's; I suspected I was babysitting when I was bodysurfing. I doubted she was lonely, at least not this week.

I wasn't lonely either. Mike came by every day and joined in the bodysurfing. He was a widower and easy company. We went to town for lunch a few times. He had rented a condo in one of the big resorts out the road so we hung out by the pool with monogrammed towels, personal cabanas, and iced tea with flower petals. He wasn't Steve; he didn't like the fancy place. He said he was going to grab my place next year. I told him he'd have to wrestle me for it.

I wondered how Steve was getting on in Mexico; his mother must be happy. I didn't know if he'd ever even mentioned me to his family. I called Eric and Anna to break the news that Steve was gone. They were disappointed, as in heavy sigh, when will it all end, disappointed. And they're my biggest boosters. I called my mother and told her too.

"I'm sorry, Hannie. We really liked him, we thought he would work out."

"I did too. But he couldn't get past Stroud."

"Are you talking about Alan?"

"Yes. We might have survived it if he'd been a doctor, lawyer or Indian chief. Steve really hated the whole truck driver thing."

"I can see that."

"You can? What if Daddy had been a truck driver?"

"I wouldn't have married him."

"I'm not talking about marriage, Mom."

"I don't know. Aren't you lonely there all by yourself?"

"Not yet," I lied.

I woke up on Christmas Eve and decided to go to Jon's place for dinner. Mike had been encouraging me to go. He said I'd know at least two people. The only thing I had to wear was a crazy black sarong dress with big red flowers and hair sticking out all over the place. I had to pull it together. I opted for hyper-crazy hair like I meant it, and then threw on my pearls to confuse the message.

It was an interesting mix of people from the all over the country, ex-pats from city living, a few locals. There was a couple from Seattle with an asset eating coffee plantation, and two women physicists from Cal-Tech. One wore a baseball cap that said, "Blah Blah Blah." Jon hosted in a wildly colorful shirt. He was with a beautiful young woman who turned out to be his daughter Chana. She was completely at ease in the group. She'd obviously known most of the people for years.

Live slack key music came from the corner. Everyone talked and laughed and swapped chairs through a dinner of platter after platter of Hawaiian morsels. Mike introduced me to everyone. It was a fun and lively group. He mentioned to one of the physicists that I was going to India. She said they'd been, that it's a wild place for a Western mind. He kept introducing me as someone who worked in the movie business. He was twinkling. He knew I thought it was silly. But people who didn't know better were enthralled with the business, even some in the business.

Everyone was sent home with a bottle of champagne and a

box of chocolate covered macadamia nuts painted with red flowers. It was a tradition, and a great touch. I tore open the box of candy as soon as my car headed back to the cottage.

I got home and sat on the deck with my feet on the railing and watched the moon on the waves at the end of my tunnel. The view was blocked by a figure walking my way. A tingle of L.A. fear ran through me, but it was just Jon.

"You want to share?" he held up a champagne bottle. "We didn't get a chance to talk."

"Is this because Grandma's gone?"

"No, it's because I was busy and we didn't get a chance to talk."

"Sorry. Bad joke. Let me get some glasses."

We sat with our feet up on the railing and toasted the Christmas that had just spun through the cosmos to us.

"That was a lovely party. Thank you for including me. I've never been alone on a holiday like this."

"Mike took care of you. I thought he might be here."

"No, sorry. He gets a kick out of saying I'm in the movie business. He knows the effect it has on people."

Jon said his daughter was graduating from high school and considering colleges; UCLA was at the top of her list. The physicists were pushing for Cal Tech.

"UCLA is my alma mater," I said.

"I'm not sure she's ready for L.A."

"In my business, L.A. is like the center of the universe. Unless you're from New York."

"Then maybe I'm not ready for her to be ready for L.A."

"That sounds like algebra. But I don't blame you, I'm an old cat in L.A. who's running out of lives."

"Do you know algebra?"

"Not since high school. I majored in anthropology. As my last director said, and I quote, 'I will not be held captive by the laws of mathematics'."

He wanted to know if I was more Margaret Mead or mummies. I told him I hadn't been able to decide, so went into production design instead where I gathered intense knowledge about slices of life for brief periods of time.

"I know a little about a lot of things," I said. "What the Sufis might describe as digging shallow holes, but it's never boring. Brushing dirt off shards in a museum basement could get old."

We poured the last of the bottle and sat in the balmy silence.

"A cat?" he said.

"It looks like you're having fun."

"Having fun?" He looked at me, then at my hair. He probably figured they'd stopped the shock treatments a little short of the mark.

"I didn't mean that in a bad way," I said. "At least someone is having fun."

"You're not?"

"According to my mother, I'm a cat in a world of kittens. My window of opportunity for finding the right man is slamming shut."

I could swear he was considering my hair again. I doubt it looked like right man hair. "Do you want to find the right man?"

"Of course, I don't want to spend my life banging bar rats. But apparently I have no idea how it all works."

He was quiet; I glanced over at him. "Sorry, that was incredibly crude. I didn't mean to go all L.A. on you; we have a tendency to spew our little stories. And I have a tendency to say stupid shit when I'm drinking champagne. I won't bang bar rats. I don't intend to bang anybody."

Okay, obviously I'd already had too much champagne. I was

not only saying stupid shit, but I was saying bang and shit while I was at it. My parents would not approve.

"I should go to bed. Now I'm saying banging shit with my stupid shit. I can hear my parents clucking their tongues. Thanks again for inviting me tonight. I was feeling lonely and it was a perfect Christmas Eve. And thanks for sharing; it was really thoughtful."

"You're welcome."

I could swear his hair was sticking up even more than usual. He headed home. I stripped off my sarong, washed my face, and took note of the fact that my hair looked like I'd pulled the bathroom light chain while standing in water. The grow out was going to be a trial. At least I'd be in India where no one would care how I looked as long as I did my job. Well someone would care. There's always a man or two on location who thinks he cares, or who has lost his moral bearings in a Bermuda Triangle of strange place, opportunity, and horniness.

I woke up with a massive hangover complicated by eating too much chocolate. I cleared the empty bottle off the porch and washed glasses then dug out the bottle of Gatorade I'd had the foresight to buy. I was hours earlier than the mainland, so I had time to get my act together before the Skype calls started. I dragged out and dove in the water. There is nothing better for a hangover than the ocean. I forced myself to body surf, figuring a little pounding might goose my system to life. Maybe I could restore my internal chemistry through osmosis. It worked, sort of. Argh. I swam out past the breakers and floated to give my stomach a chance to get rearranged. I was beginning to feel cleansed.

"You okay?" Jon was treading water next to me.

"I've been worse, though I can't ever remember being so rude to someone. I'm really sorry about that. How about you?"

"It's okay, holidays aren't always happy. I'm fine. I'm a little bigger than you and don't think I put down quite as much."

"No, that was stupid. Now I can check 'drink too much at a party' off my to-do list."

"What else is on the list?"

"You don't want to know."

"Sure I do."

"Well, chop off my hair, which I didn't even notice I was doing at the time. Talk endlessly at friends, which I have never had a tendency to do. I do it with complete strangers instead, as you are my witness."

"That's it?" he asked. "Sounds doable."

"Add take up stupid hobbies; I'm thinking wood burning, it runs in the family. The last is no joy sex with random unavailable men, that's done and done. If I can get extra-curricular credit for that one, I'll finish early."

"What about finding the right man?"

"First things first. Gotta work the program."

"That last part doesn't sound too bad."

"No, it sounds like more inappropriate blabber," I was smiling at the sky. "Your restaurant open today?"

"Yep, people don't come here to cook a turkey."

"Good, I need burger and fries therapy."

"Try the Maui onion rings, they work better than the fries."

He took off while I continued to float. I had absolutely nowhere to be, and no one to be nowhere with. That's mathematics, zero sum total. Or is it sum total zero? Total sum zero? I should have worked harder at math. Oh well, at least I could get some fatty food.

I felt much better after the swim. I sacked out on a towel and dozed with a gentle breeze consoling my skin. I slept for hours. When I woke up, someone had put up an umbrella and thrown a white sheet over me, weighted down with driftwood. There was no one around. It was strange to think someone was so busy while I slept.

I got dressed and headed in for food. The place was packed so I sat at the bar. My burger and rings arrived just as Jon pulled up a stool and sat down next to me with a bowl of chowder and chunk of bread in his hand. I was getting a little more consistent. I knew two men who ate soup.

"How you feeling?" he asked.

"Almost human. Were you the one who covered me up?"

"Yeah, the way you were sleeping out there, you would have ended up in the hospital."

"Thanks, you saved my vacation, if not my life."

"Merry Christmas," he tapped my glass with his bread.

"Merry Christmas." A wave of sadness swelled over me. I should be home with my family. Steve was probably off dancing, badly, with his new woman. I could see Stroud stroking the skin on his wife's belly, the new life poking out in places like my grandmother's bird. Nose and fists through silky skin. I wiped my eyes; I was not going to do this. Jon was watching me with interest. I smiled at him. He was odd to me; he was a little like looking in a mirror.

"Sorry, lonely woman stuff. Not enough to be stupid."

"Yeah, that's all behind you."

"You're funny," I said.

Mike came in and Jon gave him his seat. By the time lunch was over I had a pretty good handle on beer making ingredients. We made a plan to hike the Napali Coast.

I went home and Skyped Karin; she was home alone. I pulled out her gift. She enjoys watching because she never remembers what the hell she puts in the boxes she gives. She just starts buying and wrapping until it's full. First up, a book on ikebana, one of the hobbies I was going to take up in those first haircutting days.

"That's great," I said. "I can try it here."

Richard had included a hand-painted dinosaur, a raptor like in Jurassic Park. He knew those guys scared me. I hated the relentless way they moved when they hunted. He thought it would help me get over my fear, the little therapist. Callie included a pink baseball cap, something she considers a fashion necessity.

Next came a pink pearl bunny vibrator from the sex shop on Hollywood Boulevard, an old standard, the bunny and the shop.

"Obviously you have no faith in my ability to stay with the program?"

"I was thinking of it more as a diversion, until you get back on your feet, or I guess I should say your back. Did you know it comes in a bunch of colors now? I threw in batteries."

To wind it up, she had included a set of Kama Sutra warming oils.

"That's optimistic."

"The Napali Coast might get interesting tomorrow."

"I'm on hiatus. Though I will say, he's hot and very nice. I love everything. I'll wear the pink hat while I have Christmas with the bunny. How you doing?"

"It's okay for now. It's hard to deal with it with my parents right on top of us. What's really strange is the sex. I thought I wouldn't want him to touch me, but every time my parents take the kids on a field trip we go at it like in the beginning. We're all the way back to the knocking over the furniture stage. We did it up against the water heater. Then I get furious all over again and throw things at him. He seems genuinely shocked that he did it. He really wants me to know he's here."

"What are you going to do?"

"We're going to start seeing someone as soon as my parents leave. I don't know if I can get over it. I know people forgive. I can't imagine I'll forget."

"I'm so sorry."

"Yeah, it's driving him crazy that we never got married. It makes his position a little unclear."

I Skyped Eric's house and talked to everyone briefly. I could see Binky slopping wine on Anna's carpet from 2700 miles out. We made her drink white to reduce cleaning bills. I loved seeing all their faces, but seeing the old scene, I didn't miss being there. I had no sense of where I belonged anymore.

I wandered out to the beach. Jon was sitting alone in a low chair, legs stretched out under a straw hat, reading. I sat down in the sand next to him.

"Perfect lunch. Mike's so nice. We're going to hike the Napali Coast tomorrow, unless you finally get around to telling me he's a bar rat masquerading as a brewer. You'd tell me right? Not do some male solidarity thing?"

"I'd tell you. Be kinda stupid to warn you and then not warn you, don't you think?"

"I guess."

He looked at me. "Well I wouldn't, Hannah. He's as advertised. He and his wife used to come every year and he still does. She was a rocket."

"When did she die?"

"Three years ago, it was a tough one."

"Is he seeing anyone?"

"Nothing serious that I know of. You want to paddle?"

"You're like a relentless raptor. You think a hangover has me in such a weakened state, I'll sign on for more humiliation?"

"You're humiliated? All you did was drink a little too much and say shit a lot. You didn't start a food fight. The way you float around, I just think you'd like it."

"Do people do that? Have food fights?"

"They do it all."

"What else?"

"Oh man, where to start? They pass out in the booths. Full moons are good for that. They get very creative under the tables, they don't know the whole dining room can see them; and then no one wants to handle their money. The bathrooms are a big draw."

"Do they go in the stalls?"

I know, but a girl wants to know these things.

"Most people wouldn't really care if they were in a stall."

"What else?"

"Well, there are all the variations on the theme of how to get sick in a bathroom. They bitch out the bartenders for pulling their keys, then pass out before a cab comes and we can figure out where to ship them. They dump drinks on each other, pinch the waitresses; the waiters get their share of that too. There's a certain amount of slapping back and forth, usually as a result of the pinching, but sometimes because people think confessing in public after too many mai tais is going to save them from a show-down. That usually involves some drink throwing. There's lots of crying, by adults and children."

"I don't like crying kids," I said.

"They can hit some ear piercing notes," he said. "They're their own subset. Parents drag them in overtired and fried to a crisp. They scream, cry, and pee on the furniture. They run around and ram into the waiters; they're hard to see under a tray. They are experts at projectile vomiting chunks of cheese on the tables next to them. They litter Cheerios that get ground into the carpet and smashed down in the booth cushions. Last night one got a piece of crayon stuck in her ear. I'm going to have to rethink the coloring placemats. And that's the paying customers. At the moment the crew seems to be having a contest to see who can get it on in the walk-in; it can't be easy, it's really cold in there. According to one patron, who stumbled into the kitchen by mistake, they're doing a little warm up before they go in."

I was lying on the sand laughing so hard I could hardly breathe.

"Does that happen every night?" I asked. "It sounds kinda wild."

"No. We're usually able to pull off a nice experience for people. I have great crews; they keep the show rolling. They're usually the only ones who know what's going on."

"Do you get involved with the crew stuff?"

"Not if I can help it, I'd never get anything done. I'm more like a ringmaster. I don't let anyone get slapped or pinched with impunity. And the walk-in, yeah, the health department could shut us down over that stunt."

"You have no idea how much that sounds like being on location!"

"So you want to paddle?"

"Why not? Apparently I'm a saint."

I told him my banged up legs and inelegant ass hoisting reservations.

He smiled while he got the board in the water. "You're not going to have to do any ass hoisting today."

I got so I could step on with a little help and glide around. We went a little deeper. Still okay. He said I needed to relax and just breathe. Drop my shoulders and let my legs become one with the uncertainty, Grasshopper. Something like that. He needed to get to work, but we agreed to try again tomorrow, if I could still move.

I'd never been alone on Christmas but it wasn't as bad as I'd expected. It started to cloud up; the earth was spinning toward rain. Anna called to make sure I was doing okay. She was worried that I was alone. I told her I'd had a burger and rings, my first paddling lesson and was going hiking with a friend. She said Binky got worse and worse after we talked.

"She was really over-the-top this year," she said. "I don't know what's going to happen."

"Everyone says that until Ted gets on board, there's nothing we can do," I said.

Binky had passed out in the back of the car. None of the kids would sit on her, so Ted had to strap them all in the front seat. They were going to leave her there all night. That must be so strange for the kids on Christmas Eve. Everyone was anticipating Binky's damage control call. She always made a damage control call the next day and everyone pretended nothing had happened. It drove me nuts.

I wandered out to the beach; it was dark and quiet in both directions. The new people in Grandma's house were keeping to themselves. I sat on the cool sand and listened to the surf. Voices came through the opening at Jon's. I couldn't make out details but I recognized his voice. They walked off down the beach in the opposite direction; my eyes adjusted to long swinging black hair just as the darkness absorbed them.

I got up early and took my coffee and a book out to the beach. Jon was already out, back in his chair reading. I waved and set up my chair. He picked up his chair and moved down the beach next to me.

"Morning," I said. "You have a nice night?"

"It was okay. You?"

"It was fine. I started a new book. What are you reading?"

"Christmas gift from Phyllis the Physicist. Essays by a guy named Michio Kaku. Good stuff. Dark energy, parallel universes, oozing to other planets. What about you?"

"*The Wave*. The woman at the bookstore in town recommended it. Amazing really, the ocean looks different. Not quite the same as yours."

"A lot the same."

My phone rang; it was Mike. We made a plan to go at 10:00.

"You ready to try again?" asked Jon.

We went back in the water and started out with the shallow stuff. I managed to crawl on and stand up by myself. I was better. Breathing really helps. That should be so obvious. I needed to cut it short to meet Mike. I threw on hiking clothes just as Mike pulled up.

"You look rested," he said.

I told him about my paddling lesson with Jon. He asked if I'd seen Jon's latest housing project.

"A group of them build affordable housing," he said.

"I thought you were going to say fancy condos."

"No, the housing dovetails with his business. Affordable housing that they own and decent benefits keeps his key people around. That's important. He still has about a fifty-percent employee turnover rate. That would kill my business. The bookwork and break-in eats up a lot of time. He ends up doing just about every job at some point during the year. He's not as laid back as he looks. He really will make me come up with a great beer."

We hiked for a few hours along the spectacular trail and told each other our stories, or some sanitized version. We came upon a waterfall with a group of kids skinny-dipping. We smiled at each other, stripped down and jumped in. They were on Christmas break from Arizona State. They'd tried Tom's beer. And, big shock, they even knew Layla's Loft. The young women had more sympathy for Vampire Chick than Layla. I didn't ruin the ending for them. We left them and hiked to a bluff overlooking the coastline to eat lunch.

"This is so peaceful," I said.

"Between helicopters. My wife and I used to hike this trail every year. I still do."

He talked about his wife. They'd built the business together. They'd planned to have children, but she died of breast cancer before they had a chance. It had looked like it was in remission but it came back and she'd died in a matter of months. He'd dated a few people, but so far nothing had clicked. He said he wasn't on hiatus, but he wasn't in any hurry either.

"Jon said she was a rocket," I said.

He laughed. "That's a perfect description. I always thought they'd be a good match if anything happened to me."

"You thought about that? That's so generous."

"Didn't you ever think about what would happen to your husband if you died?"

"Never. I wouldn't wish my ex-husband on my worst enemy."

"That's too bad."

"What's Jon's story?"

Jon had been divorced as long as they'd known him, he guessed maybe fifteen years. He'd raised his daughter Chana. Mike had never met his ex-wife but it didn't seem like there was any animosity there. She remarried and lived on the big island. He got the impression her new husband was uptight with Chana.

We finished lunch and made our way back down the trail. He was heading back to Portland in a few days. We decided to try kayaking the next morning, see the coastline from a different angle. He invited me to visit Portland when I got back from India, experience brewing first hand. He said I could try my hand at making up my own recipe, design a label and everything.

Eight

When I got back to the cottage, there was a message on my cell from Jon asking me to call.

"Hi," I said. "How'd you get this number?"

"My assistant tracked it down."

"How'd she do that?"

"I don't know. It's a small island. Good hike?"

"It was great. I'd never been out there. It's spectacular. We went skinny dipping at a waterfall. We're going to take kayaks up tomorrow."

"He still there?"

"No. You need his number?"

"I have it. I'm going to dinner at a friend's restaurant tonight and I thought you might enjoy it if you don't have plans."

"I don't have plans. Is it another party?"

"No, just us. He wants to try out some new dishes."

"Sounds fun. What's the dress?"

"It's Victor's. There are white tablecloths, but that's about it. What you wore the other night will work. I'll get you at 7:00."

He picked me up wearing a really silly shirt covered with grinning moons dancing around in leis and flip-flops.

"That looks like something my father would wear. Drove my mother crazy."

He looked at the shirt and smiled. "It was clean. Chana gave it to me for Christmas."

Victor's is only about four doors down from Jon's restaurant, but it could be in Paris. Jon's exotic girlfriend Kaia was the hostess; they hugged in greeting.

"He can't wait to feed you," she said.

She led us to a small table tucked in an alcove overlooking the water. Chef Victor came out to greet us; he kissed my hand which was very courtly for a big Samoan in a toque. Kaia came over and slung an arm over Victor's shoulder.

"So you ready?" she asked.

"Yep," said Jon.

They went back to work.

"Are Victor and Kaia related?"

"They're married with five kids. I'm pretty sure that's related."

"I thought she was one of your girlfriends."

"And that I invited you to dinner here? Sounds like someone hasn't been very nice to you."

"I guess. What's their last name?"

"Last names are a moving target."

"Mine's Spring."

"Mine's Moon."

"I deserved that. What is it really?"

"Moon."

I was looking at him and the shirt, thinking about the name. He looked up. There was that mirror again.

"You've never met a Moon?"

I got a pingy rush and started laughing. He smiled.

"I bet you get some serious mileage out of that line. But no, I've never met a Moon. It's nice. It suits you."

"Spring suits you. I'm pretty sure I've never used that line before."

Kaia brought us chilled Lillets with the barest wisp of orange peel. It boded well for a meal free of pineapple in undercooked cornstarch.

"Mike said you raised your daughter. That must have been difficult."

"It was fine."

"All the single mothers I know say it's like having leprosy when it comes to men."

"I know, a lot of them work for me. Kids are like bait for men. Everyone wants to rescue us."

"Is that what made it easy?"

"I wouldn't call it easy. But making my own schedule and having enough money made it doable, the bait part just made it strange."

"Strange?"

"Women auditioning to be mom, talking to her in squeaky voices. She has a mother."

"You're immune to feminine wiles?"

"Wiles are a lot of work, especially when it came to her."

"No wonder we get along. My aunt says I'm wileless."

"Being subjected to wiles, as you put it, is about as interesting to me as watching boys surf is to you."

"That can't be true for most men. They seem to love wiles."

"Or they're willing to wade through the bullshit. I just try to get through dessert so I can escape. I try to not be too rude."

"Dessert? Or dessert dessert?"

"Dessert."

"I'm surprised."

"Shocking I know," he smiled.

"Well it's totally different for single mothers. Men stay for dessert dessert, but can't wait to get out the door before the kid wakes up."

"We're not big on raising someone else's kids."

"Have you dated a woman with kids?"

"Sure."

"Were the kids a problem? My aunt says my mother never remarried because she was stuck raising me."

"I doubt it was you. I got pretty involved with the kids. Chana liked the situation. It needed to go to the next level but I realized I was more involved with the kids than I was with their mother. It wasn't a good scenario."

There was hope for Karin. Maybe she wouldn't have to raise the kids alone.

"My mother has a man now. He stayed through dessert, then breakfast, lunch and dinner."

"She doesn't have kids to raise."

"That's debatable. Mike said he always thought you and the rocket would make a good couple if anything happened to him."

"Mike's a good guy. Anything there?"

"It's comfortable, he's easy. I'm going to visit him in Portland when I get back from India. It feels sort of neutral, a good start for now. We're leaving early tomorrow so I have to skip paddling."

"Never neutral. You probably remind him of his wife."

"I've hardly been a rocket. We've just been having fun. We just roll along. No pressure."

"I don't think you understand about rockets."

"That's no surprise. Did you think about that? Who your wife could marry?"

"She figured it out on her own."

"I always thought my husband would go back to his old girlfriend; he never really gave her up," I said. "But he didn't. That wasn't the point..."

I looked out the window remembering just how miserable

it had been. My husband had held out his old girlfriend as an example of everything I wasn't; then acted like I'd broken his one true love heart when it was over. I was embarrassed that I'd said it. I needed to learn to stop talking. Jon was looking at me.

"You want to try this?" he pointed to his plate.

"Thanks."

We traded plates and talked about food and paddling. By the time the spectacular meal was over Victor had been out three times to quiz us about the various dishes. We stayed so late we were the only people left. Victor came out sans toque and had espresso with us while we passed three different desserts to taste. Kaia was busy closing out the bank and releasing the staff.

I put my fork down and smiled at Victor, "That was the best meal I've ever eaten. You're a master."

We said goodnight.

It was a shock to be jettisoned into reality after such a lush trip in food land.

"Do you mind if we stop in at my shop?" Jon asked.

"Not at all. Maybe we can catch the walk-in warm up act."

"I hope not. I walked in on the cocktail waitresses the other night. They were dancing on the bar, singing and shooting each other full of lemon vodka and Reddi-wip. Luckily we were closed. When did girls start climbing all over each other?"

"Shooting each other full of Reddi-wip?" I have a vivid imagination. Women climbing all over each other and shooting Reddi-wip was a head full.

"Into their mouths. It was a rough night. They were just blowing off steam."

"Wow, you really got me going! I know what you mean though; the young girls are all over each other. I don't know what it's all about. Is it sexy?"

"It's disturbing. Chana's Facebook page is full of it. I've known most of the girls since they were little. They're all pouting and sticking out their asses. It's gotta be like live porn for the young guys."

"You look at her Facebook page?"

"She set up a page for me, then friended me. I'm trying to keep ahead of things. So far all she has posted are cartwheels and good waves, petitions to save the whales, that kind of thing. I don't like the cartwheels. You on Facebook?"

"I was for a while," I said. "It got to be a time suck addiction; a parallel universe. I went cold turkey. I got the shakes and everything. I kept reaching for the app. You'll see if you ever try to give it up. How many friends do you have?"

"One. I don't think I'll bother trying to give it up."

His restaurant was quiet but the bar area was slamming with a bachelor party. He parked me at the end of the bar, while he went in back to talk to the staff, and undoubtedly take a peek at the walk-in. One of the cocktail waitresses was working the rowdy bunch of men; I heard her say, "What the hell are you doing?" Uh oh.

Jon must have a third ear for that kind of thing; he came out of the back in two seconds flat and went over to the group. I watched as he talked to the cocktail waitress who was wiping her shoulder with a napkin, then to a guy who was sitting back down. I heard the guy say something about Fifty Shades of Grey. Oh boy, this could get good. He didn't look like someone who read chick porn, but men are full of surprises. They stood around for a while. The cocktail waitress and the Shades of Grey guy seemed to be in some kind of negotiation. The other guys were egging it on; Jon just listened. Grey pulled out his wallet and handed her some money and they all went back to business as usual. Jon looked at the bartender, a signal passed between them.

"What was that?" I asked.

"I'll tell you in the car. Let's get out of here before something else happens."

He took my elbow and rushed us out the door and into the car to make our getaway.

"So?" I asked.

"The guy slathered her shoulder with a lime slice, sprinkled on salt, and started licking it off before she knew what hit her. He was drinking shots."

"Wow. That happen often?"

"It's a new one. Cost him forty dollars."

"Forty dollars?"

He looked over at me, "It was only her shoulder."

"I would have taken twenty."

"Not with me standing there you wouldn't."

"How do you handle this with your daughter?"

"She's been in the culture all her life. She knows what's what. We've taken care of her."

"Nobody licking salt off her?"

"Would your father let men lick salt off you?"

I started laughing.

"That's funny?" he asked.

"Listen to us," I said. "Salt licking men, like it's a big population."

He smiled and shook his head.

"Oh god you make me laugh," I said. "I have no idea what my father would or wouldn't let happen. I was on my own with that one. I'm pretty sure there's been some licking, salt and otherwise, he wouldn't approve of. But I don't know, I just found out he had an affair."

He asked me where my father was. I told him the story.

"That must have been hard," he said. "But don't confuse his

affair with taking care of you."

"You know about that?"

"I know a lot about that."

We were back in front of my place.

"I had so much fun, thanks for inviting me," I said.

"You came to mind."

"Luna's. Moon in Latin."

"Yep."

"So passion fruit moon beer?"

"I think we'll stick with Liliko'i Luna. "

"I like it as long as they don't stick *Lager* on the end. Night, luna."

I leaned over and licked his ear. Really, Hannah. Now what?

He smiled sideways at me. "Is that where the cat thing comes from?"

"I have no idea where that came from! Forget I did that. Too much sugar or something."

"Be hard to forget."

"Well do. It was only your ear, Jon. It must have been the whole licking conversation. I'm so sorry. Erase, rewind, whatever!"

I fled the car and slammed the door. He called good night. Crap! I flapped a hand at him without looking back. He waited until I was in the house before driving next door.

Nine

I was happy to be going kayaking. I didn't want to face Jon after the licking incident. I so hoped he hadn't mentioned it to Mike.

Mike and I had a great time and then stopped for a late lunch before he left to pack. He didn't mention licking. He gave me a very nice good-bye kiss. He was looking forward to my visit to Portland. He was an unselfconscious and happy man who looked great without his clothes on, but I didn't have an urge to lick him.

I spent the rest of the afternoon reading. No Jon sighting. I figured he was off with some sane woman, his ears safe. I hoped it was a one-off and that I wouldn't have to add ear licking to strange small talk and singing the wrong lyrics.

I talked to Karin. Her parents had gone home and she sounded stressed now that they were seeing a marriage counselor and they weren't forced to be cheerful in the face of her potentially gloating parents. She was in a down, shit-throwing phase of the cycle. Oscar was starting to feel like maybe things should start to lighten up a little. He was sorry, he loved her, and he wasn't going anywhere.

The school had started calling; Callie was acting out and getting bossy, she'd started wearing black. Richard was going the opposite direction and getting more serious. Karin and Oscar might be battling for the power, but they were able to bury the hatchet when it came to helping their children. She wanted news from cat-land.

"You licked his ear?" she said. "The Napali guy?"

"No, the flippin' boy next door," I said. "Totally bizarre."

"It sounds like you need to go a few rounds with the pink bunny," she said. "Take the edge off."

"Oh stop! The guy has more women than China has pigs."

"People."

"People?"

"Than China has people."

"Whatever."

"I meant your edge, not his."

"So embarrassing. Why would I do that?"

"Oh I don't know, but I'm guessing he could stand in for the bunny."

"I'm on hiatus!"

"Self imposed. I got the picture from dinner the other night; you two look like you're related. His hair even sticks up a little. He's blonde; you've always gone for the Steves—tall, dark and handsome."

"He's handsome, and he's the same height as my father. Stroud has blue eyes. Anyway, I haven't gone for him."

"Yeah right. He's your father's height, and you're licking him like a scoop of blue-eyed pineapple ice cream. Haven't even thought about it."

"Glad I could cheer you up. I'm hanging up now, bye."

She was laughing when I hung up.

Next I called Anna for an update. We didn't laugh. Leaving Binky in the car overnight on Christmas Eve had been a tipping point for the kids. Sam and Sam looked numb. Amber was throwing frantic tantrums and leveling every single thing in the house. Ted was floating. I'd only been gone a little more than a week. If I were there I could take the kids out. Now that Mom wasn't drinking, we had a chance at an intervention. Anna would talk to Eric and Arthur about it. Ted would be the sticking point.

Jon was out the next morning with his daughter's board for me. He wanted to cover some miles so I could get a sense of the possibilities. He took the boards out past the breakers and I managed to stand up in less than half an hour. Even in that shallow water, it was dreamy to glide over the bottom and check in with everybody. I told him about the sugar cube and my theory that millions were doing the conga on every grain of sand. He said I was really into parallel universes. He was right. Why else would I get involved with men with two names and work in the film business? All we did was dream up parallel universes. My mind started to work on that idea; something was whispering in the background as we slid across the water, but nothing took form in my mind.

"You okay?" He startled me out of my reverie. We glided to a stop while I rocked back and forth and regained my balance. I looked at him and had the weirdest premonition that I was going to look at him a lot.

"That was weird. I was flying with my father one day. We ended up in a sky sandwich. That's what he called it. It happens sometimes on cloudy days; you end up flying in a band of clear sky between layers of clouds. You can't see up or down, you can't see what's going on except right where you are. This is different. We can see other universes. I have no idea what I'm talking about."

"We can see them." He smiled. "But we can't go there for very long without help."

"Like a plane?"

"Or air tanks," he said. "We should turn back. You're going

to feel these swells in your hips tomorrow."

We got back and he read while I rolled up in a sheet like a mummy to nap.

My voice was muffled through the fabric. "Did you understand what I was talking about?"

"When?" he asked.

"On the water."

"You mean about living in our own universe?"

"Yeah."

"I don't know," he said. "Did I?"

"Yeah. It's safe to leave me here. I'll steam but I won't broil."

I unrolled an hour later sweaty and squished. He was still reading. I sat up and peeled wet hair off my face and tried to dislodge the sand stuck to my chest with sunscreen and sweat glue. He watched me go through my monkey antics.

"I need to wash off," I said.

"You want to go to Victor and Kaia's for a pig roast tonight?" he asked.

"Sounds fun," I said.

I tried to blow my bangs off my forehead; I'd already rubbed sunscreen into my eyes trying it with my hand. He reached over and brushed them loose.

"Thanks. I'll never get lonely the way you keep including me."

"Victor suggested it," he said. "I gotta tell you though, if you get out of hand and start licking people, you're on your own. It'll be mostly Samoans, way out of my league."

I guess that little blip wasn't going away any time soon. I ignored the licking comment.

"I haven't been out of hand in years," I said.

"You miss it?"

I had to think about how to answer that. The short answer

was, yes. The long answer was, yes but.

"I don't miss a lot of it. I was young," I said. "They were less wild than stupid. But I miss thinking I was free, if that makes any sense. How about you?"

"Same. Though I felt free, at least until Chana was born. Chana's good; she came out of it."

"Yeah, I missed that," I said.

"You don't think you'll have kids?"

"No, not now."

"Right, it's all behind you."

"What about you? You want more kids?"

"It's a little late for that."

"Yeah, old man with one Facebook friend. Chana Moon is a beautiful name, be hard to match that anyway. What time's dinner?"

"It'll be up to the pig. I'm going in to work for a while, we can head over about five."

I went to town, bought flowers and spent the afternoon experimenting with ikebana arrangements. I was short on supplies so used a square Tupperware container that I wrapped with a black napkin and filled with rocks and sand as my base. I gathered greenery from around the cottage. I set it on the kitchen table.

Jon came over to get me and nodded at my first attempt. "That's nice."

"Hobby number one."

"What happened to wood burning?"

"I can't believe you remember that. This felt right for now."

Victor and Kaia's was only about a ten-minute walk down the beach. It was on stilts, much more exposed than my green shrouded den. The colors were faded; the many-paned windows had mullions peeling with generations of paint color whims. The finish on the floor was completely gone, the wood soft and worn. The steps in front and back sagged. The tin roof looked like it could Frisbee away any second. They had a huge fire pit on the waterside; we could smell the pig passing over.

It was all locals. There were lots of kids and dogs. Victor's upper arms were banded with tattoos and he'd switched out his toque for a headband. Kaia had her hair braided, probably to keep it from sweeping through the fire. Everyone was talking and laughing in the glow of red coals. A band of light bled out the kitchen window and folded its way down the stairs. A tabby cat with a stiff shivering tail paced back and forth through the light, waiting for that pig. Someone passed a joint. Jon introduced me around. The food was Victor delicious.

A couple of the women decided I needed to learn to hula. I guess they thought it would be amusing to see me try. They'd never seen me drive; I have great rhythm. They rolled my skirt down around my hips and tied my blouse in a knot. Ha! I did not embarrass myself. It was pure novice for sure. I couldn't get the whole belly jiggle thing going; but I could get off a pretty good hip pop. We bonded over my trying. I lost track of Jon. It was still early but it was starting to cool down and people were beginning to drift away. I had my blouse untied and skirt pulled up and had put on a shawl.

"Ready to go?" His voice near my ear sounded like a seashell.

"Yeah. Where were you? Hiding while I was trying a stoned hula. That pot was crazy."

"I was right here."

Kaia invited me to go to the locals' beach the next day and the waterfall the day after. I was making friends. I could see myself coming every Christmas. I needed to talk to the owner, get my dibs on the cottage before Mike.

It was dark walking back. The moon lit the sand enough to see. Jon said the paths around his house were crushed shell that the moon illuminated so they glowed. I smelled like smoke and roasted pig from head to toe.

"You want to take a hot tub? I'm smoky."

"Sure," he said. "You ready to drink your champagne?"

"Great idea. We'll celebrate my not making a complete ass of myself. Cut me off if I start saying shit."

I lit a hurricane lamp and put it on the porch. Jon opened the champagne and came out with two glasses. He clicked off the kitchen light.

"How do you want to do this?" I asked. "I'm okay naked if you are."

"That's fine."

We got in and clinked our glasses.

"You should have been dancing," I said.

"I've done the hula, it's not my dance."

"Oh boy, I'd love to see that."

"Catch me at a local wedding, I've been known to put on quite a floor show."

"Do you like to dance?"

"Sure, just not the hula."

"Are you any good?"

He laughed. "I have no idea."

"So you weren't embarrassed by your little haole friend?"

"The only person who can embarrass me is me. I know enough to not hula in front of Victor, I'd never hear the end of it. You've made a friend in Kaia. I think you can drop the haole. They weren't expecting that."

We put our heads back to look up at the sky. Papery leaves rubbed against each other and whispered in a gentle breeze. Night birds called. The ocean was off in the distance; the moon glittered on the surface like a path to the universe. White water rushed toward us then swept back out again. Champagne on top of pot. Crazy!

"How did a mathematician end up in the restaurant business?" I asked.

"I started out waiting tables. I needed the extra money to support my family."

"Your wife didn't work?"

"She wasn't my wife when she got pregnant. But no, she threw up for nine months, then Chana was born."

"So you worked two jobs?"

"For a while. My best friend, a biologist slash waiter, and I decided we should open our own place. We borrowed money from our parents. It was a juggle at first. She helped out then, until Chana jumped her corral. It worked. We ended up with five."

"That still seems like a huge stretch."

"It's not. I don't know many people who grew up dreaming of opening a restaurant. Most are like me, came at it sideways. It's an interesting business; it's always changing."

"But you have three restaurants now."

"And no partner. He has the two big ones and Chana's mother."

"Ouch."

"It's okay. I don't have a problem with it. He might."

"Mike said he's uptight about Chana."

"Yeah, that's been too bad, can't unwind children. He was with her mother first. It was pretty casual between us. We wouldn't have ended up married, but she got pregnant."

"Why didn't she have an abortion?"

"She'd had one with him, that's why they broke up. She was worried she'd never get pregnant again."

"That's not true."

"I know. I think it was more that she was mad at him for not wanting a baby with her. She always loved him. Then I came along. She felt ganged up on, maybe a little unappreciated. There might have been some payback."

"Unappreciated? How about pregnant and unloved?"

"I liked her, but he loved her. He just wasn't ready at the time."

"But you raised Chana."

"Not at first. They couldn't have more kids, she was right about that. Chana was mine. The tension was bad, bad for Chana. Her mother made a choice. That's where we are."

"Do you think the first one was his?"

"None of my business. It wasn't mine, I know that."

"I can't imagine not raising my daughter."

"She's a good person, Hannah. We were all young. She never stopped being a mother."

"It sounds like a soap opera."

"It was our stupid days. You want a glass of water?"

He went in for glasses of ice water and got back in the tub.

"I don't mean to sound critical," I said. "I don't know what I'd do. I was with a man who married a woman he doesn't love because she got pregnant. He didn't think she could do it alone."

"I love Chana, but trying to stay married would have just compounded our stupidity."

We were quiet in the steamy tub.

"I love this place." I was looking up through the leaves to a slice of starry sky. "I have no idea what India is going to be like. Physicist Phyllis says it's going to be wild."

"You'll fit in."

"Is this about the ear licking again?"

"No. I just think you'll melt in like you have here."

"Well, I'm trying to be a grown up. I'll be working anyway; it's a totally different thing. There's very little energy left over for wildness."

"What about the misbehaving crew?"

"There's always that. It's true for any gypsy business; same as yours I imagine. People used to party like rock stars, but that's toned down now, crews are smaller. We'll be using mostly local people. But lots of marriages still come apart on these long shoots."

"Why do people do it?"

"I guess because when you're in it, it's like rubbing up against something shiny. It pays well with great benefits. It's creative. We become just like a family, good and bad. It's hard to leave it. And if you do leave, you can't go back."

We were quiet for a few minutes.

"You tired?" I asked.

"A little, I'm okay. Why?"

"You're so quiet. Did I insult you again?"

"No, I'm just listening to you. You?"

"I'm a little buzzed, but I'm not tired."

"What do you think about now?" he asked.

"About now?"

"Does this feel right for now?"

"If you mean what I think you mean, if we do, I just want it to be two friends."

"It'll be what it'll be," he said.

"What's that mean?"

"It means we'll see what it means."

"Is that some kind of double talk thing that works on the lonely women who come through?"

"You need to drop the insults. I don't like it."

"Well, would you like some man talking to your daughter like that?"

"You're not my daughter. But if he were here now, it would be fine. It means it's wide open."

We were quiet. I got out and held out my hand to him. "It means we're just friends."

We put the cover back on, then dried off and took the hurricane lamp in, leaving it on the kitchen table. We stood looking at each other by the side of the bed while our eyes adjusted. My breath kept catching. He sat on the edge of the bed and pulled me down on him. I wrapped my legs around his waist. There was no overture. It was a strange beginning; I must have looked frightened.

"It's okay, Hannah," he said.

We stayed like that, looking at each other.

"I didn't want this to happen," I said.

"I know, let's just make the best of it."

I started laughing. "Make the best of it? We don't have to do this; we're not marooned here. We could go dancing instead. Oh god, I'm actually laughing. And I'm afraid to move."

He smiled. "You haven't stopped moving."

"That's just the laughing."

"I don't think so." He reached up and ran his finger around the edge of my ear. "I'm pretty sure we have to do this."

He was right. My mind may have been resisting, but the wild animal part of me had leapt ahead, and had been rolling and rollicking with him in complete abandon. Stroud's hot and otherworldly creature was on the loose.

It felt all new and like we'd known each other for lifetimes. At one point he knelt down between my legs. I reached for him but he pushed my hand aside and said, 'uh uh.' I don't know where his nose was, but I know where his tongue was. He held down my hips when I tried to push away from the intensity of it. When it was over he slowly dragged his tongue up my body to my ear and said, "Needs more salt." I started laughing again. He rolled me over and I thought of Steve. He slid his arm down along mine and followed along like he was reading Braille, then nudged my hand aside and took over. I was doing the same things to him. We learned, experimented, we played. I said "ouch," he said "sorry."

At one point I said I thought I'd met god. Another reason to not mix pot and champagne. Not the god part, that was true; but the saying so part. Sheesh. We fell asleep tangled like one; there were no protruding bones, no uncomfortable spots, we smelled better mixed together than apart.

I was completely surprised to wake up with him. Like I'd had a dream and there he was. He was still asleep with his arm thrown over his eyes. Soft hair swirled in his armpit. I knew it was soft; I'd spent some time there. He didn't smell like citrus or bay rum or Beverly Hills. He just smelled like a clean sexed up man who I knew. I lay looking at him while my psyche chewed her lip. I put my nose under his arm. He wrapped an arm around me as his other hand played with my electrified hair. He didn't open his eyes.

"That felt a little wild," he said.

"As compared to what?" I laid my head on his chest.

"Not going there."

He opened his eyes halfway and pulled me up to lie on top of him.

"Your rendition of 'Great Gig In The Sky' is something to hear," he said.

"It's a good song for me, no lyrics. I always get the words wrong."

"So no god?" he asked.

"Okay, that's embarrassing in the light of day."

"Yeah?"

He put his mouth to my ear and repeated back a few of my choicest lyrics from the night before. It was like hitting the play button. We slept another hour after that.

He went to work and I hiked out the red dirt trail to the beach. The locals had hung a swing in a tree so you can swing out over the water. If you time it right, you can jump out into a swell. Kaia and several of the other women from the night before had been in. I climbed over the rocks to the swing. I watched the rhythm of the swells then launched. Perfect timing. I hit the fat part of the wave and plunged into the warm water.

I surfaced and looked out. It looked like a set was going to start breaking a little father out; I swam toward it. I didn't want to get caught inside with wave after wave of soupy foam rolling over me. That's just confusion, water up the nose, and fighting for air. I dove just as the last wave broke. I didn't make it. I was slammed to the bottom; pinned to the sand. I grew up in the ocean; I knew I'd be okay. But there are always a few seconds, right before Mother Nature finally lifts her hand, when you think maybe this time she won't let you go on. I marked time. Crowds of laughing and unworried bubbles came to visit. With a life span of a millisecond, why worry? Mother's fingers rippled across my back. Sand and shells brushed past each other in scratchy conversation. I could see blue sky and air above me through salt-water eyes. Down there, it's like checking into a dream. The force passed overhead with a muted roar, the hand lifted, and I kicked for air.

A dicey shorebreak had developed. The waves were rearing up, sucking all the water with them, then slamming back down on the drained sand. From the beach it always reminds me of kittens leaping straight up, suspended for a beat, before pouncing on imaginary prey. But from the water it can be a problem. If there isn't much undertow, you're only in for one good spanking on the sand before you crawl to dry land. The kids do it for fun. But if there's a strong undertow like today, it slams you on the sand then drags you back out before you have a chance to get away. Then it keeps lifting and slamming you to earth until it gets bored. It can play the game for a long time. It's dangerous, exhausting and hard on the optimism.

People had run down to the water and formed a chain. They were pulling out stunned humans as they washed up within reach, a tug-of-war with Mother Nature. I got in line and took my smacking. I washed in dazed and confused and grabbed the hand that reached out for dear life. It was Jon. He was on the way back from picking up Chana at the airport and thought they'd stop to say hello. I had to pull my top down over my breasts, pull my bottom out of my sandy butt crack and then shake a blob of sand out of the crotch lining. If toying with the ocean isn't a metaphor for life, I don't know what is.

"I hate when that happens," I said. "At least I didn't lose my suit."

The guy next to me was fencing with the shorebreak wearing nothing but a band of white skin, and a dark patch of pubic hair. His trunks were washing in-and-out. When he finally grabbed them everyone yelled, "Ole!"

They stayed a few minutes while the women asked Chana how her Christmas had been with her mother. It was nice to feel the group of women holding her in their circle.

I went home. Jon was going to be at work until closing; he wouldn't be coming over. I checked in with Karin, nothing had changed which I took as a good sign. I told her I had skipped the pink bunny and cut to the chase, and that it had an added dimension I couldn't quite describe. That I'd not only licked his pineapple ear, but that I'd met a higher power.

"You called him god?" she said. "Not just 'oh god, oh please please baby, oh god'?"

"I didn't call him god, I said I'd met god," I clarified. "I think I said the other stuff too."

Boy do I hate it when I open my mouth and my mother falls out. I was really parsing the point. She hadn't said she drinks too much; she said I said she drinks too much. Ack.

"Crap, now I sound like my mother," I said. "Can you imagine what he must be thinking? He made a point of saying he wouldn't see me tonight. He'll probably hide now until I leave."

"Or show up in flowing robes. He's probably growing a beard."

"Oh my god. Or, oh my higher power, will I ever learn how to do this?"

"You met god, you're doing it. I gotta run, I locked the kids out, they're attracting the neighbor's attention."

I called Mom and heard about her new dress and comfortable shoes for New Years. Anna and Eric weren't home. I fell asleep sitting up reading in bed. When I woke up the next morning Jon was asleep beside me; he'd turned off the light, put my book aside and slid me down. I peeked under the sheet, no robes.

"How'd you know I wasn't here with someone?" I asked.

"Mike's gone so I took a chance. All your lights were on when I got home. Your door was wide open and you were sound asleep sitting up, lit up like a scene in a horror movie. It's a good thing I'm the only one who wandered over. You were out of it."

"Thank you, my neck would be killing me. I don't know why I'm so tired."

"You want to meet god again?" he asked.

"I didn't mean god, it was more like a higher power."

"I'm pretty sure I know what you meant. I saw some white light."

"White light?" I asked.

"Shhhh," he said. "Let's just do this."

We had a little more spirituality before fruit and coffee.

We hiked out to the waterfall. It's all very Tarzan. There's a rope swing and a slimy ladder made of branches to climb back up to the top and swing or jump off again. My arms were getting tired and I mistimed my last swing. I landed in a full court back flop. Ouch. Not exactly me-Jane material. It felt like the entire universe had taken it upon itself to spank me out of my last breath. Jon was already in the water.

"That must have hurt," he said.

"I'm sorry. I can't hear you making fun of me over the ringing in my ears."

"Come on, Hannah, move your arms and legs. I want to see you're okay."

I wiggled my fingers and toes; apparently my spinal cord was still intact.

"I think I am. I'm sure my posture is better."

I rolled over and treaded water. Everyone had been watching in silence from the rocks. When I finally moved they rained down on me from the cliff, sending cannonballs of water my way and howling with laughter.

"It's a good thing you landed so flat," said Chana. "People have died here doing that."

"Always a silver lining," I said.

We ate a picnic lunch in the warm blowing mist of the falls and hiked home. Jon ran his finger down my spinal column; he said I looked sunburned. They invited me over for an early dinner, then Chana was going to spend the night at a friend's and Jon was going into work for a while.

I found a piece of driftwood with a hole that fit a used glass jar perfectly. Then rooted around the cottage for greenery and a few flowers that I turned into a modest ikebana arrangement to take as an offering.

Jon put it in the middle of the table and Chana lit a few tealights around it. Their house was similar to Victor and Kaia's, but in much better condition. Everything that should have sagged had been reinforced. Jon had scraped all the paint off the mullions and painted them white which contrasted nicely with the dark green exterior and the soft neutral color on the inside walls. The bare floors were sanded and sealed. The furniture was eclectic and spare. For some reason I had imagined a 1970s surfer pad with hatch cover tables under heavy resin. Far from it.

The kitchen had been remodeled, but he hadn't gone overboard. He'd used a restored O'Keefe & Merritt stove with all the bells and whistles circa 1950, and a white refrigerator.

"That stove is great," I said. "I would have guessed a Wolf."

He smiled. "It belonged to my grandparents. I can go to work any time I feel the need to clean grease off stainless steel."

The bookcases were jammed with books behind well-used reading chairs and good lights. There were piles of magazines sitting around. They ranged from *Surfer* to *Scientific American* to *restaurant*. Chana had a pile of *Teen Vogue* topped by a calculus textbook. Laptops and cords wound around on the floor. CDs spilled out of a box by the sound system. Except for the slack key music and the sound of surf through wide-open windows, it reminded me of Margaret and Ed's apartment in New York.

I leaned against the kitchen counter and listened to them kid comfortably while they fixed dinner. The refrigerator was covered with photographs; lots were of Chana, a few looked like they were Chana and her mother. Lots were of Jon with various women. My heart pinched over those. I must have gone still because he was looking at me, his expression unreadable, when I broke away from the montage and looked back at him. I don't know how my face looked; it felt slack. I smiled at him, it didn't reach my eyes. Chana glanced up and looked back and forth between us.

"Salad's ready," she said. She held up red-stained hands. "That's the last time I use pomegranate seeds."

"I'm sorry, I'm just standing here. I should have shown you how to do it underwater," I said. "It's much easier, no mess."

We sat down to dinner. We ate and made small talk. Chana planned to major in engineering at either UCLA or Cal Tech. I said I thought it was no contest; I'd go for Cal Tech if I could get in. She wanted to know about L.A. I started waxing poetic about how much fun L.A. can be; about the music clubs and getting henna tattoos on Venice Beach. I told her the only downside was that the water in Santa Monica Bay was pretty funky. Jon was frowning.

I switched over to telling her Cal Tech was in a great part of town. She could live in Pasadena, hike the Sierra Madres, and dip in and out of L.A. without the hassle. Jon was nodding along in the kitchen as he rinsed dishes. We finished clearing the table and I headed home so they could take off.

I was reading when Jon came over a few hours later with a whole passion fruit pie.

"We didn't offer you dessert," he said. "Sorry it was so rushed."

"It's okay. You two get along great, you're a good team. It was nice to see your house. It isn't what I expected."

He filled me in on work while we ate pie. People were behaving just fine on Kauai, but the other two places were cutting loose.

In Honolulu a woman had been blowing out the candles on her birthday cake when her hairspray caught on fire. Fire had flashed across the surface of her hair like a sparkler then was gone. Besides gaping mouths, a few singed hairs were the only evidence. The restaurant had provided the candles; there could be a lawsuit. There had been a small grease fire in the Maui kitchen.

He was leaving the next afternoon to make the rounds and meet with the insurance guy. He invited me to go; we could ring in the New Year on a different island. I thought it sounded fun, but I reminded him that I needed to get back to leave. He said he needed to get back to check on Chana.

"You're as busy as a bigamist with the restaurants," I said.

"You got that right," he said.

"Where are the other two?"

"The big island. We thought they'd be raising Chana. It would have been less hassle for them."

He looked at my back, "This still looks upset. Is it okay if I stay over?"

"I'm okay, Jon." I said. "I'm just a little tired of all the knocking around. Do you think the universe is trying to send me a message?"

"I don't know about the universe, hula girl, but I'm about to."

"Are you going to call me hula girl the rest of our time?" I asked.

"Not if you don't like it."

"I could do without it."

We were lying in bed facing each other an hour later; messages had been delivered both directions. Mine was from a distance, his was cautious.

"Do you think it's possible to fall in love in three days like my parents? Or was it just lust and they lucked out that it lasted?"

"I think it's possible."

"I didn't really believe it."

"Hmmm."

"What's hmmm mean?"

"It means we'll see what it means."

"Yeah, that's what I thought." I rolled over and started to slide away from him but he wrapped his arm around my waist to pull me back. I felt caught in my usual brand of stupid.

I took his arm away. "Please don't do that," I said. "I don't like it."

I lay on my side looking out the window and listening to the ocean. I hadn't made an ass of myself doing the hula, or even talking about god, but I'd managed to do it falling in love with another unavailable man.

"Chana cleaned off the refrigerator door," he said. "She said designers don't do that. I hadn't noticed how cluttered it had gotten. That stuff fades into the background."

"She shouldn't worry about it," I said. "There aren't any rules about designers. The next one could love French Country."

We didn't talk again. It didn't feel like he was asleep. I hate lying in a tense bed so I wrapped a blanket around myself and went out on the porch to sit for a while.

I was still sitting there at three a.m. when it felt like I'd been stabbed in the stomach. My first thought was that a huge spider had bitten me. I jumped up and shook out the blanket. I couldn't feel anything that felt like a bite, but I felt woozy and threw up the pie over the railing. Then the pain started, wrenching spasms of pain. I curled up in a ball in the chair, then I walked down on the sand for a while, rubbing my stomach. I wondered if a hot tub would help, my low back was killing me. It kept going into spasm.

"Is there anything I can do?" Jon had put on pants and was standing on the porch.

"No, I think it's just horrendous cramps. I get them. The back flop may have turned up the volume."

I went into the bathroom. I was bleeding. The pain kept coming in waves with only brief reprieves. I'd never had cramps that intense. I got in bed and curled up. There was no more throwing up, just pain. There was blood on the sheets. Jon was rubbing my low back.

"You should go home," I said. "You won't get any sleep."

"I'm okay."

It kept up, the bleeding picked up, something was wrong.

I whispered to Jon, "Are you awake?"

"Yeah."

"This isn't right, I think I better go to urgent care or something."

"Let me make a call."

He made a call and went to get the car. What a mess. I couldn't even figure out what to put on. I decided on a skirt. Chills were rolling back and forth under the prickly skin on my back. I got to the car and sat on a towel. A woman doctor he knew was meeting us at her office.

"Oh god, this pain is incredible."

"We're almost there."

He pulled up to a small medical building. We went to the second floor and into the office of Patricia Loring, M.D. Patricia led me to an exam room, told me to get undressed and lie down.

She closed the door. I could hear her talking to Jon. She came in a minute later wheeling a machine, a chart folder under one arm.

"I told Jon he could leave and we'd call him, but he prefers to stay," she said. "Is that okay with you?"

"I guess so. I don't know what's going on."

"That's what we're going to find out."

She did a quick history, then an exam. She peeled off her gloves, and washed her hands. She took my legs out of the stirrups and tucked the blanket around me again.

"Okay. Based on what I just saw, and the dates, I suspect you're having a miscarriage. In fact, I'm about ninety-nine percent sure. I think it's straightforward, but I'm going to do an ultrasound to rule out complications."

"A miscarriage?"

She looked at my chart and at the calendar; I was only about three weeks along. Steve. She said when it happened that early the woman frequently didn't even know she was pregnant. I wished I were one of those women. She did the ultrasound, everything looked fine. One option was to do a D&C in the office, have it done with. That's what I wanted.

She moved me to a room with a bed and gave me drugs. Her nurse was on the way in; it would only take a few minutes. After a rest I could go home.

"Jon wants to see you. Is that okay?"

"It's fine."

The drugs were already taking effect when Jon came in. He looked worried.

"I'm sorry for dragging you into this."

"I don't know what you dragged me into, but it's okay. I'm not the one in bed."

"I'm having a miscarriage. Patricia is going to take care of it when her nurse gets here."

"Do you want to call someone?" he asked

"There's no one to call. I need this to be over. And you need to go, this isn't your problem."

I fell asleep. The drugs she had given me were amazingly potent for something that doesn't knock you out. I don't know what the actual procedure is, but I can tell you that even with the distance of heavy drugs it had a quality of pain that is hard to describe. It was a sharp and bitter scraping. It was in my core and out of my control. It felt sadistic. It was angry making. I could hear myself growling. I tried to fight it off, but her nurse held my legs down. She kept saying it was almost over, but it wasn't. It stretched to eternity.

I woke up an hour later and stared at the ceiling, the dropped panels had an embossed flower pattern. I slept another hour before the nurse came in with my hula skirt and angel wing tee shirt. Jon must have brought them. When I took off the thin gown the warm scent of the Kama Sutra oils was released into the room. The universe was going to just keep on mocking me. I had to wash the blood off my flip-flops; it had run down my legs.

Patricia came in a few minutes later and pulled a stool up to the bed. I said I was feeling stoned but fine. She said it had gone well, that it was unlikely to ever happen again. She said no sex for two weeks.

"Do women actually have sex?" I asked.

"Women do everything you can possibly imagine," she said. "Every story is different. This was out of your hands. Don't be hard on yourself."

She said I'd feel almost normal the next day, but to take it easy and call at the slightest sign of fever.

Jon was waiting for me, looking strained and tired. I couldn't look at him. Neither of us had anything to say on the ride home.

He came in behind me with my bag of bloody clothes.

"You changed the sheets," I said.

"You didn't need to come home to that. Patricia said you need rest."

I was glued to the spot. A combination of drugs and shock swarmed through me. I felt immense self-pity that I'd somehow landed back on this spot. It wouldn't ever be okay. I could barely stand up. I hated that he had to help me get into bed.

"This isn't home," I said. "This is just another place."

"She said you'll be fine."

"Whatever that means."

I told him to leave. I was rude. I was gone. I slept most of the day, then took a shower and put on fresh clothes. When I opened the door to let in some fresh air a coconut rolled in with a note wrapped around it.

It said: "Patricia says to eat this. Call me."

He'd left a hammer. I thought about using it to just pound on things. I didn't dare pound on the coconut; it would vaporize. I knew he'd gone to visit the other islands. I doubted I'd see him again. I was a little sore, but it wasn't any worse than the skin on my back. The universe hadn't spanked just breath out of me. I considered calling Steve, but let it go. This was punishment enough; I didn't need to hear the relief in his voice. I stepped over the coconut, went inside, closed the door and got back into bed. I was in the sliver of space between the drugs, pain and stress, and the loss that I knew was coming.

I woke up to a tapping sound. Jon was sitting on the back porch tapping the coconut.

I stuck my head out the door, "What are you doing here?"

"I'm cracking the coconut. You should eat this, it's some healing thing."

"I thought you were leaving."

"I'm not going anywhere until we talk about it."

"You're incredibly stubborn."

"So I've been told."

He started pulling the meat away from the hard shell. He'd drained the milk into a glass jar. "You coming out? Or are you going to hide from me?"

"I'm not hiding from you."

"Then what are you doing?"

I went out and sat on the step. He handed me a piece of coconut, then sat with his back to the railing, stretched out his legs and looked at me like he planned to stay awhile.

"I can't stand that we were..." I said.

I stopped. I didn't want to say making love; it hadn't been that for him. I didn't want to say having sex, it seemed like more than that, even for him. I didn't know what we'd been doing.

"That we were what?" he asked.

"Whatever. That it was waiting under the surface."

"I don't like it either. Is this someone you're going back to?"

"Do you want the truth?"

"Probably not, but I don't want anything else either."

I told him the story. He glanced away over the night Steve had pinned my face to the bed, it had probably been that night, and again over the last night of slurs. I didn't go into any real detail, but he seemed to understand the story. I'd traded a few nights of chemistry for what might have been a long-term relationship. The long-term relationship didn't take it well.

It was interesting to tell the truth. It moved the focus from a frittering brain trying to paint a prettier picture, to the shame and pain stored in the gut. Unlike the frittering, it was a relief when it was over. The sound of waves washed in and out over our silence. He handed me the jar of milk and I drank some; he drank the rest. I felt completely drained.

"I'm sorry, Jon. I had no idea. I would never have done that."

He wiped his hammer on the paper bag he'd been using as a cleaning board, then folded the coconut up in the bag and handed it to me.

"Eat this," he said. "I need to head out this afternoon. Take care of yourself."

"You too."

He picked up the empty jar and walked away. I didn't go to bed right away. I thought about calling Karin, but I was back to that place where my throat had closed up and the back of my tongue felt so fat I was sure I couldn't speak. I finally gave in and went back to sleep.

I woke up in the middle of the night; the cottage was dark and empty. I remembered. I was hungry but nothing sounded like food. Jon was gone and I needed to be home where the familiar walls could hold me together. I turned on all the lights, packed, and then got on-line and found a flight at noon. I left a note for the cleaners to take the food and left them a tip under the dead ikebana arrangement on the table.

New Year's Eve travel should be easy. I drove in before dawn, dropped the car, and sat around in the airport watching smiling couples come and go in matching all-terrain sandals. It would never occur to me to wear matching shoes, but I guessed that was what happy people did.

Ten

New Year's Day in Los Angeles and it was colder inside the house than out. I started a fire and opened windows. It's hard to make the transition from hot to cold. I made tea and walked around my two worktables, reacquainting myself with work. I still had a month before we left for India. I decided to pack all the material and move it down to our workshop at the studio on Monday.

I'd turned off my phone so I could get some uninterrupted sleep. I turned it back on and it rang almost immediately; it was Eric.

"Happy New Year," I said. "I tried calling, but you weren't home."

"We got the message," he said. "Where are you?"

"Home," I said. "I got in last night."

"You need to come down here," he said.

"Now? I just got back, I'm fried."

"There was an accident last night."

"What accident?"

"Binky was killed in a car accident." His voice was catching. "Amber too."

I sat down in a chair. I was having a hard time understanding English.

"Amber?"

He handed the phone to Anna.

"Hannah, I'm so sorry."

"How's Ted? The kids?"

"Mom and Arthur are there. It's not real yet, for any of us."

Binky had been at an afternoon New Year's Eve party with some girlfriends. She was drunk. She'd picked up Amber from a little program that her jump rope team, The Skippers, had put on at a convalescent hospital. It struck me as so odd that Amber would be doing anything that generous. Binky had pulled on to the freeway going the wrong way on an off-ramp. It was dusk, that confusing time of day. She'd always had a hard time with the light that time of day; her eyes were damaged after our childhood of long days playing in the sun. She'd driven down the freeway going the wrong direction. A semi-truck had slammed into them. As far as anyone knew they were both killed instantly.

Ted had been at work at the hospital when the bodies were brought in. He didn't know who they were until he recognized Binky's wedding ring. I had a vision of Binky driving in a stupor, blinking the way she did, while Amber screamed at her. I could almost hear Binky saying, "Oh shut up, Amber." Amber must have died terrified.

"I'm having a hard time understanding this," I said. "Was anyone else hurt?"

"No, just them. Can you come down?" asked Anna.

"I'll be down this afternoon."

"Do you want me to send a car?"

"No, I can do it."

"Be careful. It's a shock."

I had to move, get on the road. I dumped my suitcase out on the unmade bed and threw Hawaii in a pile on the floor. I started packing again. I didn't know what I would need. I packed the suit I'd worn to my grandmother's burial. I added my book of Emily and my pearls. Bettina and I had been given pearls for our eighteenth birthdays. I damped down the fire, stirred the ashes, and even went so far as to sprinkle water on it to be sure it was completely out before leaving. I never did that. I wasn't sure what mattered to do and what didn't.

I emailed Margaret to let her know what had happened. I blind-copied Karin. It was a crude way to deliver the news, but I didn't have a phone call in me and I knew she'd understand. I was on the road by noon.

I drove for miles and miles without awareness. I needed to pay attention. I tried to force my mind to focus, but it wanted to run the Bettina movie. Not the Binky crash movie, but the vivacious young Bettina movie. The smart big sister who told me I must be growing up after I told her I had a hankering for butterscotch pudding. She said knowing what I wanted was the first sign of growing up. I felt so proud of myself over the taste of butterscotch that had spontaneously bloomed on my tongue.

We used to have a monkey tree with needle leaves in the backyard. Binky used to say she was the doctor and poke me with them. She kept saying she wouldn't really poke me this time, but then she did. I always fell for it. I wanted her to like me.

One day she decided to fry donuts while our parents were gone. The grease caught fire. Instead of putting the lid on the pan, she ran screaming through the house with the flaming pot of oil, through the garage, and then poured it in the street. My parents weren't as upset about the fire and burned up kitchen, as they were about the fact that she'd drunk two shots of whiskey before they got home. She'd seen Mom do it.

Her drinking years had been a nightmare. She was so unhappy. She'd wanted to go to college and be a doctor, to poke people for real. But she'd been trapped in Mother's dream catcher of how life should be.

Eric opened the door. His eyes were red-rimmed with crying and fatigue. His shoulders sagged under the burden of being a responsible man. Anna's nostrils were chapped; she looked plain and worn out. Their kids, Adam and Grace, were quiet and sticking to themselves in their rooms. They were good friends with their cousins Sam and Sam; they were close in age. They had taken their cousins to the beach where they just sat around. They'd picked bits of dry seaweed out of the sand until it was clean, and then let the warm grains run through their fingers, over and over, like an hourglass. Anna said the kids hadn't said much.

Eric was on the phone with the funeral home, but nothing could be done New Years Day. It's a busy night for the coroner. No one in the family had buried a child since our grandmothers, two generations before. We needed to learn how to do that. Would there be two services? Two burials? Could we even stand that? There would be no viewing; the damage was too great. I wondered if that was better, to not have that last image of a stranger called by your sister or niece's name stuck in your memory.

Anna and I went over to Binky's where Mom was passing time cleaning out the refrigerator and making homemade soup. It smelled like a hundred Sunday afternoons growing up. Arthur was playing a video game with Sam. Samantha was in her room with the door closed. Ted was wandering around. Samantha came out of her room and then went back in a few minutes later, carrying her mother's jewelry box. I smiled at her, she didn't smile back. She closed the door. I'd have to tell her I still had my father's.

No one was watching football or reruns of the Rose Parade. I knew what they were doing; they were living in a shocked ground fog, suspended between then and the unknown of what would come when the sun burned through the haze. I thought of a sky sandwich, of Jon saying we can't go to those other worlds without some help. But they would, they would somehow get to the next place like we all do, with or without help.

I hugged Ted, he was stiff; he thanked me for coming. He was going to need to do a lot more than wander in the years ahead. I hugged my mother and she started to cry. The fabric on my shoulder was completely soaked before she ran down. I was crying on her shoulder. It felt like we were literally steaming with grief.

Anna and I didn't stay long. There would be days and days of it to get through. We started home. I told her about the miscarriage. She reached over and held my hand and started crying. I felt cried out. I said she needed to pay attention to her driving or she'd get us killed too. Black humor was creeping in. We drove down to the beach, parked and just sat together. Eric called to check on us. We went home. He needed us too; we sometimes forget that about him.

None of us were hungry. I said I thought being hungry confused the issue so Anna defrosted homemade lasagna and heated rosemary rolls. We devoured it. I wondered if they felt the same twinge of guilt I did, for enjoying food when Binky and Amber never would again.

Friends and neighbors would start arriving with food at Binky's tomorrow, as soon as the word spread and their New Year's hangovers were behind them. We would stop calling it Binky's soon, and start calling it Ted and the kids' house. I wondered if Ted would remarry. I thought so. I hoped he had better luck.

I checked my email. Margaret and Karin had both responded with concern. Margaret said not to worry; we would be fine no matter how much we got done before we left. Karin was shocked and said to call when I got a chance. Jon hadn't called. I tried him, but it went to voicemail. I hung up. I knew I couldn't get through leaving him a message. I didn't even know why I was calling him.

I took a long hot shower and put on my nightgown. I felt like a little girl in a red and yellow flannel nightgown in my brother's house. My mother had given it to me for Christmas with the note, "red and yellow, catch a fellow." She hadn't met Steve yet. But when I was only fifteen she'd given me sets of red and black lace underpants and bras. I didn't know what to make of it at that age. She can be so out of synch.

The next days were a blur of arrangements. We picked out caskets and shopped for funeral clothes with the kids. We talked to the minister and listened to music for the service. We picked prayers. We picked photographs to have enlarged.

We took turns being the hostess at Bettina's. Food, flowers, strained conversations. I made a point of being the one who ferried food back and forth from neighborhood freezers so the kids didn't have to do it. They'd find out soon enough that they were aliens in a changed land.

Ted and the kids wanted one service, one burial. After Grandma's burial Bettina had announced that she wanted to be buried in Altadena too. Ted was torn between burying them close so the kids could visit, and honoring Bettina's last request. He opted to buy new plots, side-by-side. No one got on their high horse about Binky's last wish. We knew it didn't matter. As far as I knew no one in my family had ever visited my father's grave. I decided to ask Eric to do that with me. I emailed Margaret and Karin progress reports. I knew they were sitting out there loving me.

Eric and I went to our father's grave. We wondered why people do that. We had Filipino friends who set up a whole

Christmas tree, and Hispanic friends who took picnics. Presbyterians are called the frozen Christians; we don't go in for graveside partying.

"Anna told me what happened, I'm sorry. We hoped you'd have a good time over there," he said. "Get a fresh start."

"It's the most fun I can ever remember having, but it wasn't meant to be, none of it. I guess it was a fresh start in a way. The alternative would have been a nightmare. The boys next door were sleeping in a hut they built. Do you remember the forts Binky built for me?"

"Yeah, especially the pink sheet tent. Then she served you graham crackers and mandarin orange slices for two days until you threw up and Dad put a stop to it."

"Warm mandarin slices. I still can't even think the word *mandarin*. She saved me from the boy up the street when I was nine, did you know about that?"

"What boy?"

"The Taylor boy, not boy really, he was probably eighteen. I was over playing with his sister. I didn't even know she had a brother; he just appeared one day. He took me in the den and stuck his hand down my pants and rubbed me. He told me to wear something silky next time. I didn't know what he meant. I was still wearing cotton underpants with smiley faces."

What I didn't tell Eric was how it had felt good; his voice in the dark room was hypnotic. I felt guilty at age nine without having any idea why.

"That guy was never a boy, he was a fucking freak." Eric was looking off in memory. "He was always being hauled off somewhere for reprogramming."

"I told Binky about it at a swim meet. I can still see her in her shiny blue bathing suit and one of those horrible caps that tear your hair out. I swore her to secrecy."

"Binky never kept a secret in her life," he said. "God, could she blab."

"She must have blabbed to Mom and Dad. The guy disappeared. No one ever mentioned him again. I still played with his sister."

"Dad probably took him half a tank off the coast and shoved him out of the plane."

"That's kind of mafia for a Presbyterian."

"That was a no-fly zone for him."

"That's comforting to know. I was wondering about it the other day. I've never known what would be okay with him."

"He was no Puritan, obviously. But he was dug in about people confining their activities to the appropriate age group."

"Yeah. Mom too. She hired a painter once when I was in high school. He said something funky to me and I told her. She got in the car to go to the office, then drove around the block, came in and kicked him out of the house."

"Mom. Took her a trip around the block to decide to fire him before the work was done. It's hard to find a painter."

We ended up on the ground laughing. It's good to laugh when you're burying your sister and niece. I asked him why Aunt Asp wasn't around. I couldn't believe she'd miss a chance to be cruel to her sister over the death of her daughter. They were traveling in China; it was too much to come home. Nice sister, but better for Mom that way. We were lying on the grass looking at the sky, taking a break from adulthood.

"What kind of truck was it?" I asked.

"Mack."

"A John Deere would have been too weird, wouldn't it?"

"Yeah, but as Anna said, stranger things have happened."

"What did Binky keep of Dad's?"

"I don't know."

"Oh come on, Eric. She told you everything. She had to blab."

"She wouldn't tell me that. I can't even guess."

"Does his watch work?"

"No. The crystal was broken, it could probably be fixed."

"What time is it?"

He was quiet; he knew what I meant. "Eighteen-thirty-one. You were right. I looked it up. It was sunset."

"It's hard to see that time of day," I said.

"For this family at least," he said.

The world turned and the day of the service finally got around to us. Ted and the kids looked like a set of papier-mâché death effigies on sticks. Their clothes hung off them. Samantha was wearing Binky's pearls. I was wearing mine. Mom was in a black suit with some room in it; she'd lost weight. Her skin looked pale and flakey through a hole that was starting in the back of her black pantyhose. Adam and Grace sat with Sam and Sam, next to Ted. Arthur and Eric flanked Mom, who looked out of focus. Anna and I found space to fit in.

We got through the service. Eric did the eulogy; he had borrowed part of our graveside conversation. Not the hands down the pants guy, but he talked about swim meets, and pink tents, and how Binky never could keep a secret. Everyone smiled a remembering smile. Amber's Skipper team came; they wore their team tee shirts with the rainbow jump rope logo. They sang "Somewhere Over The Rainbow" and we all sobbed. Ted could probably have told stories about his wife and child, but that was too much to ask.

The burial was private. Two shiny black limousines followed a black hearse with Binky, and a white hearse with Amber. Their caskets didn't match either. Binky's was a soft metallic grey with silver trim. Amber's was smaller. It was white with little girl trim edging the lid. It looked like multi-colored pastel jump rope. The sweet pastel colors flashed soft flares of rainbow color across Binky's metallic grey as they carried them across the lawn to be lowered into the ground. The plots were under shade trees. It would be a nice spot for them on hot summer days. The minister said a few words. Then I read Emily's poem "Hope."

Hope is the thing with feathers
That perches in the soul
And sings the tune without the words
And never stops at all

And sweetest in the Gale is heard
And sore must be the storm
That could abash the little Bird
That kept so many warm

I've heard it in the chillest land
And on the strangest Sea
Yet never in Extremity,
It asked a crumb of me.

As I read my mind was panicky with the realization that hope had nothing to do with the situation. It was the wrong poem. My voice kept faltering as my brain tried to run on two tracks. No one said anything. I doubt they were listening. Binky wasn't there to roll her eyes at me.

They lowered them into the ground. We each threw a handful of dirt and a flower on their boxes before turning away to the cars. The raggedy burial boys who had been standing back in the trees started up the coughing backhoe. Diesel fumes drifted our way. Eric looked back at them and they shut it off.

We were halfway to the cars when my mother started making a low growling sound. It reminded me so much of the sound I'd made during the procedure it made my gut spasm, like I was back on the table trying to fight off the scraping. She started keening and sobbing. Arthur tried to take her arm but she wrenched it away and threw herself with pounding fists on Ted. He stood like a statue and took the beating.

She was screaming at him, "Why didn't you do something, why didn't you do something? You just let her die. You let them die. You killed your own daughter."

Eric and Arthur together couldn't get her off him; she lashed out at both of them when they tried. She scratched Ted's face. Somehow he stayed on his feet and took it. The children were horrified. Anna and I were saying "Mom Mom Mom," over and over and trying to reach her. She kept twisting away. She finally ran out of strength and dropped to her knees on the grass.

She was sobbing and chanting, "My baby, my baby, my first baby." She clawed at the grass.

Anna and I were crying. We murmured at her as we tried to lift her to her feet, but she was dead weight, heavier than dead weight. Eric looked stricken. His eyes were full of tears, his nostrils were flaring; he was trying to keep it together. Ted put his arms around his children and walked them to the car. Adam and Grace were frozen in place to see their grandmother like that. Arthur watched quietly.

We finally got her to her feet; her stockings at the knees were smashed in with mud and grass. She allowed us to lead her back to the car but she kept looking back at the holes in the ground. The burial crew had started to remove the flower sprays from the caskets, but thought better of that too.

We got her to the car. Ted had left with the kids. Mom and Arthur had come with them, so we had to all squeeze into one car. Eric sat in front with the driver. Arthur was rubbing the top of Mother's hand with his thumb. She was looking out the window. I doubted she could see. Tears were running down her face, her nose was running unchecked, her muscles looked slack. She daubed at her face with a saturated and dirt smudged linen handkerchief. There was an "S" embroidered on it; it was one of my father's. She had dirt under her bare nails. She looked twenty years older and yet somehow like an angel. There was nothing to say.

We arrived back at the funeral home. We had planned to eat together at Eric and Anna's, but Mother asked Arthur to just take her home. We drove home in silence, unlocked the door and walked in dropping our purses as Eric dropped his clattering keys on the kitchen counter. He said he was going for a run; he was good at pounding it out of his system. The kids disappeared together into Grace's room. Anna and I made tea and sat in our burial suits in the living room. Our stocking feet touched on the ottoman we shared.

"Do you think she'll start drinking again?" I asked.

"She already has."

"Have you talked to Arthur?"

"Eric talked to him this morning. It's under consideration."

"What's to consider?"

"Whether Arthur is big enough in her life to outweigh what losing Binky and Amber means to her right now. It's not something any of us can know at this point."

"That's up to Mom," I said.

"I know," she said. "We figure she has it under consideration. Arthur won't stay; he's made that clear. But he loves her, they've been very good together."

"What's his timeline?"

"He's debating. Pretty quick I think. He understands how it works."

"I was so hopeful for her."

"We all were, and for Arthur. It seems like they've been together a long time, but it's only been a little over a month."

"I was so happy she'd found someone. Judith told me that Grandma referred to me as a gangly cat after Daddy died. That she told Mom no one would want a woman with a cat instead of a cute kitten. Have you ever heard that?"

"She didn't say you were a cat. She said Mom should find someone while you were still a kitten."

"That makes me sick. Why would she talk about me like that?"

"She was worried about you both. She couldn't admit Mom drank. She dragged out what she had."

"I thought she loved me," I said.

"She did. She used to brag about you to everyone in the family. She always said you were the most like her. Such a strong little girl."

"She never said that to me."

"They never do."

"This family is exhausting," I said.

"Well you know mine, they're the same way," she said. "We're always the last to know."

I was feeling so raw, I grabbed onto that little shred. The idea that my grandmother thought I was strong. I was leaving in the morning; I was now down to three weeks. I'd had a few inquiries about subletting my place and I needed to get that settled so I could pack up. I knew losing Binky and Amber would come in waves. There was just no way to rush it; it had to be lived through. We'd all discover in time what it meant to us. If my father's death had taught us anything, it's that we'd keep discovering what it meant, for the rest of our lives.

Eleven

I got home at noon the next day and started the coming home process again. I washed or threw away my moldy clothes from Hawaii, then settled back in with work. I'd lost so many mental threads along the way and I couldn't pick them up. I needed boxes. My mind wanted to talk about the last two weeks; my heart just wanted to hear Jon's voice. I'd left him another message telling him I'd be home. He hadn't called. I wondered how long it would be before I was released from wanting him.

Karin and I met for lunch. She looked wan. I caught my reflection in the restaurant window; I did too. The whole thing, especially Amber, horrified her. It hit too close to home with Callie the same age. I told her about the miscarriage. She was glad I hadn't had to grapple with Steve over an abortion; he wouldn't have wanted it.

"I thought it was love, Karin," I said. "With Jon."

"I know, you sounded so happy," she said. "I'm sorry it had to all come crashing down like this."

"I think the worst part of the whole thing is this feeling that I got caught out again not having any idea what was really going on. It felt so right. It was so easy. I imagined that I knew him from some other time. It was like we understood each other. He hasn't even called me. I feel like the whole world knows something that I don't, like there's some big secret to all this. I'd really like it to slow down long enough for me to figure it out. I'm beginning to think arranged marriages are the way to go. I really don't trust myself."

"I don't know if there's a big secret. If there is I obviously don't know it. Your mother would have arranged for you to marry Steve. I don't think you'd be happy with that. It can't have been easy for Jon to go through that with you. Especially if he loves you."

"He doesn't love me, Karin. That last night, before it happened, I told him I loved him and he said we'd see what it means."

"See what it means?"

"Yeah, that was just one of his dodges. He said it the first night and I ignored it. I guess I just didn't want to know. I told myself we were just friends. I shouldn't act so shocked. The warning signs were flashing at me."

"Maybe. It's hard to see when we're under the ether."

"Did you have any inkling about Oscar? I remember you saying you just thought he was having an affair."

"I already knew. I was like you, trying to not know. And we were past the ether stage. According to him he's surprised he did it."

"Do you believe him?"

"Not really. So far he hasn't said why. He hasn't blamed it on me though; he's been good about that part. That alone might save us. Remember when Melissa's husband said it was because she needed to lose weight and have a facelift? She's only forty."

"That guy was an asshole from day one. We could have all told her that was coming. Did you know when you were pregnant? That early."

"Not the first time. I was tired, but the way we were going at it every second we weren't at work anybody would have been tired. With Richard, Oscar knew it before I did. He kept saying I was pregnant, that I tasted pregnant. I thought he was crazy."

"I thought I was just tired," I said. "Tired and happy. What am I going to do?"

"There's nothing to do, it just takes time. It's really good that you're going to India."

"My heart won't let him go."

"I know. I have the same thing going on with Oscar. I think it might be easier if he was in Hawaii and I didn't have to be around him. See him with the kids and all that."

"I have no reason to hang on. You have two good reasons and a life together. I hope you guys survive this."

"We'll see."

We parted company. I had arranged to meet with a couple of guys interested in subletting my house. Their project synched up almost perfectly with mine. They loved the idea that the place was a party house with a pool. I didn't even need to pack up; I could just store my stuff in the closet. That sealed the deal. I ran out for boxes. If I couldn't focus on work, I could start clearing out and storing.

I spent a few days doing that. Tears kept making the emulsion gooey as I sorted old photographs. Binky helping me ride a bike. There was a picture of her shaking her hairbrush at someone; she did that a lot. I hoped she had found some peace at the end of her struggle trying to be Bettina and still be the Binky that our mother loved. Anna and I talked almost everyday. Eric was better. He had turned his focus to Mother; it wasn't going well. Arthur had stopped seeing her. It was showdown time. I hadn't gotten any calls from her yet; I dreaded that.

Jon called.

"Hi Jon."

"I didn't expect you to leave, Hannah."

"You left. It was time for me to get back to reality."

"What's reality?"

"So glib, Jon. Reality is me here, work, India. My sister and niece were killed in a car accident."

"Why didn't you call me? I would have come back."

"I've been calling. I was in the air, I didn't find out until I got home."

He was quiet on the end of the line. Hearing his voice had unleashed a tsunami that swept along fragments and splinters of broken up lives. I got hoarse trying to not cry. I did not want to cry anymore.

"My mother started growling at the burial," I said. "It sounded just like me when I tried to fight off Patricia; they had to hold my legs. Have you ever been held down while someone hurts you? She beat my sister's husband; she said he'd killed his own daughter. She was talking about herself; we knew that. I don't want to end up clawing at the earth to give me back my baby. Binky saved me from a bad man. I was only nine. Binky told. She never stopped blabbing. My father did something. I had to live thirty-two years before I could know he'd throw him out of the plane. She saved me and I couldn't help her. I should have done something. I just stood by. They buried them with a back-hoe like they dig in trash at the dump. They threw their flowers on the ground. There was no viewing; they were crushed. Crushed. Samantha is wearing her pearls; Binky's skin is spun around the silk cord. They're her color. Pearls become the color of us. I didn't even want it. I just kept thinking I could do enough to make it work out okay, to be what he wanted, to fill it all in; to fill the hole. That somehow it would work out. I didn't even know you. Then all I wanted was you."

I sounded like I was being strangled from the effort to say it all; it was tumbling out so hard. The phone was covered with tears and snot, but I had stopped crying.

He was saying, "Sh, sh, sh, it's okay, it'll be okay."

"Don't shush me! Oh my god, don't do that. That's just what you do. You say it's okay. My sister and her baby are dead and you're saying it's okay. Nothing is okay! This is real. This is what it is and it's not even remotely okay, it will never be okay. How can you even say that?"

"I didn't mean them dying, Hannah. I meant what happened to you, between us. There are no words for what happened to them. I know it will never be okay."

"I can't stand this right now, Jon. It seems so unimportant. Maybe if we'd talked about it then, when it still mattered. But you just accused me of hiding, then walked away when I told you the truth. I know it wasn't pretty; I didn't want to talk about it. I know you didn't love me. But for some reason I didn't expect you to be careless with me. I didn't see that coming; the just walking away. It feels like everyone leaves without saying good-bye. But it really doesn't matter any more. Thanks for calling."

I hung up on him. I hated that I did that. But I was afraid he'd keep talking and I'd somehow get sucked into feeling hopeful. Or worse, that he'd say good-bye. I couldn't do that right now. He called back. I ignored it.

The next morning I packed for a while and then met Karin. Lunch was quiet in each other's reassuring field. My hair had grown out enough to try to make some sense of it. She called and hounded our guy into fitting me in. Then she went along while he did his best to even it up and get rid of the chunks of color that were growing out and leaving crazy-quilt patches all over the top of my head.

We drank espressos and paged without seeing through *People*. We had enough self-respect to talk about everything but what was on our minds. It was a struggle, but we both understood the futility of running around in words that would get us nowhere. We'd say a lot of meaningless things that we didn't believe. We were two people at a no answers place in our lives.

The pink-stick pedicurist bounced over and said hello. I envied her what seemed like her oblivious state. My hair ended up shorter, but it was smooth. I looked like a blonde version of Aunt Judith when she was young. I wondered if I'd end up just like her, a bitter woman making excuses.

I talked to Anna at the end of the day. Arthur had taken Mom to an AA meeting and everyone was holding their breath. Adam and Grace had taken Sam and Sam to the latest comedy movie; they'd laughed. Anna had aced her entrance exam. I knew she would. We'd have a lawyer in the family. Eric was running miles and miles; he was training for a yearlong schedule of 10Ks.

We covered the checklist; Binky and Amber were not on it. There were empty lines. We didn't poke at "the Binky problem," we didn't shake our heads over Amber's tantrums. The hope for them had come to an end.

Jon left messages asking me to call him. I wasn't ready for that. I might never be. I couldn't just be friends with him, not while I loved him. I'd read somewhere that love passes in eighteen months. I needed time to pass. I hoped it passed more quickly when only one person was involved. I hoped nine months in India would be enough. I wanted to just go away.

I was done packing away my things. After giving away the clothes that I never liked, dropping books at the Goodwill and sorting old files, it all fit in a row of boxes along the top shelf in the closet. I was leaving everything else in place; the guys were just bringing clothes.

I made neat stacks of all the old photos and put them in my father's box, the overflow I put in Grandma's box. I folded my father's tee shirt full of holes on top of the boxes. I threw away Stroud's card. I'd found that and more in Jon, and lost it.

I hadn't even thought of Steve in the last week. All the pain and energy and it was as though he had never happened. I'd felt the same way after kicking out my husband. How did I do that? Keep tricking myself into thinking I knew what I was doing. Investing so much energy trying to make nothing seem like something.

Margaret emailed the location of our offices on the lot and said she'd see me there when I felt up to it. I decided to move everything down the next day and get back to work.

I called Mother early the next morning. According to Anna, the meeting had stuck; she was back in AA and Arthur was back in her life.

"How are you doing, Mom?"

"It does help. The one-day at a time."

"We were so worried about you."

"I know, but there's no salvation in going backwards, that's what someone told me at a meeting. I can't change the past; I've already lived there. It's hard to understand that sometimes. I know we have a lot to do. How are you doing?"

I told her about the miscarriage that had slammed me back to earth with a mouth full of wet sand. I wasn't worried anymore about her telling Binky and having Binky blab to the universe. Binky was probably doing that anyway, but at least it was out of earshot. She was sorry, but sounded almost philosophical when she said I was probably right about not having children just for the sake of having children.

I asked her if she knew about the Taylor boy. She said my

father had threatened to kill him. The police said they'd have to prove damage. They hadn't wanted to put me through that. They had settled on sending him away and watching me. I told her I hadn't even remembered it until a few weeks ago. She laughed full out over Eric's idea that Daddy had shoved him out of the plane over the ocean like a mafia guy. She said the wrath he was in, she wouldn't be at all surprised if he had. It was good to hear her laugh over Daddy again. It was good to know about the wrath.

I asked her if she knew what Binky had kept from our father.

"She kept his office coat. The one embroidered with his name."

"His white coat? Why?"

"I don't know, Hannie, I never asked her. She didn't know I knew."

I knew why. Binky had her doctor's coat, one way or another.

"She wanted to be a doctor, Mom."

"I guess she did."

"I'm glad you made soup that day."

"Soup?"

"Yeah, you made soup that first day after they died. It was comforting to have that smell in the house."

"It was all I could think to do."

"I know. It was a good idea."

I called Eric and told him she'd kept the coat. "Her dream coat," I said. "I bet she would have worn it the first day."

"Dr. Spring," he said. "Does this shit ever end?"

"I don't know. I don't think so."

"Me either. Take care."

"You too," I said. "And stop swearing. We're starting to sound like a couple of Camp Pendleton Marines."

"Fuck that."

"Yeah, fuck that," I hung up. That felt like the first decent good-bye all year.

I called Jon; it was stupid, but I told myself it was time to pack him up too. Whatever that meant. It rang and rang before a sleepy woman answered. I realized it was still early there. The phone got fumbled around a little and Jon got on. He sounded tense.

"Hi Jon, it's Hannah. Sorry to disturb you. I wasn't paying attention to the time. I'm just leaving for work here."

"It's okay. How are you?"

"I'm fine. I felt bad about just hanging up. I was upset. I know I didn't sound very rational. It's been a lot, but I don't like that, the just hanging up. I wanted to say good-bye. I need to get to work."

"I'll call you later."

"Don't worry about it. I'm super busy now."

"I'll call you later."

"It's okay, it's all fine. I just didn't like that whole hanging up thing. I'll be back in a year and we can catch up then. Tell Chana I'm still rooting for Cal Tech. Bye."

Fuck that would have been better. I walked around on the stone floors. Some part of me hadn't believed it. He really had moved on. Why had I called him? I was acting pathetic. I said the words about not knowing what was going on, but apparently even I didn't believe me. Well I'd gotten what I deserved.

Maybe it was time to call my therapist and ask for a reminder about who I was. Or just confess to a massive relapse; that I'd tried to fit not one, but three, of the wrong men into my life over the holidays. Maybe I could live with her in lock-down clueless rehab until I left. My exploding heart set off shockwaves. I wondered just how long it would take for the time glue to dry and stick the broken pieces back together. It didn't feel possible.

I hauled boxes up to my car. I had no will to drive to the studio and go through the motions, but I had told Margaret I'd be there. In our business, even with people as close as Margaret, you show up and act interested.

Margaret was on the phone when I arrived. She had a guy there setting up tables for me and moving things around. He helped me unload the car. Just being in motion in the familiar surroundings of a back lot helped. Margaret opened my boxes and pulled out treasures.

"This is great stuff," her voice was muffled at the bottom of a carton. "I'd burn some incense to get us in the mood, but it would probably set off the sprinkler system."

"I've been burning it at home, it's a little shrill." I must have sounded bird shrill myself; she looked at me over her glasses.

"How are you?" she asked. "Maybe you should have stayed home."

"I can't think of a time when I've been worse. Other than that, I'm fine."

"You want to talk about it?"

"No. It feels like too much right now. I wouldn't know where to start or how to stop. It feels like all I do is cry. I'm sick of me. It feels good to be here, to work."

We unpacked the rest of the boxes and divided it up by topic. I had files of photographs, artwork, artifacts: anything that might help us decode the zeitgeist of India circa 16th century.

We worked and made lists; we went to the commissary for lunch. We sat in the harsh winter sun with our pads and laid out an order for the work. We weren't at a cold start; Margaret had already been working on the project for months. She wanted me to handle all the night time work. She was passing the really fatiguing work on to me as the younger member of the team.

It was a vote of confidence. Our days went on like that for the next week. Work, lunch, sketching, planning, endless phone calls tracking down material in India while dealing with a 12-hour time difference. The production office was up and running over there. People were more than happy to stay up all night and take our calls.

Going out on location is different from personal travel; it's like moving with an army. They'd provide all the support we needed so we could go into battle each day, then return to camp. We'd have runners and messengers and a general in our director. The only thing missing would be carrier pigeons. For all I knew about India, we'd have those too. Our camp would have Ed at the cook stove sipping gin.

I fell into a pattern. I swam laps in the morning, then called Mother while it was still early. Some mornings she cried, but so far they were sober tears. I talked to Anna every few days. They were negotiating the household workload now that she was back in school. Their sex life had taken a turn to the wild, like New York in La Jolla. She'd never talked about their sex life before.

All of us had been roused from the going to work and making dinner trance of our lives. Death is like an earthquake, it reminds you to pay attention to life. Throw some extra shoes and a bottle of water in the trunk of the car, and get ready for it, for a while at least. Like everything else we try to prepare for, the day the earthquake comes the shoes have turned to stone and the water has leaked out and left a dried up stain.

I was up early on Saturday morning when Jon called. It was 5:00 a.m. in Hawaii. I couldn't not answer.

"Hey, Jon. You leave before the kid woke up?"

"I didn't want to miss you again. How are you?"

"Busy, we leave in a few weeks."

"I want to see you before you go."

"Don't be ridiculous. I'm barely getting through the day."

"I'm going to fly over."

"Don't come here. We don't need that. I hate the whole talk it to death thing. That's just code for you wanting me to apologize for something. I know all about that. I'm willing to make amends, but unless I'm completely crazy, I only inconvenienced you a few times. You seemed to have a good time; it was a fair trade. But seeing you, talking about it, it's never going to happen. I'd rather go flog myself on Sunset Boulevard."

"No apology. You know that wasn't it."

"What was it then?"

"It felt like a bomb had dropped, Hannah. I went from worrying that you were going to die because I took you to the waterfall, to hearing that story. I wanted to kill the guy. That's all I was really thinking about. How to track him down and kill him for doing that to you. I got in that stupid place. I didn't mean to be careless with you."

"He didn't do it alone and he sure didn't do it to you."

"You didn't listen to yourself. But he wasn't just careless; I've been there. Sometimes it's just easier. But I didn't want to hurt them. He cared about hurting you. That's something else."

"I know, Jon. It took a while, but I got that part. I don't appreciate you talking to me like I'm your daughter. I did my part. I cheated on him instead of just breaking up; I wanted it both ways. I let him talk about having children. We almost had a child."

"You could have stopped that."

"But that's just it, I wouldn't have, not without him agreeing. That would have felt dishonest. I realize now how incredibly stupid that would have been. I am so lucky. I don't think I even liked him."

"Then why won't you see me?"

"Because I thought it was love with you. I'm so furious to be in this place and still so clueless that I can hardly stand it. You moved on and I need to do the same. I can't be friends, not yet. I need time and space."

"I haven't moved on."

"Jon, when a woman answers your phone in bed, you've moved on. I've never done that."

"It didn't mean what you think. It was nothing."

"Why do men always refer to women as nothing? Do you tell her she's nothing when you're making love to her?"

"I'm not doing that. I have no idea why she answered the phone."

"Not making love to her? She answered the phone. I don't think she knows that, Jon. You sure had me fooled. Though to be fair, I just fooled myself. Even so, I wouldn't have answered your phone. You so-called good guys are worse than the bar rats; you're all voodoo spin. She probably thinks it means something."

"She didn't."

"Really? Grandma back in town? You never told me about that. She had some serious wiles. Introducing me as Calypso, what insulting bullshit. You ate it up. And I sat there wide-eyed through your wading to dessert mumbo jumbo."

"For christssake, Hannah, do you ever stop talking? It was none of your business. I'm never going to talk to you about that kind of thing. It's history. It has nothing to do with us."

"There is no us. Anyway, you'd tell me when you're pissed."

"If I was going to tell you when I'm pissed, I guarantee you, I'd be telling you right now."

"It doesn't matter. But tell me, Jon, how many men are going to refer to Chana Moon as nothing after she's generous or naïve enough to share herself with them? Because she will, we all do.

I don't care how much you think you've got that covered. We're just as interested as you are. That's the truth that never gets spelled out. We just have so much more to lose. You still feel free, we just feel knocked up or used. I have to go."

He didn't say anything. I didn't want to just hang up.

"I'm going to stop talking, Jon. Believe it or not, I'm sick of hearing my own voice. I'm sick of the whole thing. So do me a favor and just say good-bye. I don't want to keep hanging up. It's impolite."

"I'm going to hang up but only because I'm too pissed to keep this up," he said. "But I'm not going to say good-bye. You may be done talking, but I'm not."

"Whatever," I said. "Honestly, I don't even know why you're calling me. It's going to be okay, you said so yourself. We're both nice people. It was what it was. That's all."

We hung up without saying good-bye. I started feeling like I could breathe again. It almost felt like I was taking the first breath of my life. I was wrathful and weirdly calm, like the eye of a hurricane.

I don't know why it was Jon, but he had gotten a maelstrom of pent up fury directed his way. I had no right to be so angry with him. We'd had a brief sex thing that I took to heart, right before I tried to bleed to death in his car. He'd helped me and it wasn't even his problem. I wonder what had happened to the towel I sat on. Maybe I wasn't quite as over the miscarriage as I thought. I thought about calling Steve, but that wasn't it either. I was relieved to be spared paying for my dishonesty with him.

I was just mad at men. I'd lost count of the number of men at work I'd heard whine about being used for their meals and their money. There's a cosmic difference between the outcomes of sticking your hand in a pocket versus in a pair of underpants, though maybe not in their minds. Only a shoulder licking? Who knows what that meant to the cocktail waitress? She could have been held down when she was nine, licked by a sick neighbor or abusive stepfather. She could have gone home from the bar that night feeling violated all over again and wept with helpless fury. Forty dollars just makes that worse.

Boing boing boing. My hurricane needed a name. Maybe it was *Hurricane Clueless,* or maybe *Hurricane Finally Lost Her Fucking Mind,* or maybe just *Hurricane Had Enough.*

Twelve

I swam laps and had a shower and coffee before 9:00. The conversation with Jon was hamster wheeling through my mind. Until I'd said it, I hadn't realized how naïve I'd been to buy his no wiles talk after seeing him with Candace. I could not wait to leave for India. The phone rang.

"Hi Mom, I was just going to call you."

"Hi Sweetie, I thought maybe you could come down and spend the night so we can see each other before you go."

"Tonight's my only night. I'm going to be working straight through after this weekend. Does that work?"

"That's great, I'll fix dinner."

I said I'd be down by early evening. I threw a few things in a bag and called Anna; we made a plan to meet in Del Mar in the morning for breakfast.

I ran to the market and bought a week's worth of healthy food. I even bought a coconut; I have my own hammer. I stopped at Karin's for a quick lunch. Oscar was just leaving to take the kids to a game. They both seemed okay, but Oscar wasn't blue-black jazzy and Karin wasn't all Chicago gum-cracking. They sounded overly polite with each other. They seemed older. Their lightness was gone.

"How are you two doing?" I asked.

"It's smoothing out. I still don't know if we're going to end up flat lining. The kids are doing better in school; that's our barometer at this point. I've taken a toe tag crime drama project in town. How about you?"

"Jon called this morning. He said the woman in his bed was nothing."

"Yeah, they never are. How are you feeling? You all recovered?"

I caught her up on news.

The phone rang while I was unpacking groceries. I didn't recognize the number. We had a lot of hunters and gatherers in the field since the project had gotten underway.

"Hi Hannah," said Steve.

"Oh, I didn't recognize the number."

"I'm in New Mexico. I called Margaret this morning. I'm sorry about your sister and niece."

"Thanks. You called Margaret?"

"Yeah. I wanted to know how you are and I didn't think you'd take my call."

"Well the number flew under my radar. I'm fine. Have you started yet?"

"Next week, everyone is arriving now. How's your mother doing?"

"Okay so far. I'm just walking out the door. I'm going to see her a last time before we leave."

"Would it be okay with you if I call her? Send flowers?"

"I guess. It's not like you really knew her, but do what you want. Her name's Jackie."

"I know her name, Hannah. It was good to hear your voice."

"Okay, I need to get on the road."

"Have a great time in India," he said. "Let's have dinner when you get back."

"Why would we do that?"

"I loved you, Hannah."

"You had a strange way of showing it."

"So did you."

"We can talk when we both get back," I said.

It was only 2:00 in the afternoon and the day was running away from me. I closed up and headed to San Diego. For the first time that I could remember, I was looking forward to seeing my mom. She can be one of the silliest people I know when she gets going. We'd always enjoyed each other's sense of humor.

Traffic slowed then came to a full stop over an old mattress that had flown out of the back of someone's truck. A dog cowered on it like it was riding a tattered magic carpet. People were stopped all over the road, trying to coax the snarling terrified dog to safety. My phone rang again, Steve.

"I can't talk, I'm on the freeway."

"Why didn't you tell me?"

"Tell you what?"

"About the baby. Your mother's upset about losing a grandchild."

"That's infuriating. There was no grandchild. That's just crazy. I had a miscarriage. I had no idea I was even pregnant. I should never have told her."

"Hannah."

"Hannah what? I can't have this conversation on the freeway. You have no idea what it was like. I've never been through anything so painful in my life. I thought I would die."

I hung up and turned off my phone. It felt fine to hang up on Steve. So she'd turned it into her very own lost grandchild drama. I guess some things might never change. I couldn't believe she'd reverted to her self-absorbed suck so soon after Bettina and Amber died. I looked forward to screaming at her, while she was sober and would remember. That would be a first.

Someone finally got their belt around the dog's muzzle and dragged it off the road. The truck driver picked up the mattress and threw it in the back. He drove off and left the dog behind. Bon voyage lucky dog.

I pulled into Mom's driveway at dusk. A few lights were on. I used my key to unlock the door and called hello. No answer. I switched on some lights while I walked around calling for her. There was nothing going on in the kitchen except an empty wine glass. I got to the hall and saw one of her shoes, a few feet away was her second shoe. I followed her breadcrumbs and found her passed out cold on the floor of the den. What a familiar picture. I stood looking down at her. I didn't feel like the helpless little girl who had done the same thing so many times before. I felt sad for her; but I was frustrated as hell that she'd managed to avoid hearing me scream about her lost grandchild bullshit.

I went into the kitchen and found her notepad and calculator by the phone. Then I sat down at the kitchen table and did the math. I was twelve when my father died, and nineteen when I left home for college. I'd actually stayed home an extra year thinking I could help her. So 7 years times 365 days. I kept it simple. I figured, roughly, that for 2555 and one nights I had stood by helplessly while she disappeared from my life. I dug the black Sharpie fat tip for marking boxes out of my purse and went back into the den. She was snoring softly; she hadn't moved a muscle. I pulled up her sweater and pulled down the front of her pants to expose her belly. She'd lost so much weight since the accident, her hipbones were sticking out. She wasn't wearing her Arthur jeans; she was back in sweats. Using my best production designer graffiti lettering I wrote: Hannah Was Here 2555 & One Nights.

It needed embellishment. At first I thought of enclosing the message in a heart, but that didn't feel right. Instead I drew a round head and added two pointy ears, eyes, two soft swoops for a nose, and cat whiskers. I thought of the terrified dog on his mattress and drew a magic carpet under the head. Unlike my grandmother's rudimentary wood burning, I drew in perspective. I added scrolling designs like Indian henna patterns to the carpet, plus fringe. I surrounded it with swirling stylized clouds. I drew a sun peeking out from behind one hipbone, and a moon rising behind the other. I gave them both eyes that were swiveled down in alarm on the scene below. I got a little carried away. I thought about how lucky she was I didn't start in on her forehead like a Hindu bride. On second thought, I added swirls to the backs of her hands and down her fingers. Then brusque bands like Victor warrior cuffs around her wrists.

I sat back on my knees and waited to be sure the ink was dry. I blew on it a little and tested the densest spots with my finger. The mantle clock my father had built from a kit chimed five o'clock. She was right on schedule. It occurred to me that I looked like someone in a psycho killer movie. I pulled up her waistband and put her sweater back in place. Then I backtracked. I turned off the lights and locked the door. I called Eric as I drove away.

"Mom's drunk and passed out on the floor of the den."

"Oh shit, here we go. Are you still coming down in the morning?"

"No. I'm headed home."

"You're going to just leave her there?"

"She left me there 2555 and one nights. She'll be fine."

"Okay, you're right. We'll miss seeing you before you leave."

"She told Steve about the miscarriage."

"Oh Jesus. Well Binky came by her blabbing honestly. Is that why you're leaving her there?"

"No, I'm leaving because she invited me for a visit and then didn't show me the courtesy of staying home."

"Drive carefully."

"I will," I said. "Give everyone my love."

I turned off my phone again and was home in less than two hours. I had been trying to convince the family to do the Sharpie art on Binky for years. I couldn't stand the way she always called the next day pretending she hadn't ruined whatever family event we'd had, and how everyone played along. I wanted her to wake up covered with messages from the family, written while she was in one of her near-death alcohol comas.

One Christmas all the kids had received fruit-scented markers; I thought they'd be especially good. The more senses the better. Everyone thought it was too mean. I bet they were grossed out by the idea of drawing on her flabby belly.

I wonder if it would have made a difference. Mom would be contemplating her navel for a few days at least; that ink wasn't called permanent for nothing.

I had a good night's sleep. There's nothing like drawing a flying cat head in perspective all over your mother's stomach to make you feel like you've gotten some work done.

Steve called the next morning. I was sure he'd sunk his teeth into the scene and wouldn't stop calling until he was satisfied with his version of events.

"What happened?" he asked.

I told him the story, or the part that was any of his business.

"Are you sure it was mine?"

"Yes I'm sure."

"And you didn't have an abortion?"

"Of course not, what a thing to say. Did you hear anything I just said? You can be such an asshole."

"I guess I wouldn't be hearing it from your mother if you had."

"I wouldn't put it past her, but I didn't. I thought you'd be relieved."

"We got pretty fucked up, but I wouldn't be relieved."

"What about your lawyer? Talk about complications."

"We would have figured something out."

"Figured something out about a child? I don't want to figure out complications before a child is even born. I feel like I'm in a nightmare. What happened to no child of mine will be born outside of marriage? I can't believe we had a relationship."

"We were good."

"We were not good. I don't know why you keep saying that. We were never going to be good."

"You thought we were good when I was taking you to Paris."

"You think I was sleeping with you for a trip to Paris? You call that good? I introduced you to my family."

"I'm not exactly a truck driver."

"I never met your family. That would have been awkward if we'd figured out a child."

"Who knows? I loved you, Hannah. I thought we could get past the families. Past the other people. I'll call you."

"You loved someone who used you for trips? You're crazier than I am. Don't even think about calling. Just blow me one last kiss."

"What are you talking about?"

"Which part didn't you get?"

"That blowing kiss part."

"It's a song. Look it up."

I hung up before he could ask me the lyrics, which I so didn't know. I swam laps until it felt like my lungs would burst. Then I lay on the hot patio stones and took note of the soaking hot sun on my body as wispy chills of cool air tried to sweep it away. That's all I did. I checked out. I hadn't dodged a firing squad; I'd dodged an atomic bomb.

Eric called. Mom hadn't shown up at church. He couldn't stand it so he'd driven up to check on her. He found her in the backyard gardening and crying. Arthur was sitting in a patio chair drinking coffee and watching. Neither of them had much to say to Eric. He didn't know what to do. He didn't know the protocol for having your mother fall off the wagon again. He didn't say anything and neither did they.

"Was she wearing gardening gloves?"

"Yeah, I guess so. Yeah, she was. Why?"

"Just wondering. So you don't know if she told Arthur?"

"No. It was pretty damn strange though. Arthur was watching her with the same look he had when she was beating up on Ted. I figured he knew. What's with the gloves?"

"Oh, I got a little carried away."

I told him what I'd done.

"You are fucking kidding me. She's supposed to go to a luncheon with Aunt Asp and Anna tomorrow."

"Well I don't see that happening unless she reverts to her 1960s look of crisp white gloves. Though I guess she could wear leather, it is winter, but with the bracelets she'd need three-quarter length, not a good look in the middle of the day."

"Jesus, have you lost your mind?"

"I don't know, maybe. We should have done the same thing to Binky years ago; they might still be alive if we'd stopped hiding from the truth. Everyone thought it was too mean."

"Ted would never have stood by while we did that. I don't think it would have been too mean. Most of the time I wanted to slap her to Jupiter. But can you really imagine us doing that family art project? The kids would be in therapy for the rest of their lives."

"Now that you put it that way, I can see that it was a solo exhibit kinda gig."

"And borderline crazy. Maybe not even borderline."

"It sounds like it got Mom's attention. We don't know what Ted would have tolerated. We never tried. We never tried anything. We kept saying it was up to him. I think that whole weakest link thing is AA bullshit. She needed all of us to play along and we did."

"She didn't care about any of us."

"Yes she did, it just got lost in the wilderness of her misery. She was a good sister when we were young. We had that history. It was important to her. I'm not going to just stand around like I'm twelve anymore."

"Obviously. How long do you figure the ink will last?"

"Depends on how hard she's willing to scrub. Maybe they'll discover Arthur is into tattoos with his coochie."

"You really are crazy," he was laughing. "I'll keep you posted, you do the same."

I got the coconut and a hammer and set up shop on a paper bag on the warm patio stones. I was wearing my angel tee shirt. The sun heated the metallic ink so I could feel the outline of the warm wings on my back; my grandmother must have her wood burning tools out. If she really had hated my mother, I imagined her with a rare smile while she drew my wings.

I went to work tapping all over like I'd seen Jon do. My phone rang in the house. I ignored it. It rang again. It kept up like that, a steady ringing at even intervals. I doubted it was Mom; as Eric said, she was more into machine-gunning it with autodial. I finally got up and looked at caller ID.

"Please, Jon, stop calling me."

"You wouldn't answer," he said.

"Not answering is an answer. Leave a message. I thought we were going to talk when I got back."

"I never agreed to that. I plan to talk to you every day."

"Is that a threat?"

"It's a promise."

"Oh brother, you sound like a bad gangster movie. I'm not going to call you again at dawn; you don't need to worry about that. In two weeks I'll be on a different planet. I'm going to take up with a nice Indian man."

"Call any time you want, I'll be calling you."

"So it's payback?"

"No. I want to hear your voice."

"Really? Haven't you had enough? You said I never stop talking. You should know my brother just said I'm crazy."

"Why are you crazy?"

"You don't want to know."

"Sure I do," he said.

"You're like talking to a mule," I said.

"I know. You might as well just tell me and get it over with."

"I found my mother passed out and drew all over her with a black marker. I drew a cat's head. I did the math. She had passed out on me 2555 and one times. I wrote the number on her belly. I covered her hands like an Indian bride. I gave her Samoan warrior cuffs. It got all feline multi-cultural. I probably should have thrown a little Egyptian something in there. I wanted to draw on my sister for years. I couldn't think of anything else and it might have saved their lives. My brother says it would have landed the kids in therapy for life."

He was silent on the other end. It wasn't the dead controlling silence Steve could pull off; he was listening with both ears. Why was I even telling him? He felt like the most natural person in the world to tell; at the same time it felt like I was asking to get poked by monkey tree leaves.

"I've gotta go," I said. "I'm in the middle of something."

"I can't think of another person on any planet who would tell me that. I've been alone a long time. I love you, Hannah. I should have told you that the night you licked my ear."

He hung up. I called him right back.

"Yes," he said.

"Did you say you love me?"

"Yep."

"What am I supposed to do with that? I didn't expect this, even from you. I so don't need this right now. I was starting to breathe."

"You can drop the insults anytime now, I'm really not that bad. I'm just telling you I love you. I have no idea what you're going to do with it."

"Are these going to be daily hit and run calls? You don't even sound like you."

"No. I know; I hear it too."

"You haven't been alone. What bullshit, Mr. Refrigerator Door."

"How long have you been alone?"

"I've never been alone until now; and it's fine. It'll be a long time before I stick a toe in those waters again, I can tell you that."

"What about the Indian man?"

"That will just be a little cultural exchange program," I said.

"I don't want to hear about it. And I didn't ask how many people you've slept with. I hope we never think that conversation is a good idea. I asked how long you've been alone."

"I've slept with men, Jon, not people."

"Men, people, goats. I don't want a head count. How long?"

I thought about that for a minute. He was listening at the other end. I'd always been alone.

"A long time, so what?" I said.

"Yeah," he said. "You were right about the nothing comment by the way; men are assholes. It's almost true, but it's still a shitty way to put it. I'll call you tomorrow, I hope you'll answer."

He hung up again. I called him back.

"Yes."

"Stop hanging up on me," I said.

We were both quiet.

"I can't let you back in here," I said.

"We don't have a choice, Hannah. We're in it; we both know it. We need to move along now. I don't think either one of us is up for all this struggling."

"I don't know it."

"Yeah you do."

"It's too soon."

"Too soon for what? It is what it is."

There must be a thousand reasons why it was too soon, but I couldn't think of one. That was the biggest problem with Jon. He scrambled my brain into thinking I wasn't wrong about him. I understood him and it drove me crazy.

"So just like that?" I asked.

"Yep, just like that. I'll call you tomorrow. What's a good time?"

"After work, seven I guess. Is that good for you?"

"It's fine. Any time is fine. Have a good night."

"Why do you tap the coconut all over?"

"I was just trying to wake you up gently. I used to do the same thing with Chana when she was a baby. She hated waking up."

"I don't hate waking up."

"Okay, now I know to just pound on the door."

"Jon."

"Yeah, not now, it's good. We're okay. Tomorrow. I'm not hanging up by the way, I'm just signing off."

I went back to my coconut and gave it my normal big fat smack. It broke open and the milk ran across the stones and into the pool. Oops, I forgot about that part. I dug out the meat and munched while I used the shell to scoop water and rinse off the flagstones. Tick tock, tick tock.

I felt a tad manic with the surge of relief energy. Jon had sounded a little crazy too. I wondered if the next thing I'd find out was that he's completely nuts. I hadn't picked up on that at all, but people find their own water level, and my family thought I was nuts. Where had he come from? I knew he'd say Santa Barbara. All I could think of was the cosmic soup. The wild animal was humming while a little voice kept screaming at me to wake up!

I still hadn't heard from Mom. I called her and Arthur answered.

"Hi, Hannah, your mother's in the shower."

I couldn't help it. The relief after talking to Jon mixed with the vision of her scrubbing struck me so sideways, I started laughing out of control. Arthur hung on as long as he could, but then he started in too. We were both choking; I had tears streaming down my face.

"Oh Arthur, how's she doing?"

"It will take some time. That ink is on pretty thick. I think she got the message."

"I'm surprised she showed you."

"I was supposed to have breakfast with you all. She was sitting on the bed in her underwear crying when I got here. She wouldn't have been able to hide it for too long. We're past that point. I would have seen her hands anyway. The cat really bothered her."

"It just came to me. She's always telling me I'm not a kitten anymore."

"I know. And it may sound out-of-line coming from me, but cats are more fun."

"Thanks for that, Arthur. What do you think?"

"I don't know. She's fine for now. I'm taking her to a meeting tonight. She won't go out to dinner with her hands like that. It's not easy to get sober after Bettina and Amber, but she has a good sponsor."

He'd tell her I called, but he had no idea when she would call me back. I liked Arthur; he was a straight twelve-stepper. I'd met some real whack jobs at Alanon. People can really complicate a simple spiritual path with crazy shit. If anyone could survive Mom with equanimity it was Arthur.

I hummed around in the sun, eating coconut and scooping leaves out of the pool. It was 4:00 in the afternoon and my entire cosmos of people was out there somewhere besides with me. There was no one to turn to and just talk, no one to answer my phone when I was in the shower, no one under my roof, or in my time zone. Jon, who I guessed was in my cosmos now, was living at 2:00 p.m. It was 4:30 a.m. tomorrow in India, not a time to call anybody about anything. I knew Karin and Oscar were struggling in their own time zone. I was afraid to ask her what she thought, she might not be having one of her philosophical days and she'd point out how nuts I was. I felt like I was coming down off a sugar high. I called Jon. I could hear surf in the background.

"Yes," he said.

"I'm lonesome. Where are you?"

"I'm sitting in front of the house reading. I'm headed in to work in a few minutes."

"I don't know if I can do this."

"Which part?"

"I don't know if I can be out there alone, but I can't just give up my career. I need to think about the future. It scares me to think about being left alone. I don't trust this. My mother had to start from scratch with kids. They didn't see it coming."

"I won't pretend I don't know what you're talking about. I don't expect you to give up your career."

"How do people do this?"

"I don't know. But if we want it, we're about to find out."

"I know I shouldn't say this, but I have such an immense longing for you. It never went away, no matter how angry I got. I really don't know how to fill up the next hour. I feel aimless. How is that going to work for nine months?"

"We better say it if we're going to get through this. I'll come there for a few days before you leave, or you can come through Honolulu and I'll meet you."

"Let me see what I can do," I said. "Jon, why didn't you tell me that night?"

"I thought maybe it was just a licking thing. That was a new one. It seemed soon to start throwing around the word love. I didn't want to make a mistake with you. I didn't know what was going on with Mike."

"But you had me there. You knew that. We could have lost each other."

"But we didn't. In a way I think it's better that we did it this way."

"Someday you'll have to explain that to me."

"I don't think I need to explain it to you."

"How did this happen? That we would find each other so far apart?" I asked. "Other people find people close."

"Do they? It seems pretty random to me."

"Are you sure you don't want to hear about even the goats?"

"Were they good dancers?"

"They didn't hula if that's what you're worried about."

"Let me think about it. I'll call you tomorrow."

Thirteen

I got to work early and started a pot of coffee. Margaret breezed in asking how my weekend had been. I started in. She was hooting with laughter at the body art and the idea of Mom wearing gloves to the luncheon, through the entire meal.

"It's that kind of inspiration that sets you apart," she said. "Did Steve get a hold of you?"

I told her the story, that Steve would have wanted the baby with some kind of working things out agreement. She said someone must have been looking out for me.

"Blow me one last kiss?" she asked.

"It's a Pink song. Jon walked in on the cocktail waitresses dancing to it on the bar. It's a fuck off song, just how I felt talking to Steve. It was like I was talking to a better-dressed version of my ex-husband. I would have stopped at blow me, but I didn't want to encourage him."

She was subdued listening to the story about the burial, about my mother's wailing and beating on Ted. I told her about Jon and that I planned to stop in Honolulu on the way to India.

"I'm sorry for your mother, it's out of order," she said. "Jon sounds real."

"I hope he is. I keep wondering if I'll ever turn that corner."

"It sounds to me like you finally have. We'll run it by Ed." She actually winked at me. She'd never winked at me.

"How did this happen, that he should be there?" I asked.

"Or you here from his point-of-view. I don't know why we get dished these things, but in our business, in some ways, it really doesn't matter. It always has to be worked out. It's like the military. We spend a lot of time in different time zones."

"How did you and Ed work it out all these years?"

She was quiet as she looked out the window of our big workroom.

"It wasn't a bed of roses. We kept a lot from each other and we always will. It's not ideal. But we both loved our work, or thought we did, so that was the accommodation we made. We survived, most people didn't. At a certain point, you realize that you made it all the way through."

"Would you do it again?"

"I have no idea. The road not traveled or whatever it is. I don't know how the people who took a more traditional path did. We can't know what the inside of marriages are all about."

She thought it must have been easier for the children with a mother and father at home. Their children were mildly estranged; they were more attached to Ed or Margaret depending on which one was home the most when they were young. They called them Margaret and Ed, not mom and dad.

"But you were both happy in your careers," I said. "That had to make your life more rewarding."

"It did. And we've always been each other's best friend. We made choices. There were some wrong ones."

"Did you two have affairs?"

"I didn't. There were close calls of course. I don't know about Ed. If he did, he better not get a deathbed urge to confess. I'll put a pillow over his head."

I told her about Karin and Oscar.

"They're at a deciding moment," she said. "I wish them well. I've always liked Karin."

Our producer Dede came by with paperwork. She had my contract to sign and our passports stamped with visas.

"Did you tell her?" asked Dede.

"I haven't had a chance," said Margaret. "She's going to Hawaii on the way."

Dede handed me my contract. She said to review the credit language and money with an agent.

"Call the production office, they'll change your tickets." Dede answered a call and headed out the door.

An agent? I didn't have an agent. I flipped to the credit section; Margaret had decided to share screen credit. She had pushed me above-the-line. I was stunned. That was what we all worked for. Not only did it mean a big jump up in pay; it meant she considered me an equal in work. It said it to the whole world. It was the nicest thing that had ever happened to me in our unsentimental business, where even your best friends guard their credit. And it meant that I was in a financially stable place for the first time in my adult life. I could pay off my credit card; I could make plans. I looked at Margaret.

"I don't know what to say," I said.

"There's nothing to say," she said. "You've earned it, you're gifted, it's time. Don't ever feel like you haven't earned every last thing that comes your way in this business. Believe me, even I wouldn't give you the lift if you hadn't shown 150%; it would reflect poorly on me."

We worked the rest of the morning. Ed came by with lunch; his cooking for us had begun. Margaret gave him the lowdown on Jon. He agreed with her. It sounded like I'd made the turn to a grown up man. He was basing his feeling less on Jon, who he didn't know, than on the fact that I not only understood what Steve was all about, but that I'd told him to fuck off in such a stylish way. He wanted to know if Jon played golf. I didn't think so. He said he'd have to remedy that; he loved the idea of playing golf in Hawaii. Sigh. Now my love life was a vehicle for golf vacations. We wrapped our day on schedule.

Jon called right at 7:00. I told him I was coming and about my career boost.

"I've been thinking," he said.

"About the goats?"

"No. Well, yes. I have to admit I'm curious until I remember I'm the one who brought them up. But it was about your nothing comment," he said.

"You worried about Chana?"

"Yeah."

"She'll be fine, just get her to marry her high school sweetheart like my sister-in-law. Although I'm not sure she got through completely unscathed."

"Her boyfriend's an idiot, but you can chew the chemistry. Women must have nothings."

"It's mostly nothings in the end. But we call it regrets."

"Do you get over it?"

"Not so far."

"I'm sorry it's that way."

"What did you mean when you said it's almost true for men?"

"I don't know."

"Come on, Jon."

"It's never absolutely nothing, once you've crossed that line. It's not possible. But that doesn't mean it's anything either. It's rarely even interesting a few minutes later. We are assholes about that part. "

"I think you've switched into calculus. Do men regret it?"

"Not unless it's a psycho. We're different that way, but we

don't forget either."

"Oscar says he regrets it."

"He involved his family."

"What happened to your marriage in the end?"

"We involved our family. It wasn't real to start with. She switched back to my partner, long before I knew it. I just switched. Neither of us regrets it."

"I don't want to have this conversation again. It was easier thinking nothing was nothing."

"Doesn't it feel better knowing that we're all in this together?" he asked.

"Not really, I don't want to be in it with all your other women. I know it sounds childish, but I can still hear her voice answering your phone; that stuck. It doesn't feel like history."

"She only answered it because I left it in there. I was asleep on the couch."

"Why?"

"I didn't have a car. It doesn't matter; the point is nothing happened. I admit I tried. You were there, yelling at me every time I managed to get you on the phone. It didn't feel too promising. I wanted to move on. You still got in the way. I couldn't put it together in my head. It was all off notes."

"I thought we were going to tell each other the truth."

"That's the truth."

"Is that for real? I've never heard of that," I said.

"It's a new one. We are human," he said.

"So you claim. Why didn't you tell me?"

"You wouldn't stop talking. I thought my ears would fall off. I got pissed and the moment passed. It's not the easiest thing to put out there, especially after you dragged Chana into it. I thought it wouldn't matter, it sounds like it does."

"So a real nothing?"

"That's one way to put it. After that, you could be my only option."

"So now everyone is going to pity me?" I asked.

"You know what? You're like wrestling an octopus," he said. "I'm the one who deserves pity. You're only pitied in Ottumwa."

"Is that where she's from?"

"Some "O" place."

"Jon."

"Don't, Hannah. It just doesn't matter. I don't even know her last name."

"That doesn't mean it was nothing."

"Fuck me. Pull up now. Please. I can't take this. It's like being trapped in some rogue algorithm."

"Okay, you're right. I don't want to get you swearing. So what's the difference?"

"Besides the fact that I couldn't get it going?" he said. "That is extremely extremely different."

"Besides the bragging. We both know that's temporary."

"Everything. You? Besides god."

"I just like all of you. I felt the real free."

"You'll get over liking all of me. Feel free to do that."

"Not you, you're required to keep liking all of me," I said.

"I know how it works," he said.

"I don't want to talk about us anymore, I don't want to jinx it. You know, except when I do."

"Fine with me."

"I wish I had some magic answer about Chana, old dad. It isn't fair we get stuck with regret. Tell her the mistakes are okay. Hearing that from you will be important. I think it would have helped to hear that from my father. The next few years are the hardest. Are you sure her boyfriend is an idiot?"

"Yep, I hope he drowns before he becomes a regret. I'm

thinking about hooking him up with the Maui wall riders; speed up his demise. I figure I'll comp them free meals for life."

"That would break Chana's heart."

"He's a menace in the water. She can ride rings around him. She's going to be embarrassed when she comes back to earth."

"Leave him alone, she'll figure it out. Do you play golf?"

"No, do you?"

"No. But Ed says he's going to get you playing."

"I'll try if he tries paddling."

"I don't have a big picture of that. May I ask you something?"

"Unless it's a history question."

"How do you know it's not something you should see the doctor about?"

"I tested it. I have a scenario worked up that involves that black dress of yours. Doesn't take much."

"Am I in the dress?"

"The whole time, plus or minus."

"Mine's more impressionistic."

"I don't have time to hear it now, I'd never get to work. I'll call you the same time tomorrow. Put some words to it by then. Bye."

"Bye."

What more was there to say? He's fast, just the way I like it. I was beginning to feel uneasy about it all. My track record said fast, right before the crash. On top of that, I wasn't feeling charged up about going to India anymore.

Margaret and I spent the rest of our time packing up and sending our material to the first location in Udaipur. They were going ahead to Delhi to get acclimated, while I went through Honolulu.

I met with Margaret's agent about the contract; I knew he

was a straight shooter. He said the deal was clean, to just sign it. I did. He welcomed me to his stable and said I was very lucky and very young to break through. On top of being tired of the horse analogy, I could really hear the depreciating creep directed at women in his voice. I decided to take a page out of Margaret's playbook and told him there was no luck involved; I'd earned it. I realized Margaret was teaching me how to be in the world. It's a father's lesson, and not one my mother knew how to teach. She was all about apologizing and not firing painters.

"You are Margaret's protégée," he said.

Eric and I talked a few times. I told him about Jon. He wasn't holding his breath. Who could blame him? He did like the fact that he went by one syllable. Mom had finally come out of hiding. Her hands were back to normal; he had no idea what was going on under her clothes. He talked to Arthur; she was still going to meetings. She had started talking about Bettina and Amber in the present tense; she might be in some kind of denial phase. She still hadn't called me.

"Do you think I should call her?" I asked.

"It's up to you. Anna and I don't have any idea how it hit her. She mentioned at brunch that she imagined you were off to India by now. We told her you are still home. Maybe just call her to say good-bye. If nothing else, you'll have swept your side of the street."

"Where'd you hear that street sweeping thing?"

"Anna and I started going to Alanon. You've gone. We figured it was time we went."

"What do you think?"

"We're surprised there's an alcoholic under every rock. Listening to the people has made us realize how much harder it was for you to be there alone. I told the Sharpie story, that okay?"

"It's fine. How'd it play?"

"Buy stock in Sharpies. I wouldn't be surprised if we start seeing a lot of gloves around town."

"Oh boy. You have to keep me posted!"

"Are you taking your cell?"

"I'll have it in Hawaii. After that I'll be in touch."

"Have a great time," he said. "Anna can't wait to see you on the front end of this picture."

Jon and I talked at the same time every afternoon. We told each other bits of our life—past, present and future. I tried to put words to my fantasy; he was quiet on the other end. He was interested in Grandma's canary and appreciated "Wild Nights." He liked the part about being done with a compass and chart. He was a full out romantic. Conversations unfurled like ribbons.

I told him the family story; how my parents had gone out for three nights in a row and he proposed. That they'd seen the movie *A Man And A Woman* on one of those nights, and that I'd been weaned on the image of a woman running around the French countryside in a garter belt and smoking Gauloises. Which, in light of my father's affair and the black lace bra at age fifteen, didn't sound all that far-fetched.

His parents had taken a more rational approach; they'd dated all through college and still lived in the house where he was born. His father was a banker, his mother taught freshman English. They played a lot of beach volleyball and were crazy about Chana. His grandparents raised his mother after both her parents were killed in a car accident. She'd been in the car. He would tell me more when he saw me. He had a brother and sister-in-law, both psychologists. They had two kids. He said he'd take a pass on the smoking, but he liked the garter belt idea.

He talked about the housing foundation. He hated that we

ran off and threw money at Haiti, but had such a half-assed response to Katrina. He only got involved in projects where he had some say over how his money was spent. That was a whole side to him that you wouldn't know looking at him. It must be what Mike meant about him not being as laid back as he looked.

We voted the same way. I know people on opposite sides of the fence can get along, but why try? He had no idea why anyone cared who married whom, or what they did in the privacy of their bedroom or family. He tried to integrate environmentally sound practices in the restaurants, but he didn't make it his mission. They were making a bigger point of it in their next housing project. They had a new Board member, a retired management consultant who was pushing them all outside their comfort zone for fundraising, but it was paying off.

He wanted to hear about my job, what my typical day was like. We agreed we lived similar lives. We spent our days swinging back and forth between repetition, and problem-solving on the fly. Between seriously tedious people and genuinely interesting people. It was always different. It was challenging.

Some days he filled in tending bar when only one sad drunk showed up. Some days I spent hours running around town for minutia props that were only going to be on-camera for two minutes, and then only in the corner of someone's eye. He needed to be behind the bar. I needed to find the prop. Did any of it matter? When I thought about it, what seemed to matter was that we both said we would, so we did. We both showed up.

I told him Mike had called a few times to check in. He wasn't ready to think about Mike and me in some future widower/widow scenario. To me it had felt like Mike could take it or leave it. It was a different and surprisingly calm place to be. A year ago I might have felt insulted, but it just felt reasonable. I didn't tell Jon any of that. His refrigerator door was going to take some time to process. I wasn't stuck on it. But I needed it to fade into my background too.

I called Mom; she was never home. I finally left a message that I would call from Hawaii and hoped that she was well. It was time to leave. I put the key to the house under the Buddha head, and took a long look at the party house and pool. I closed the gate and patted Sparky on the way by; the guys were going to use her, maybe they'd fall in love with her. I got into the town car the studio had sent and was away.

Fourteen

Jon was waiting for me at the exit gate. I hadn't seen him since he'd walked down the steps at the beach cottage and disappeared. I hadn't seen him since burying Bettina and Amber. Or drawing on my mother. Or since telling my new agent that I'd earned my way. I wondered if he would be romantic in the theory of distance and long phone calls, not so much in the practice of being there in person.

"Aloha," he said.

We stood looking at each other. He was warm muscle and bone dense against me. All the wildness of the first night was still there. I was struck again by how nice it was to not have someone towering over me.

He put his nose in my hair, then ran his hand over the new smoothness. "This is different."

"Not wild anymore. You like it?" I asked.

"I like it, I liked wild, really doesn't matter."

He smiled and put his arm around my waist and pulled me close. "That okay?"

"Yes."

He took my carry-on and we headed for baggage claim.

"Good flight?"

"Except for the bounce on approach."

"Yeah. That gets the tourists wailing and moaning. Not as bad as Maui. You hungry?"

"Not for food."

He smiled. We drove in quiet to a small condo complex where he let us into an airy studio with a jungle-like balcony overlooking the water.

"Is this yours?" I asked.

"Victor and Kaia's. They come here to escape the kids. Or make them, unless my math is failing me. I have one on Maui, we swap them around."

"Does he have other restaurants too?"

"Yeah. Not like the place on Kauai. He runs a string of Spam and pineapple wagons. He calls it soul food."

"I forgot about the whole Spam thing. Do I need to learn to love it?"

"You might have to choke it down from time to time."

"I need a shower."

"That's an interesting segue. There's one on the balcony." He opened the heavy sliding door. A light breeze ballooned the curtains; he turned on an overhead fan that looked like palm leaves.

The balcony shower was enclosed with translucent shoulder high panels so you could see the water beyond. The air was so balmy; it was like there was no difference between the warm water and the warm breeze. It's a blissful feeling to lose the edges and melt into the air around you. A sloppy afternoon rain started washing the air. He got undressed and then dragged a teak chair into the shower. He pulled me down on his lap just like the first night.

We made love off and on for hours. We ended up on the floor on top of a sheet, under the sweeping palm leaves. We'd both fallen asleep. I woke up to him looking at me.

"What happened to not watching?" I asked.

"I'm living my life. Are you hungry now?"

"Starving, and thirsty."

"I'll bet. You can really sing."

"Is that good?"

"It's like my nervous system is riding a sine wave."

"That doesn't sound so good."

"It is."

I put on the black dress and we headed to his restaurant.

I gathered from the double takes that they were used to seeing him with someone else. We sat at a small table by the window and had Liliko'i margaritas. It was a strange combination, but anything would have tasted good.

A waitress came over.

"Can I get you guys anything else, JT?" she asked.

"We're good, Sara," he said. "This is Hannah; Hannah, this is Sara."

Sara and I agreed that it was nice to meet each other and she went back to work.

"They're like family. You can be sure they're all talking about you. I've never brought some one in."

"I just figured I was a new woman."

"Nope."

"Is it going to be okay?"

"As long as you don't throw a drink at me. I'd hear about that for a year."

"That's oddly tempting," I said. "Even after this afternoon."

"I know I deserve it, but can we agree to do that kind of thing in private? My command of the situation is usually a lot sketchier than it looks."

"I can't see myself doing it at all," I said. "So, JT?"

"Jon Thomas. My father is Thomas Raymond, his father was Raymond George; it's a pattern, the middle name thing."

"It's nice, they work together. I like JT. I can imagine everyone calling you that. I don't know if we have a family pattern, unless it's widows with kids starting over."

"That's a sobering thought. Let's eat. How about sushi? You probably shouldn't eat that in India. There's a good place down the street."

We headed out.

"How do you know that?" I asked. "About sushi in India?"

"I've been reading about the place. I want to know where you are."

"You're ahead of me," I said.

We had a platter of sushi then headed back to the condo. Jon looked over at me as he drove; his blue eyes flickered thoughtfully in the streetlights as they rolled off my face and down over the black dress.

"Ah, man," he said.

He turned down a dark residential street, parked, and shoved his seat back.

"Push your seat back," he said.

"What's wrong?" I asked.

"Nothing's wrong."

He managed to get on his knees on the floor in front of me then pushed up the dress. He made a low growling sound when he hit my underpants. Their resistance was futile, he'd figured out a way to include them in the action. He was so fast it occurred to me that they were probably always in the scenario.

I was kind of surprised he had it in him after our afternoon. But then I still had fuel in the tank. He seemed to sprout four hands, on top of everything else. I threw myself into keeping them all occupied.

I tried to be quiet, but I ended up taking the fat of his palm in my mouth, like biting down on a bullet while getting your bone set in an old Western. Not that it felt anything like getting a bone set, I don't think. I've never broken a bone. From the sounds he was making, I couldn't tell if I was helping him or hurting him. He wasn't trying to get away. A dog barked along with us, then broke into baying and woo-rooing.

When the baying and rooing was finally over Jon put his head down on my shoulder. Our hearts hammered private code back and forth through our chests as we caught our breath. His head and shoulders were shaking against me. He squeezed warm tears out of his eyes onto my bare shoulder. Oh boy, how sweet is that? I thought I was the one who cried.

I stroked the top of his head and planted little kisses in his hair to comfort him. He started making that back of the throat squeaking sound, like people make when they're trying to not laugh about their mother's coochie in church. He sounded suspiciously like my brother, but I hung in there.

"Are you okay?" Asked the ever solicitous me.

He heaved and choked a few times. He wasn't crying crying, he was laughing crying. He was just using my neck to try to smother the sound. He turned his head to the side to get some air. One of his tears ran down the back of my shoulder. He took deep breaths and made that high "ha haa haaa" open mouth gasping sound you make when you're trying to get it under control but you can't breathe. Then he started back in with the wheeze squeak thing and shaking against me.

"I hope you had your rabies shot," he managed to get out.

"Oh my god! That wasn't me, that was the dog!"

Someone turned on a blasting yard light. Maybe it was my "oh my god!" that did it. We squinted away from the white glare. It flooded the car and revealed more bare pineapple ass than was seemly for Jon's mother's little boy. It really glowed. It was, literally, a luminous moon rising from below his dark horizon tan line. It would have been right at home climbing out of heavy shorebreak sans trunks, but the front seat of a car is a totally different story. It was quite scenic. His ass has some rockin' sculpted muscle scoops. He could give Michelangelo's David a run for his money. Well, if David could run and Jon was seventeen feet tall.

A man stepped out onto the porch, took one look at my man's dazzlin' ass and my whatever was showing, called Max the dog in, shut the door and turned off the light. I imagined him sending the women and children into the jungle for safekeeping.

"Do you think he'll call the police?" I asked.

"Maybe." Jon was still going for air and trying to not laugh. And not being real successful I might add. He pulled his head back; he was smiling like the oldest brat alive. He kissed the end of my nose. "What are they going to do?" he asked. "Call our parents?"

"Or my owner. Woof woof. You could be in real trouble at work now. And you mooned that man. I know there's a double entendre in there, maybe even a triple. He's probably waiting for his daughter to come home from a date and now he's in there having a heart attack."

"Or loading his shotgun."

"You would go there, dad. I mean it. This story could have real legs with Sara and the gang. Howling at a rising moon ass."

He was back laughing again.

"Rising and setting moon," he gasped.

"There is that. Oh my god, I hope he wasn't watching. Total time lapse nature film with his dog doing voiceover. David Attenborough is going to be pissed. There's enough material in this to keep the crew talking for years. If they're like my crews, they'll howl at us. We'd never live it down."

He finally lost it laughing. Apparently getting busted banging in a car wasn't going to cost him any mojo at work. Getting me to howl, even though it really was pretty much the dog, might even add value. Just another way in which boys and girls are so so different. I looked around to see what, exactly, we were riding in.

"Oh my god, Jon, we're in a Corolla." I said, "This will kill my mother."

He dove for my shoulder to bury his laughing. Max the dog yelp yelp yelped inside the house. The yard light clicked on again. We didn't waste any time. Both our minds had tripped over to shotgun. I stuffed my underwear in the door pocket and yanked my dress around to cover up. Jon was back to only two hands. He used one to zip his pants, while he steered with the other. His foot was a little random on the gas while he zipped. We lurched and wove down the street.

I got on my knees on the seat and looked out the back window at the man and his dog silhouetted in front porch light. They probably thought I was getting ready to top off Jon with a $20 blowjob. I doubted that Max the dog cared, except that he'd miss another three-way, but I wondered if the guy had gotten our license plate number. We couldn't be good for the neighborhood.

I bent over to give Jon a hand with the top button on his pants. He slid his hand up, way up, the inside of my thigh, grabbed a fistful of coochie hair and gave a little tug while he pressed a kiss down deep on my scalp.

"Thanks," he said.

"Any time," I said. "Do you want a blowjob before I button this? It's only an extra $20 for repeat customers."

"Do I ever, but not now. I know a guy who totaled his Porsche doing that."

"This is a beater, Jon."

"Yeah, but it's Kaia's beater. Talk about having some explaining to do. I've got nothing on Victor that's big enough to keep him from telling that story to our kids."

We sat on the beach in front of the condo and listened to the surf. There was a torchy tourist luau with flaming batons going on down the way. The sounds of drumbeats and blowing conch shells were adrift on uneven wind waves. We stripped down and floated side-by-side in the water, holding hands so we wouldn't drift apart in the darkness, then we sneaked naked up the stairs and rinsed off in the shower before getting into bed.

"I'm sorry about your hand," I said. "I don't think I broke the skin."

"It's just bruised. It was worth it. I didn't even notice it at the time," he said.

"It sounded like I was hurting you."

"I'll let you know if you're ever hurting me."

We fell asleep with the door open to the clicking and clacking of palm leaves in the breeze.

The morning after was mellow. I slid down under the covers and woke him up with the deluxe $40 valued customer version. I kissed his hand and his eyes, and let my tongue have a long silent conversation with his ears. Then I fixed coffee and fruit while he got dressed. He left for work with an odd smile and loose limbs. We probably said ten words the whole morning, and it was fine. I read on the balcony until he came back a few hours later. He had a bag of groceries for dinner, and a sack with fish sandwiches and beer to take to a beach up at the end of the island.

It was windy and wild, and remote from the metropolis of Honolulu. It was a flat beach with no trees, just row after row of breakers pushing onto the stony shore as the wind tried to blow them back. He said the spray blowing off the backs of the waves was called liquid smoke. We sat looking toward India while people flew gliders silently in the updrafts overhead.

"This isn't a little thing," he said. "We're going to need to be careful."

"I know. But I have to go. I'm committed. It's a huge deal for a first time credit like this."

"Of course you do. I just want us to come back to this."

"Do you think we can do this?"

"I think so," he said. "But we need to decide one thing now, that no matter what, we can be sure about each other. We're not doing this with a lot of time behind us."

"Can you visit?"

"No way. I can barely get to the mainland. Chana still needs to do some interviews."

"We'll have email."

He smiled at me. "A satellite ping isn't what I had in mind."

"I'll leave you something. I kept my favorite aunt's pillowcase for months after she visited."

"I wasn't thinking of a pillowcase."

"You can have whatever you want."

"Good," he said. "Let's head back."

I hadn't taken my phone; it was ringing when we walked in the door. Aunt Asp.

"You going to answer that?" asked Jon.

"No. I've answered it too many times already."

"Maybe it's important."

"It's not. My brother will call if it's important. She's just calling to be cruel. I just this second realized what my therapist meant years ago when she said I could go home on my own terms. I'm home. I don't owe her another chance to run me down."

"What would she run you down about?"

"Never can tell, that's part of her charm. But my guess is

the miscarriage. I'm sure my mother told her. My mother can no more resist giving her sister ammunition than I could stop agreeing to being stuck by the monkey tree."

"Stuck by the monkey tree?"

I told him about Binky and the monkey tree. How I always fell for it, just like my mother always fell under her sister's spell.

We decided to go swimming before we cooked our first meal together. We started dinner and I looked in the refrigerator. "There's a can of Reddi-wip and a bottle of Grey Goose in here."

He smiled at me. "Grey Goose is decent stuff."

"Seriously? I thought you didn't like that."

"I don't like it splattered all over the bar a few hours before the mimosa crowd shows up. I didn't say it didn't look interesting."

"Does that include pouting and sticking my ass out?"

"You're the production designer. I'm an easy audience."

"You said you've known those girls since they were babies."

"It's just us. I'm pretty sure I can keep it all straight. I just grabbed it; it's no big deal. My feelings won't be hurt if you don't want to climb on me covered in whipped cream."

"Oh boy."

We had dinner, then went to bed with the can of Reddi-wip. It was one of those nights that starts out self-conscious with rattle can shaking and stuttering spatters on eyelashes, and ends up in total hot fantasy. Then it's sticky.

"Will you stop licking me," I was squirming. "I feel like I'm in bed with a golden retriever."

"I'm almost done." He lifted my breast and ran his tongue along the crescent underneath. "I take back what I said, that was a scary big deal. I actually got a little nervous like I was fourteen again. I'm getting chocolate next time."

"Well then you better get dark sheets too."

We tried to ignore that we were stuck together and smelled like used dessert plates, but we had to get up, take a shower and change the sheets before we could get comfortable.

"The last time you were nervous was when you were fourteen?" I asked. "I'm so behind, you're my first nervous boy."

"I doubt that."

"It's true," I said.

"Okay, forty-one."

"You're forty-one now."

"And I was nervous," he said. "You're officially caught up."

He had his arm around me when I woke up the next morning. I'd had a nightmare about Aunt Judith. She'd been a black snake trying to bite off my legs while my mother stood by. I rolled over to face Jon; he was awake looking at me.

"You okay?" he asked. "You were really tossing and kicking."

"I'm fine. I had a nightmare. I guess just seeing my aunt call is enough."

I slid out of bed and started coffee, then got back in beside him.

"Do your parents fight?" I asked.

"Hmm, I don't think I've ever heard them fight."

"Are they nice to each other."

"They are, very. They've been married a long time. They seem happier now. She is for sure, happier than when we were growing up."

"Were you brats?"

He smiled. "We were boys. But it didn't have anything to do with us, though we didn't know that at the time. I think it took her a lot of years to even out after the accident. She was always afraid something would happen to us. I think it was harder for her than most parents. She was always screaming and chasing us around the block trying to swat us with a broom. She had quite a reputation in the neighborhood."

"She was in the car?"

"Yeah, her father died immediately. I guess her mother lived for a while at least. She's never talked about it. What we know, we know from our dad."

"I can't imagine that, or maybe I can. Do you worry about Chana, besides the boyfriend?"

"All the time. I never got out the broom. She might not agree. I have a habit of showing up unexpectedly when I'm worried. She hates it. I worry about you all the time. If we have children, I'll worry about them all the time. It's the family disease."

"It sounds like you've been to therapy," I said.

"I probably should have. But I only caught it after Chana was born."

"So much death to get over."

"In direct proportion to life to live."

"Oh boy. Are you going all ying/yang?"

"I'm going basic addition and subtraction, but it's actually a variation on something my father used to say to my mother. To remind her she had two sons to love."

"What about parallel universes?"

"That could throw off the calculations. I'll have to think about it."

I got cups of coffee and got back into bed.

"So did your parents fight?" he asked.

"Not that I was aware of, but I was so young when he died. They must have, he had the affair. I just remember them being happy together. It's a good memory. They had fun. Did you and your wife fight?"

"She threw a lot of stuff, which was stupid. It wasn't like we could afford to buy new dishes every day. And I got in her face a few times just to make it stop. But we never solved anything with it. We didn't know what we were doing, we didn't know yet there was nothing to solve. How about you?"

"No. I don't like to fight. He did a lot of throwing and wall bashing. I just seized up. Jon, we shouldn't talk about having children before we talk about getting married."

"Then let's talk about getting married."

"That's so romantic."

"I love you, Hannah. It's real simple and it's real complex. I plan to marry you as soon as you get back."

"I feel the same way. I plan to marry you as soon as I get back."

"Was that romantic enough? If you need me on one knee, you'll have to wait until I put on some pants."

"Skip the pants."

"I thought about a ring, but figured you'd pick your own, if you want one."

"I just want a band. You?"

"Yep, I want the whole thing, in front of everybody.

"So it's wide open?"

"Within reason. I'm not sharing you with Mike if that's something you have in mind."

"No sharing. God, no sharing. And no sharing god either."

"My mother is going to give everyone in your family a needlepoint pillow with their initials."

"That's so old-fashioned."

"That's what happens when your grandparents raise you. She needlepoints on the beach between games. She'll do one with our initials and wedding date. The sand will fall out all over the place for months."

"Do you think your family will like me?"

"They already do. Chana's been shooting her mouth off ever since I told her you were coming. I keep expecting my phone to overheat and explode from all the texts. If they knew our location they'd be milling around outside the door."

"It's that clear?"

"Crystal. Chana sent them pictures from the waterfall day."

"Why the waterfall day?"

"She had fun with us."

"Are we going to start wearing matching shoes? Hey, Chana knows where we are."

"She won't tell. I threatened her, said I wouldn't pay her tuition. I explained about massive student loan debt."

"Is that good parenting?"

"I don't see a downside. If she spills, I'll retire and travel with you. If she doesn't, I'll be broke, but she can support us in our old age."

"Has she narrowed her choices?"

"She's on Cal Poly now, I think that's it. She'll be close to my parents. My mother can worry up close. I told her she can drag it out as long as she wants, the first four years are on me."

"Oh brother, you are such a dad!"

"I'm just going on instincts at this point. Realistically I think we're looking at grad school too."

"Will her mother help?"

"They'll kick in half, that's never been a problem."

"You all sound so civilized."

"Now," he said. "The lawyers made some money."

He slid me down next to him, "I don't want to pressure you. I know you might not consider me suitable for the purpose of reproduction, but let's get in some more practice just in case it goes that way."

"The way we practice we could end up with a baseball

team."

Our lovemaking wasn't laughing and playful and covered with whipped cream. We were groaning and whimpering. Our teeth hit. We were quiet and watching. We memorized each other. We struggled, trying to imprint enough of ourselves in the other to carry us over. It was like trying to climb inside each other. His face had the strained look I'd seen when he thought I might die.

"What did you mean about matching shoes?" he asked.

"I noticed all the intense couples in the airport wore matching all-terrain sandals. It doesn't appeal to me."

"I hope not, I don't love you that much."

"You do too."

"Don't test that theorem."

We made love again, without all the sadness and struggling.

"I can't go yet," I said. "I need more time like this."

"You need to go so you can come back."

"Did it feel like I was a screaming woman chasing you with a broom?"

He smiled. "A little. You can really get going."

"It felt like I found you and then you vanished. I didn't think I'd find that again."

"I'll be right here when you get back."

"Worrying?"

"Every second. I'll survive."

I pulled the black dress out of my suitcase and dangled it at him.

"Maybe I'll get married in this," I said.

He nodded, "You should leave that with me."

I handed it to him and we headed to the airport.

Fifteen

Except for a tiny man in a purple turban and gold curled-toe mojari shoes who kept calling for "whiskey, whiskey", then hocking up and spitting in the aisle before he finally passed out, the flight to Delhi was uneventful. On our final approach, the Indian woman next to me asked if I could smell it. She could smell her country already. I couldn't.

We were let loose into a cavernous room with a row of visa entry desks lined up at one end. It was worn and utilitarian, all scratched metal, chipped tile, and echoes under fluorescent light. The turbaned agent eyeballed back and forth between my passport and the real thing. He stamped it and pointed toward another big hall. I became part of a crowd that was funneled into an exit chute lined with chain link fencing. A mob of people was pressing in on both sides. They shouted names and craned for glimpses of their beloveds. I couldn't focus. The chute opened into another big room where drivers were holding signs for pick-ups and people were falling on their loved ones to make physical connection. It was not New York. New York feels like a monastery compared to the chaos that engulfed me. I could see past the exit doors to what looked like yellow fog. It was nighttime, I guessed.

"Hannah!" was shouted over the pandemonium.

I tried to focus on the direction the sound had come from. A familiar looking arm waved above the heads; it was Margaret. Ed was standing next to her. He was almost a foot taller and smiling. I pushed my way to where they were, and they caught me in a three-way hug.

"This is insane!" I said.

"You'll get used to it," she said. "You just need a few days rest. Let's go find your bags."

She turned to a smiling Indian man. His name was Chahel; it means good cheer. He was assigned to us for the duration. He had a beatific smile as he put his hands together like a prayer, with a slight bow. Our souls were greeting in a pranam. It was real; I was in India.

"Namaste, Miss Hannah," he said.

I gave him my luggage checks.

"You exhausted?" asked Margaret.

"You know me."

I am the worst when it comes to the first few days of long distance travel. I'm like a zombie. I wander. I've gotten into some very strange situations. I could write a book about my misadventures in the surreal world of jet lag.

"We'll keep an eye on you," she said. "We're going to sleep here tonight, then fly out in the morning."

"Is Chahel going to call me Miss Hannah for nine months. It sounds so colonial or slave trady."

"No. He's just being polite. He started out by calling us Mrs. Margaret and Mr. Ed, which just made us think of that old TV show with the talking horse. I don't think we were ever able to explain the talking horse part to him. Just ask him to call you Hannah. He's a lovely man and very resourceful."

Margaret was dressed in loose purple pants, a loose white tunic top and sandals. A sheer purple and green scarf embroidered with gold thread was draped across her breasts and thrown over her shoulders; a good look with her mix of blonde and gray hair. Ed looked regal in Indian man pajamas and leather sandals.

A white Ambassador car pulled to the curb. We piled in with me between Margaret and Ed like a little girl. Good thing. We lurched off like we were on a Mr. Toad's Wild Ride. I was squeaking and eeking, and saying "Oh Jesus" and "Oh Shit" non-stop. They laughed like we weren't about to die.

Our driver was Dilip; he would be with us the whole time too. He beamed at every profanity like I was quoting Emily. He asked me how I liked India. I said I loved it so far. He smiled another beatific smile in the rear view mirror. It would be the most asked question over the next nine months; Indians love their country.

"Just don't yell Holy Cow," said Ed. "It makes Dilip flinch, it could cause an accident."

I looked through the dirt clogged window screen in my hotel room and down onto a deserted street. Pale yellow light lit a skinny white cow standing alone on the sidewalk. I was crashing. I was so lonesome for Jon I felt hollow. Like the energy field that bound me was missing. He was too far away. I'd made a choice; it felt like the wrong one. Nine months is a long time. I hoped I'd feel better with some sleep. The bed was more like a pallet with sheets and a folded blanket. The pillows were so flat, one plus one didn't add up to one. I took a sleeping pill.

I looked out in the morning to a sea of people. A few cow buddies had joined the first skinny guy. Barefoot people opened and closed around them like water around rocks. Bicycles glided through like fish.

I met everyone downstairs for breakfast. I felt queasy from

the shock of traveling from the first world to the third world in less than twenty-four hours. From the world of the shaka hang loose sign, to the pranam bow for meeting souls; from *Aloha* to *Namaste*. That's the kind of transition better made at mule speed.

We were flying to Udaipur in a few hours. Margaret and I took a walk and bought clothes in a local stall. My work uniform would be like hers: baggy cotton pants, a tunic blouse, with one scarf draped backwards across my breasts for modesty, and another to pull up over my head. That, plus sunglasses and learning the shorthand namaste, which is just a one-hand brush to the forehead, a little shake of the head and keep moving, would buy me some space in the crush of people.

"This is going to be so much fun!" said Margaret.

She loves adventure. She asked about Jon. She looked thoughtful when I told her about the marriage conversation. Her throaty chuckle enjoyed the whipped cream and baying dog stories. I told her I'd left my dress.

"You're getting married in black?" she said.

"With red flowers," I said. "But he said his mother will probably needlepoint me a dress full of sand while I'm gone."

"We better have wardrobe send her a pattern, maintain some kind of control," she said. "And you better go into training, it'll weigh a ton."

We got back to the hotel where Ed and the guys had the luggage loaded for the trip.

"Ed," said Margaret, "Hannah's marrying Jon when we get home, in a needlepoint dress full of sand."

"That'll never happen," he said.

"Why not?" I said. "He's the one."

"I'm sure he is," he said. "But we're in India and I know you. I'd bet my right arm you'll be in a sari before this is over. I'll never forget that yodeling outfit, and we were only in Switzerland five weeks."

"They were lederhosen," I said. "The director said he liked them."

"He was sixty and they looked like hot pants," he said. "You were giving all the old guys flashbacks."

"Sheesh," I said looking at Margaret, "someone could have told me."

"That was our first job together," she said. "There was so much to tell you."

We flew to Udaipur on an Indian airline. The climb out was through air that looked scratchy on the throat. We broke into clear sky and tracked across a red desert. There was something wrong with our final approach. Instead of what my father used to describe as a gentle ass dragging over the ground, we were diving, like Udaipur was a bulls-eye and we were a dart. We were way too close to the ground to have a pilot for whom the word *flare* was a second language. I started bracing myself and got a death grip on the armrest. Like sitting there braced in seat 10A could help. Margaret asked what was wrong. Ed flashed his eyebrows at me. He'd flown in Viet Nam, he knew too, but he was relaxed. It was out of his hands.

"This guy doesn't know how to land," I said.

Margaret looked at Ed and he raised his eyebrows at her too. He took her hand and gave it a reassuring squeeze. She pried my fingers loose and passed it on. We finally landed, or I should say hit. Everything flew around the cabin. A few overhead bins popped open and carry-ons spilled out into the aisle. We fish-tailed down the runway before finally stopping and pulling up to the terminal. A tire was thumping with a flat spot. I was amazed the nose gear was still with us. Nobody applauded. Nobody even seemed to notice; they just went about the business of getting their stuff out of the aisle and off the plane.

"That's what happens when they send them to flight school for six weeks," said Ed, "then stick them in the left seat with the fancy hat."

"I'm going to feel that in my back for a week," said Margaret.

My father always said that if you can land, you can fly. Like death, but hopefully not just like it, landing is inescapable. I wish I had Ed's calm acceptance of that which can't be changed. It isn't my nature. I doubted his neck got the same jolt mine had.

"I'm shocked to be alive," I said.

They pulled rolling stairs to the door and we deplaned directly onto the tarmac into clean desert air.

Chahel was already at baggage claim; Dilip was off getting a car.

"How'd you like that landing, Chahel?" I asked.

He did a perfect Indian head bobble and smiled.

"Neither one of them has ever flown before," said Ed.

"Wow," I said. "Imagine how scary a real landing could be now. It will take forever."

"We're taking the train," said Margaret.

"We are?" asked Ed.

"Don't you think, Ed?" said Margaret.

"Probably wise," he said.

"I can just see it now," I said. "Cars piled on top of each other in the dark. Fires and torches. Steam hissing, people screaming. Barefoot people swathed in fabric and topped with turbans, scrambling over massive hot metal screeching cars as they teeter, threatening to squash everyone. Everyone trying to drag their loved ones through shattered windows. It might be worse than a plane crash, it would certainly take longer to die."

I looked at them; they were smiling.

"Sounds fun," I said.

Dilip pulled up in another Ambassador. I love those cars, they're so Casablanca to my Western eye.

We twisted and turned through streets barely wide enough for a wood-laden donkey. Wild snakes of electrical wires writhed loosely overhead, culminating in massive nests, all held aloft by unsure looking poles. Our new home was at the top of a street and overlooked the lake. There was an elephant standing in front; Lakshmi was her name. She looked like she'd worked hard; her skin had huge blotchy spots. Our luggage was piled in a covered walkway with an intricate mosaic floor. The walls and arches were smooth white India adobe, not mortuary chunk.

A woman came out of the small office off to the side. It was furnished with old British military desks and slumping and torn chairs. She was dressed in a maroon and gold sari, and backless sandals. She was pleasant, but didn't offer a beatific beam like Chahel and Dilip. A postcard with Lord Ganesh was slid under an electrical cord that was snaking down the wall. The hotel had been there long before the electricity. A calendar with mogul scenes printed with gold ink accents on onionskin paper was stuck on a nail, too high up on the wall. Cooks worked in a kitchen off the entry courtyard; that would be Ed's new home part of each day.

"That's not our elephant is it?" I asked.

Margaret hugged me. "No. We'll teach you about tuk-tuks when you finally get here."

The interior of the hotel was open with a heavily carved staircase running up the center. A walkway circled each level. There was an open view to the lake at each level with rooms in a 'U' shape around the stairs. Most of the above-the-lines and actors were staying at the Lake Palace which floated in a lake below us. Ed hadn't liked the idea of having to take a boat every time he felt like a wander. Like a lot of experienced people, they carved out privacy on location. The roof at the top of our place had heavy rafters painted with elephants and armies, lovers and flowers. It reminded me of a painted church ceiling in Hawaii, except for the elephants and lovers.

Our top floor rooms opened onto a patio with a table and chairs where we would eat and work. My corner room overlooked the lake. The heavy black door had a huge dungeon looking lock hanging on the outside. The key was the size of my hand. The room was spacious, the walls painted in a deep saffron color with scenes of moguls and lovers parading around over the bed. It had a Western bathroom.

The bed was a bigger pallet than the one in Delhi with four of the same slap-flat pillows. But the main event was a huge window seat that spanned the entire width of the room. It hung out over the lake. Divided from the rest of the room with carved arches and pillars, it was covered in purple fabric and piled with brightly colored pillows. What a perch. I could see living just there. I could see endless things with Jon there.

I wandered out and found Margaret and Ed having chai on the terrace. Their room was identical to mine and directly across the way.

"We don't have wi-fi here," said Ed. "But there's a place a few doors down. And you can always use the production office."

I walked down to the internet cafe with Chahel and emailed Jon. I tried to paint a picture for him. I tried to write a little fantasy about us in the window seat, but I was only two days in. I wasn't gone from Hawaii yet and I wasn't in India yet. I was in a sky sandwich. I couldn't find lucid words. I could only find troubled, lonesome and longing words. I didn't want to worry him. So I told him we had an elephant in the front yard and that I hoped he was home safe.

I dropped a note to Karin and Anna, and asked Anna to pass the word to Mom; we had never connected.

The next morning Margaret and I got in a passing tuk-tuk with about ten other people. They're the three-wheeled Indian taxi version of a clown car. In theory they seat as many people as a golf cart, in practice they seat as many people as are willing to cram in and hang on. It's one place where the whole touching thing goes out the window, or would if there were windows, which is one reason so many people can hang on. It's quick cheap transportation.

We spent the day at the City Palace location making lists and talking to the facility liaison. The trades were setting up; the director had just flown in from her home in Mumbai. I may have been imagining it, but I could swear everyone was massaging their necks, probably the same pilot.

The director looked like the royalty who had once lived in the palace. She had a salt and pepper bun. She wore a salwar kameez in deep blue with metallic gold accents. A dime-sized red bindi floated between her large dark eyes. I hate to say they were penetrating, but that's what they were, maybe even entrancing. She was considered a top director. I knew her eyes could see. There were stories about her crews; they became like devotees who would do anything to make her happy. I had a vision of them throwing themselves over a cliff for her.

"I don't think anyone's done that yet," said Margaret. "But the cameraman on her last picture almost got run over by a train trying to get a shot for her."

"That sounds like every cameraman I've ever known," I said.

"I know," she said. "But she'd already called off the shot as being too dangerous. She's not a crazy director; she never asks for something you can't handle. That's another thing, she wants us well ahead of her. She wants to hear about problems in advance."

The key people walked the sets and discussed problems and solutions. The work rhythm felt familiar; I grabbed onto work like a life raft.

Dede was flying over for the start and had arranged a dinner for the head people that night. The director arrived in a glorious swirl of red silk sari. I was itching to buy a sari.

The next morning I was up and out on our porch for chai with Ed. Margaret was tired and sleeping in for a while. She was okay. He thought she was letting down a little knowing we were sharing the load. He said to go ahead to the location; she'd catch up. I negotiated my first solo tuk-tuk ride. Chahel was already there, standing by for anything I might need. The Director swept in. We waited, metaphorically, for her baton to drop. It began. Margaret hadn't been there for the start of the symphony; that was odd. The Director was good and we made every shot scheduled for the morning. Margaret pulled up with Dilip right in time for lunch. She was rested and her usual cheerful self. The afternoon went off without a glitch.

I stopped at the internet cafe. Jon had written back. He must have heard my subtext because he said to just work; to let the parallel universes take care of themselves for awhile. His words sounded so normal and grounded; he wasn't adjusting to a foreign land.

I needed to spend some time on the sets at night. Ed prepared an early dinner of California cuisine. He and the owner were doing culinary cross training in the kitchen. A few Indian spices infused the lemon chicken sauce. After dinner Dilip ran me over to the location. I wandered through rooms with just the weak electric light seeping in from a few windows that weren't blacked out by the lighting guys. I could sense the lives lived in the shadows. The whisper of silk and intrigue, bare feet on worn marble floors, the soft sounds of bangles and bells, murmuring behind closed doors, furtive lovers, men's voices planning adventures and defenses, women's voices doing the same, children playing at both. The walls and furnishings smelled of incense, spices, bloody births and bloody deaths, and the smoke from oil lamps. Our husband and wife characters, trapped in their arranged marriage, made me think of Stroud. It was nice to feel no charge. I didn't regret his interlude; there would be no Jon without Stroud. I hoped he was happy.

I was beginning to think there are no accidents. Despite Jon's admonishment to let the other tracks take care of themselves, I was spending my days and nights slipping in and out of the parallel universes of India and our Western crew. It's even more convoluted when you're consumed with creating a foreign world inside itself, separated only by time, where the actors answer to two names. Both worlds were places where there is only the barest space between religion, philosophy, and fixing dinner. One nice thing about working in India, there are still a lot of things on the shelf that were there hundreds of years ago, even thousands of years ago, if the modes of transportation were any indication. It was easy to find all the little things that would indicate that people were alive and well in the world we were creating.

A month passed in a blink. I smelled like India. I was dusty with India. I was sweating India. I drank chai instead of coffee, lemon soda instead of wine. My clothes came back from the laundry wallah clean and pressed, and smelling of India. I left my sandals covered in monkey, human, and cow dung outside my room door. Every few mornings they were clean; someone had washed them while I slept. At least half the crew was holding tight to the West. They dressed in Western clothes. They hung out in the most Western bars they could find and complained that they still couldn't find a decent club sandwich. I don't believe in going native, but their superior attitude toward the Indian crew and help was annoying. How could they not make room in their heads and hearts for all that surrounded us?

One day bled into the next, then days into weeks, weeks into months. Sometimes day shoots, sometimes night. Margaret and I worked while Ed kept the food and good cheer coming. Jon and I emailed daily. The loneliness swept through us like tides as we told each other about it. It helped. Sometimes he felt so distant in his steady clean world of ocean, space, and "A" restaurant ratings. Most of the time I thought I could hear his voice in his emails. He sent a stream of pictures of everything that came along during his day. It kept me tethered. He threw in a few x-rated images involving my dress, which always got me going. He sent me a picture of a coconut wearing my underpants from Honolulu, courtesy of Victor and Kaia. They'd found them in the side pocket of the car during their last trip over. They wanted to know when the baby was coming. I couldn't return the favor; my technology was shared with hundreds of people.

I followed along as he planned to break ground on a new housing project. It looked interesting; they were going native sustainable. They actually looked like huts. I told him I'd love to get involved somehow when I got back. The fifteen and a half hour time difference and our uneven work schedules made it almost impossible for us to make any sense of phone calls. We were walking a long road and we were old enough to know that we needed our rest.

I made regular postings to Dede. And kept in touch with Eric and Anna. They were completely immersed in school for her, and traveling to 10Ks for Eric. She lugged books and studied while Eric ran around. Their kids were fine. They saw Sam and Sam once a week; that whole family seemed to be getting lighter. They said Ted had laughed the first real laugh they'd heard from him in ten years.

Eric had run a background check on Jon. I didn't know whether to laugh or cry about that. Anna said he couldn't help himself; but that the good news was that Jon was solvent and had only one name if you didn't count the number of times it showed up as John instead of Jon. She said to ask him about the high school pot thing.

Eric set Mom up with email and she had started communicating with me. She never mentioned the ink job. I knew from Anna that she'd fallen off the wagon again, but had climbed right back on. She didn't mention that either. She hoped I was having a wonderful experience. She said Arthur was fine. I wondered if his patience was wearing thin.

Karin and I went back and forth; they were making progress. She was getting to a point where she could look at Oscar and the other woman wasn't her first thought. She didn't think she'd forget. I thought about what Margaret had said about smothering Ed; there are some things that should be left in the dark.

Every afternoon a little man brought around chai in a delicate wire holder, like a small milk bottle holder from the 40s, with individual clear tea glasses clinking in the slots and covered with small squares of cotton fabric.

Sixteen

Our last day in Udaipur dawned chilly with clean air; we got a last perfect sunrise shot between palace towers. The afternoon was spent striking sets. We were moving on to pick up our camel and oasis shots. There would be angry hoards stampeding around in the desert.

We were leaving most of our things at the hotel and heading out to a ranch owned by an Indian man and his Dutch wife. They had horses and were on the edge of a large reserve with a lake. Small villages, that probably haven't changed much in the last thousand years, surrounded them. We would only be there a week, camels willing. I knew absolutely nothing about working with camels. I'd been sent pictures and had been put in charge of camel wardrobe.

Working in India is difficult. The travel is hard, even with all the money and support in the world. Margaret seemed more tired than usual.

I called Jon. I'd given pretty darn good phone sex when I had the chance. He seemed genuinely touched, so to speak. I told him I might start a sideline as a call center; really go Indian. He thought I should give that a pass and just come home and work through my issues with him and a garter belt.

"Hi," I said. "We're going to be out of touch for a week. I wanted to hear your voice."

"How's it going there?"

"Good. We're ahead of schedule. Margaret is still way off, but she's soldiering on. How about with you?"

"It's fine. The usual. It's getting on to a quieter time for us."

"How's the housing project coming?"

"We hired a designer who can't hear."

"I saw the problem in your pictures. He's doing some kind of Tommy Bahama thing for your little huts. It looks spendy."

"Tommy's not going anywhere. We're already fighting the cost uptick dealing with round rooms."

"Did you get my suggestion about floating the service modules rather than going custom?"

"Yeah, thanks. We're pushing the pencil on that now. It looks good."

"You want a little talking too before I go out with the tribesmen?"

"Not now, Jesus, I'm at work. That last time was unbelievable. It took days to clear my head of the Coochie Goddess."

"Could you hear me laughing?"

"I couldn't hear anything. I'm pretty sure I was deaf at that point. All systems were focused elsewhere. It didn't even throw me off when you added in her goat consort. I don't want to think about where you learned to talk like that."

"I've never talked like that in my life. It's something about you."

Okay, so shoot me. But I didn't have to throw Coochie out with the bath water. Coochie was mine. And I did add the goat. If I had to start completely over I'd never get past square one.

"Call me when you get back to civilization," he said. "And leave the nice Indian men alone out there."

"You remember that?"

"Trying not to."

"I miss playing with you, Jon. You doing okay?"

"I tell myself you're away at war."

"I kind of am. The usual broken promise stuff is going on around me. There's going to be some public confessing and drink throwing when we get home. Not for us though."

"Nope, we're good."

"Are you going to have a bachelor party?"

"Why would I?"

"I thought guys do that, last chance."

"I'm not going to prison. I wouldn't marry you if I needed a last chance."

"I guess this whole shoot is like a last chance."

I could hear my crazy insecurity bouncing around in space. I didn't even know where it was coming from.

"What's going on H?" he asked. "You okay?"

"I don't know, I think so. I don't know where that came from. I'm worried about Margaret. I have a bad feeling about it, but no one else is worried. I think this is just starting to wear on me. We're all getting really tired; you can see it in everyone's eyes. A lot of people are sick. People are getting skinny with parasites. Tempers are short."

"We're all worried now that we're moving into an area with a lot of Dengue Fever. They're haranguing us about using the mosquito repellant they're passing out. They want us to wear special clothes they're shipping over. No way. It's all stiff slimy safari gear soaked in toxins. Nobody's shooting at us, but it's like being at war."

"How much longer?"

"Two months. We move to Varanasi after this. The story is going to play out on the banks of the Ganges. Tell me news. How's Chana?"

"She broke up with her boyfriend. I'm not sure the new one is an improvement."

"Oh, Dad. Is anyone going to be okay with you?"

"I doubt it. She wants to visit you there."

"That's probably not a good idea unless you come too. I'd love to show her the country, but I don't have a minute to spare. And I don't want her to get sick."

"You know I'd like to, especially hearing you like this, but I still need to take her for a few interviews on the mainland."

"Next time."

"Yeah," he said. "Though I hope it will be a while before we do this again."

"Me too. I miss you, Jon. I miss you in a way I don't quite understand. It was like I filled up on you and now it's almost spent. It's like even my vivid imagination is going dull."

"I don't like to hear that. We'll see each other soon."

"I know."

"Hannah, I don't want to raise kids alone."

"I'm not sure I want kids."

"I know, and that's fine too. It's just been on my mind."

"I can't think about that now."

"No. We'll talk about it when you get home."

"My brother actually ran a background check on you."

He started laughing. "Anything I should know?"

"What about the high school pot thing?"

He laughed harder. "I was going five miles an hour in a twenty-five. Dead giveaway. How'd he get that? I was underage, it's supposed to be sealed."

"Nothing is beyond his reach."

"I'll keep that in mind. What about you? What would I find if I dug into your past?"

"Nothing. I'm as pure as the driven snow."

"You mean you never got caught? Or your brother went in and deleted everything?"

"No need for deleting. Anyway, most of the stuff I did wasn't against the law law, it was against the laws of good judgment. I was always worried I'd worry my mother. I don't think she was ever worried about me. Figure that one out."

"Get some rest," he said. "I'm worried about you."

I had a small cottage at the ranch. A magnificent horse was standing around waiting for his close up. He kept sticking his head in the window to say hello. I pinched some carrots from the mess area for him.

Our lunches were delivered in tiffin boxes, but we ate dinner around a huge bonfire. Besides a few lanterns and a bare bulb in the communal washroom, it was the only light in the middle of the desert. A group of hill people came down and played music around the fire and smoked herbs, then melted back into the hills. It was melancholy and reminded me of Hawaii. I even danced with one of the women; it wasn't that different from the hula. Women all over the world pop their hips while men watch. She came back one night and painted the backs of my hands with swirling and intricate patterns in henna. Next time I would do a better job on Mom's hands, if she needed a reminder.

A group of local camel drivers arrived early with a mad assortment of camels in different camel outfits. I added some glitter and gold to their regalia, but basically they were good to go. Each had a heavy net blanket that served as ladder and stirrup. The saddles were wood and let me tell you, not easy on a girl. Going downhill on a wood saddle was the first time I'd thought of Steve in months, and not fondly. My camel was named Juli. She was polite, no spitting. Margaret and Ed went with the Director by car out to the lake where we were shooting. I rode Juli. We stopped for lunch in the middle of nowhere while the camels rested in the shade; I could imagine the place as unchanged.

Our Director was no nonsense. She seemed to sense the flagging energy in the crew, though she seemed as fresh as day one. She could bark orders with the best of them, but mostly she was quiet and everyone still worked hard to please her.

I watched Margaret and Ed walk down the dusty road we had come in on, hand in hand. She had tied on a big straw hat with a scarf, her baggy white pants and shoulder scarf flapped gently in the breeze. He wore a straw hat with his man pajamas and dusty feet in sandals. They looked more British interloper than Indian. They looked the most settled together that I could remember.

We went back and forth to the location every day. Ed was making chapati by hand by the end of day three. After all the dusty army movement, wooden saddles, and sleeping in stifling hot cottages smelling of hay and horse manure, we only had one skirmish left to knock off before we were done.

We got our last shot in that golden hour as the sun was setting. Fortunately the Director was satisfied. The sun only sets once a day. There's nothing like waiting for sunsets and weather to push a crew to the edge. It's right behind trying to get animals to perform. Which is right behind working with children. I thought of Jon trying to get people fed in peace with peeing and puking children and a refrigerator banging crew. He'd fit right in on location. He might even think it was easier. Too bad Chana hadn't ratted us out; he could work with me.

We packed up our debris and made our way back to camp in the darkness under a sky bowl of stars. My sure-footed Juli knew her way in the dark.

It was quite a shock to wander out of the desert to the news that a massive earthquake had hit Los Angeles while we were lounging by an oasis. There was very little news, but it had been big. Not Japan big, but the biggest so far, a long hard shaker. Those of us who lived in Los Angeles knew the stories would be wildly confused and inflated in the first days. We were all worried beyond speaking for our beloveds.

I had no way of reaching Karin. She was home alone with the kids while Oscar was in New Orleans on a picture. We counted hours on our fingers and toes, trying to figure out what we had been doing while they were going through the terrifying shaking when the earth reminds you it's still a work in progress. It had happened on a Friday night about 9:00 p.m. I hoped everyone was home together and not sitting in a movie theater in panic with collapsing plaster and falling fixtures. I knew my place was okay; I was on bedrock. During the last big quake it had hardly moved while refrigerators flipped over in Studio City, just down the hill. Karin's neighborhood was on pretty solid ground. I sent up a prayer for those three.

They decided to move everyone back to Udaipur that night. No one could stand the idea of being so far removed from information. We had only flashlights and headlights to pack up under the stars. The motor homes made their noisy exit. Margaret and Ed went back with the Director.

The rest of us waited for the cars in near silence, under the same moon that would go look in on our loved ones in just a few hours. The cars finally came. It took an hour to get back to town and another half hour to get back to our base. Communication lines were jammed. We would get more information from CNN India than we would if we were home.

Ed and Margaret were watching on an old black and white set in the owner's apartment. They were holding hands. Their children and grandchildren lived in L.A.

The news was pure chaos. CNN was repeating itself like an

old piece of film slapping at the end of a reel. Natural gas pipelines had exploded in a line of flames the length of the Sierras to the north. People were in the street milling in some areas; in others it looked like nothing had happened. They showed the same fire hydrants spouting like geysers; the same collapsed overpasses, and the same phone videos of shelves emptying in the same grocery stores. They showed the same people over and over. They didn't show anyone we loved. No one had been able to get through yet, forget the internet. We would simply have to wait. Like waiting for news from any disaster, even in wired in times, the people in Los Angeles were cut off and on their own.

"Let's go to bed," said Ed. "We can try to sleep. We're going to need our energy tomorrow."

I stopped in the kitchen and got a pot of chai. I soaked in a hot bath to loosen the dirt ground into every nook and cranny after a week of desert camping.

Ed and Margaret were on the terrace having tea when I got up the next morning. They'd been to the production office and had managed to reach their children. All was not well. Their daughter had been in bed reading when an armoire flipped over onto her. Her nose was broken, and the old mirror in the door had shattered cutting her face very badly. She had a concussion. They would not release her from the hospital, even though she had to sleep in the hall because it was so over-crowded. Her husband had been reaching for her and had gotten slammed in the shoulder by the same armoire. It dislocated his shoulder and broke his arm in two places. The doctors said he'd saved his wife's life by being there to take the hit first. It had prevented the armoire from shoving her nose into her brain.

Their two children were staying with neighbors while their parents were in the hospital. Their son and his family had gotten through without harm, but they lived hours of buckled roads away and hadn't been able to get up to get the kids, or to help out. Margaret and Ed's house was intact. They had already decided that Ed would fly home as soon as he could get a flight out. He would take care of their daughter and family.

I took a tuk-tuk over to the production office and waited for my turn. I got through to Karin on the third try; they were all fine. They'd been home playing Hangman with a young girl in Bulgaria. She offered to help Ed and Margaret's family until Ed got home. Her production was shut down until further notice.

She said the guys renting my place had called to see if I had been in touch. A tingle of worry ran up my spine, I hoped the glass doors had survived.

"What did they have to say?" I said. "I bet the pool was like one of those wave machines."

"The pool is there," she said. "They were having a pool party. A real bacchanal I gather; they were all naked. The waves actually tossed a few of the guys out, but the house blew up."

"The house blew up?"

Every eyeball in the room bulged wildly at me. The guys had a fire going, the stove pulled away from the wall, the gas line broke and the whole thing blew. The big prow roof toppled into the pool and looked like a sunken ship. My god. I couldn't call up what I'd lost. At least I'd brought my pearls with me; no idea why. In India, if it's not gold it doesn't count.

"My home is gone?" I said. "How can that be? It was on bedrock."

"Gas doesn't care about bedrock," she said. "Sparky is gone too, the fence caught fire and took her with it. I thought you were moving to Hawaii."

"Well yeah, but I was counting on my place in L.A. if I'm going to work."

"You're going to live apart?"

"I don't know yet. We haven't made a plan."

"Good relationships run on serendipity, I quote our counselor. You have to be in the same place for that."

"Then why is Oscar still in New Orleans?"

"Because he's under contract. I wish he were here today. Is there anything you want me to do at this end? It sounds like it was a total wipe-out; the guys had to borrow clothes from the neighbors."

I guessed there was an insurance claim to file for Sparky if nothing else. Poor Sparky; incinerated. What a way to go. There was no way to put a value on a tee shirt full of holes or a homemade box. I needed to call Jon.

He answered before it even rang, "I didn't think I'd ever say I'm glad you're in India."

"My house blew up, even my car burned up. I'm homeless. I didn't see this coming."

I told him the story, and that Karin and family were okay, but that Ed was heading back.

"You're not homeless, Hannah."

"I thought I'd have that place for work."

"I know you loved it, but there are other places. I'm sorry you lost your things."

"They can't be replaced. All I kept was what couldn't be replaced. All my memories."

"I know H."

"I can't stay on. There's a line out the door waiting to make a call. I don't like the feeling that the earth could take you away from me just like that. That I'm so far away from you."

"It could do it with you right next to me. We both know that. Get some rest, I'm not going anywhere."

I stopped at the internet cafe to email my family, but there was no way I'd get on a machine. Margaret and Ed were waiting for me when I came up the stairs. They were just glad that I hadn't been home in bed when it happened. They said the rest of it didn't matter. I realized I was whining about some old things while their daughter was badly injured. Ed was leaving in an hour. Margaret and I would go ahead and make the move to Varanasi. We already had train tickets and there was no reason to sit around watching the same cans fall off the same shelves.

We were up early the next day. Dilip and Chahel loaded our bags. Ed had taken care of giving each person at the hotel an envelope of money. Knowing Ed, they'd all gotten a year's income of $600. The train station was packed with people. Huge family groups in colorful fabrics sat on piles of luggage lashed together with rough rope; carts loaded with boxes that looked like they were leftover from 1850 were being pushed by the bent backs of sinewy men. Kiosks selling veggie cutlets and drinks, chips, cigarettes, and tobacco for bidis marched at intervals down the way.

Men carrying our bags on their heads pushed ahead of us with Chahel and Dilip directing movement. We would be traveling through the night. We found our first class sleeping berths; bench seats that would be our beds too. Each section on our side of the car was curtained off with four berths to a section; across the aisle they were single stacked berths with their own curtain. We had extra room with Ed's berth empty. Dilip and Chahel were across the way in single berths. They had never had such luxurious accommodations on a train. It was not luxury by any Western standard. They stored our luggage under the berths and locked them to sturdy hooks with bicycle locks. It felt like more of the same old British world.

Margaret and I sat across from each other on our bunks,

knees touching, and looked out the window as we left the station. The screens on the windows were so filthy it made the white turbans and sharp brown profiles that passed close by outside look like grainy film from a different time.

"Ed would enjoy this," she said.

"I'm still finding it impossible to describe this place to Jon."

"There will be a lot of that over the years. There's never enough time to debrief. Can't really. How can you describe the smells and noise? What do you plan to do about work and life with Jon?"

"I imagine we'll do what you and Ed have done. I don't know what Jon thinks. We haven't talked about it beyond this picture. Except that we need some time before I go away again like this. He says he doesn't want to raise kids alone."

She looked at me for a second and then out the window again. "Have the conversation. Keep an open mind."

We made our way to the dining car where we all crammed around a small table and had thali plates and chai. It was time for bed.

It was remarkably quiet considering the way we were packed in separated only by curtains. I fell asleep under a rough wool blanket and dripping air conditioner, swaying to the clickety clack of train on tracks. It reminded me of the palm fronds outside our window in Honolulu.

Seventeen

We awoke on the outskirts of Varanasi. Piles of trash were banked up against crumbling walls with dogs and monkeys, and naked trash-picking children. India can be hard to process.

Dilip went for a car while Chahel got porters and counted pieces of luggage. Water was up to the running boards in a torrential rain as we drove through 8th century streets that we shared with donkey carts, cars, teams of water buffalo, bicycle rickshaws, and wildly decorated buses with "Horn Please" painted on the backs. They looked like they were on a magical mystery tour from my parents' youth.

We played chicken through intersections made dicier by the addition of more skinny white cows lying in the middle of the road. Everyone had it timed out to the nanosecond. I had quit squealing and saying "Oh shit" after the first few days. Police officers blew whistles to no effect. It was incredible how fast everyone could drive, and right at each other, without crashing. We made a roundabout. In the center sat a small brightly painted yellow shrine. A goddess sat inside, huge red lips and voluptuous breasts impassive behind swirls of incense with marigolds at her feet.

We drove down to a dead-end street. The goddess Ganges slid by in front of us. She cleanses all. We pulled into a dirt lot lined on one side with cows in a makeshift pen. Across from the pens was a multi-storied white adobe building with a security gate that opened onto a small courtyard.

A short flight of stairs led to an entry area. A big room had tables shoved together to create one large table. Doors lined the perimeter of the room. One opened into a large kitchen, one into a small booth with a phone. The phone was huge; it looked more like a small 1960s computer than a simple telephone. Another small room had a computer with a listing chair. Our rooms were on the top floor and opened onto another tiled terrace.

My corner room was a monk's cell. It was just big enough for a single bed, another pallet with blanket and flat pillow. A small desk and chair under the window overlooked the terrace and river beyond. Shelves carved into the wall over the bed would serve as my dresser.

The bathroom was two steps up with a small lip at the door. I quickly saw why; there was no tub or shower. There were simply hot and cold water spigots coming out of the wall about two feet off the floor. A ten-gallon bucket and a small plastic measuring cup sat underneath. A drain was in the middle of the floor. The lip was to keep water from running like a waterfall down the stairs and into the bedroom. There was a traditional squat toilet made of institutional green enamel dropped into the corner of the floor.

The main room had windows on both walls. I could look down on a family going about the business of living to one side and onto a Buddhist center in front. There was no painting on the walls. It was all white. I liked it, an oasis of simplicity in what Jon had taken to calling the busy busy of India.

One of the workers brought a small stack of thin towels. He bowed hello and asked me how I like India. I told him I love it. He beamed.

Margaret came up behind him and peered over his shoulder at my room.

"Oops, I didn't imagine temple hotel meant anything so basic." She addressed the nice man. "Are there other rooms available?"

He did a head bobble and explained that all the rooms were spoken for over the next few weeks, but he'd see what he could do.

I swept my arms around the small space, "I'm fine. I like it. It seems perfect after having my house blow up."

He was confused by that and made a quick exit. Margaret came in and checked out the bathroom, then sat on the bed.

"This is a little rough around the edges for two months," she said. "My room is more like a room. I have a shower you can use."

"I'm fine here. It feels like a retreat cell. If it doesn't work out, I'll move in a couple of weeks."

She sat on the cot, "Well, Ed wanted to be right down where the action is."

It turned out it really was a temple; Ed wouldn't have been cooking with onions or garlic. Dilip and Chahel were staying with us again.

"Let's go up to the roof for tea," she said.

We went up the last flight of stairs to the rooftop. There were tables and chairs along the railing at the edge. Sheets were hung on lines in the breeze to soften the sun. They were already dry from the earlier rain. We were catching the tail end of the monsoon season. We would be working through daily downpours and gusty wind for at least a month. The producers had decided to use the weather as a dramatic element as our characters' stormy lives came to a climax. It would be powerful on film, but it would require a lot of plastic sheeting and tie-downs to make it happen. We'd heard that each day was getting a bit milder than the last.

The river was starting to recede. We were high enough to see down the riverbank until it disappeared into a haze. The bank of the river was lined with fantastic buildings built between the broad flights of stairs, or ghats, that ran from the street right down under the river water. Prime real estate on the flanks of the goddess.

I stopped downstairs to email Jon our new location. I told him about dancing in the desert and that I wanted him to do the hula at our wedding. I was trying to sound more upbeat despite feeling weary.

Margaret and I set out on the narrow dirt path to explore. Once we got down to it, we could see that the riverbank was an expanse of black slime-covered trash. Every morning the locals took their plastic bag of trash tied up with bunny ears and threw it in the river; she cleanses all. The seasonal tide lines were lines of trash.

We walked ghat to ghat as young girls in thin cotton dresses with faded patterns, like my grandmother's, danced their bare feet and smiling white teeth at our sides. I didn't remember Amber ever smiling like that. They sold fragile boats handmade from large leaves. Each boat had a tiny wick and a marigold. We were supposed to light one and set it afloat in the river out of respect for the goddess.

There was something different going on at each of the closely spaced ghats. In one people were washing their water buffalo, the next they were washing their hair. The women bathed modestly in saris, all except some of the very old women, who bathed with sagging bare breasts. People were brushing their teeth and rinsing off almost on top of each other. The next ghat was for laundry, women had cotton garments in saturated colors spread out on the steps to dry. The next ghat was for religious puja, rituals for the god or goddess who was looking over you. People dunked and smiled in the thick brown water. Monkeys ran along the narrow building ledges and watched. Holy men sat along the bank with their hands out. Chahel dropped a coin in one man's hand. I wondered how he chose. There were unholy holy men who looked like wild cannibals covered in human ash from the burning ghats. One carried a human skull like a purse.

I was fascinated by the idea of the burning ghats; the ceremonial cremation area. Indians dreamt of being burned at the ghats and of having their ashes given over to Ma Ganga, as one of the crew called her. People even shipped their ashes to her if they could afford it. But the ideal is to be burned on a pile of wood watched over by your loved ones. We didn't have time to walk that far, but we would go there.

The ritual is expensive by Indian standards. Some families couldn't afford enough wood, so partially burned bodies were dumped in the river. The government-bred snapping turtles could eat a pound of human flesh a day. They batted clean up, without biting the thousands of living who were in the river at any given moment.

We walked on as bands of young children trailed behind us then dropped away. Our body language was much less foreign after months of working. We moved with sureness and swept our foreheads in respectful acknowledgment of all the souls around us. We stopped on the way back and set a lit wick leaf boat adrift in the water.

I should have started reading up ten years ago. I knew I would be leaving without ever understanding much of it. I rarely study a place before I go, except as it relates to work. I let it wash over me. I'm sure I miss a lot, like not renting the audio tour in a museum. But my mind isn't busy with being busy with facts either; it's more impressionistic than that. It was fine. There are all kinds of ways to approach the world. Apparently I like to do it by feel. Eyes half open, like a meditating Buddha. Though I hate meditating. Jon had been reading. He referred to us as Radha Krishna, the divine lovers. What a romantic.

India is everything all the time. I usually dream a lot but I hadn't dreamt once since I'd been there. As Phyllis the Physicist had said, being awake in India was enough for one Western brain.

We had a few days to rest and wander as the company shook off the earthquake and made their way to the new location. People were scattered around town, we were the only ones at the temple; just the way we like it.

Dilip drove us across town to a restaurant to meet Dede, the Director, and other department heads. It was an Indian feast. I fell in love with butter masala. Dede had a message from Ed that he had arrived safely and had the kids under his wing with help from Karin. Their daughter was in bad shape; she was going to need extensive plastic surgery. Her husband would be able to leave the hospital in a few days, wrist-to-neck in a cast with pins. Ed planned to drive him to work each day and handle the household.

Margaret went straight to bed and I got a cup of chai from the kitchen and went up to the roof. I could see the flames of an evening Ganga Aarti at the Dashashwamedh ghat. We'd considered shooting it, but I'd checked it out a few nights before with Chahel. Millions of hard-shelled insects, attracted by the fire ceremony, rained down like rockets and bounced off our heads. I had to cover my mouth and put on sunglasses to keep from eating them or getting an eye gouged out. Chahel seemed impervious to the onslaught. I don't know what the bugs were, but I couldn't control them. We weren't going to grab any shots of their world without a firefight. I told the Director we couldn't shoot it. She nodded at her assistant. He'd slashed a red line through the scene in the script and went off in search of the writer. I was waiting for a replacement scene.

Dede came up on the roof and sat down. She nodded toward the fire ceremony. It looked like a huge luau at that distance.

"I'm glad you caught that early. We're switching to a sunset procession and burning effigy; apparently the bugs don't care about those. You'll have new pages tomorrow."

"Okay," I said. "I'll get with my people. Does she want to sign off on the diety?"

"No, the writer is going to give you some options, you can decide. Just let her know. Salvage what you can from the aarti plan. How's she doing?"

We'd all noticed that Margaret was really not well. Ed had been covering for her, but with him gone, it was more obvious.

"The doctor says it's parasites. She's on her second round of drugs. She hasn't had a fever or aches, it doesn't sound like Dengue," I said. "If it doesn't clear up soon, I think you should insist she go to a city, maybe home."

"That was my thought too," she said. "Ed agrees. He said he'll talk to her if it comes to that."

I emailed Jon to update him on the situation. He must have been reading email on his phone.

He messaged right back: 2 much work for u H

I answered in short form: GG Spring. miss u JT

J: dress worn out

H: 1 month

J: mike coming for Xmas

H: fun

J: ?

H: ? what?

J: u know

H: history

J: not funny

H: nothing

There was a long pause; I thought maybe we had lost our connection.

J: regret?

H: no, just naked just u

J: me 2

H: I hope Chana doesn't read this

J: ditto

H: so hula?

J: hell no

I was laughing when the electricity switched off so I didn't get to respond. The electricity was always going off; sometimes it took all day to get off a few lines between blackouts. He was used to me disappearing by now.

Margaret was barely working half days. With the fatigue of an eight-month push, Varanasi felt like a huge amount of work. Chahel and Dilip were doing triple duty. Dede told her assistant to find me some help.

The work went on. Our storybook couple was there, learning to accommodate each other after a rocky 16th century start. We hired traditional musicians and created a banquet in their music studio in the back of a falling down building. Half of Varanasi looks like rubble. It's a very old city, maybe the oldest on the planet. Our lovers ate their meal off huge leaves, sitting on silk floor cushions. We moved on to work in a weaving studio with low ceilings and a dirt floor. It needed almost no treatment except to cover a lone electrical wire and to mock up lanterns around the bare bulbs. Chahel boosted me up while I rewired a fabric canopy over the walkway.

We took over a lush guesthouse where the wife had assignations free from the prying eyes of her Indian household, or so she thought. It would be where she died. I worked extra hard to make her room beautiful for both activities. I arranged for her to have more than cookies to offer the man of her sexual awakening and ultimate downfall. Too bad I hadn't met Jon before I dressed the set for Vampire Chick; I would have done better by her.

Margaret battled on. She had an upset stomach, but only a little pain. It wasn't the bone achy stuff; we weren't worried about Dengue. She was hoarse; she said it was from the drugs to kill off the parasites. I had stopped buying it, but she wouldn't tell me the name of her doctor. Dilip was driving her; he'd been sworn to secrecy. It was very frustrating. We met on the roof every morning for breakfast and planning. She managed to get in a walk with me on afternoons when we weren't shooting.

Dilip and Chahel drove us down to the end so she could see the burning ghats without the hike. It's a quiet area. Attendants build pyres on platforms right at the water's edge. Shrouded beloveds are carried to the pyre while the men in the family watch with looks of pure joy and peace. A son walks around the pyre before lighting the fire; another important reason to have male children. I was trying to follow Chahel's whispered explanation.

The body burned for a few hours, after which the son used a pole to break the skull open to release the spirit to its next life. When it was all over the ashes and pieces of bone were given to the river. It sounds exotic, but when you witness it, it feels like the most natural thing in the world. There was no wailing or somber black; no heartbreaking jump rope casket trim, no clawing at the earth for more time. It was pure gratitude for the opportunity to meet in this lifetime.

As we watched them tip the ashes of a woman into the river Margaret turned to me, "This is what I want."

"You want to be cremated?" I asked.

"We're already being cremated. I want to be cremated like this, in the open on the edge of a river with people around. Not in some sterile oven."

"I don't know if there's any way to do that at home, you might have to join a backwoods sect. Move to some place like Idaho. Do you think the kids would bring you back here?"

"Never. They're ninnys. They don't even like the idea of cremation."

"I've never thought about it. I guess I did fill out the form; I can't even remember what I put down."

"You will by the time you're our age. We'll be cremated where we drop, then shipped home where we'll sit listening to the traffic on the freeway from inside a marble vault at Forest Lawn."

"I want to be scattered at sea in Hawaii."

"I like it right here," said Margaret.

We headed back to the temple.

"You did a great job with the effigy scene," she said. "You sure pulled that together on the fly."

"It worked. It was like dressing up a scarecrow; wardrobe was a big help. Chahel found a man who makes the heads."

We arrived at the temple to word that we had a guest arriving by dinnertime, my new assistant. Dilip picked her up from the airport.

Margaret and I waited for her in the dirt yard by the cow

stalls, like British colonialists greeting an arriving houseguest. A young girl in one crazy-ass outfit stumbled out of the car. She looked shell-shocked, probably from the wild drive in from the airport, but it could be she'd looked in a mirror.

She was about twenty and blonde. She'd stuck a jeweled bindi between her eyes, had glitter cream worked across her cheeks, and was wearing a tight t-shirt with a Buddha motif through which we could see a black bra with one eye shut. Her skirt only went to her knees, at least it was a full skirt. A skinny scarf was wrapped around her neck a la biker chick. It did nothing to knock down the view of the black bra. She'd topped it off with dangly earrings, jeweled sandals, and incessant patter directed at a confused Dilip. Something about us being "all one".

"You must be Amy," said Margaret.

"Yes," said Amy. "Who are you?"

"I'm Margaret and this is Hannah," she said. "Hannah is your new boss."

I looked at Margaret with daggers. She grinned evilly. What the hell?

We showed Amy to her room. She kept gushing about India and being all one. Margaret kept asking her what she meant. I worked hard to keep my mouth shut, both literally, and in a bitch slap kinda way. This was my assistant? We headed to Margaret's room for a pow wow.

"Who is that?" I asked.

"She's yours, unfortunately."

"What does she do?"

"Nothing that I know of. She's the niece of one of the big money guys."

"Niece niece or Hollywood niece?"

"Niece niece. It got past Dede."

"I didn't think anything got past Dede."

"Even Dede lives with limits."

"She's going to have to put on some clothes and knock off the we-are-all-one bullshit."

"She's your project," said Margaret. "I'm too old for this shit."

Amy spent her first day trailing around behind me. She went back and forth between asking questions about the stars and her all-one babble. I introduced her to Claire, the wardrobe assistant; they were about the same age. Claire eyeballed her bra and bindi and looked at me with a big fat question mark flashing in her eyes. I just shrugged. I suggested they go sightseeing after work.

I had Chahel move her over to the same guesthouse where Claire was living. No way was she going to live with us. I was exhausted from just one day of babysitting a Malibu one-love brat. I had used up half my allotment of energy dragging her by the arm and eyeball slapping the men on the crew for ogling her Buddha and lace bound breasts. Hell, I didn't blame them. They were kinda riveting, like Facebook poses. I could barely take my eyes off them myself, and I'm so not into women. Jon was lucky he wasn't there. I was pretty sure he'd have felt an eyeball slap or two.

The next morning Margaret and I were meeting in our rooftop aerie, sitting side-by-side conforming notes, talking over our day. I hadn't said anything to her about day one with Amy. Shared credit or not, I knew enough to suck it up. Our breakfast order was in. Amy pounded up the stairs. We might need to post a guard.

Margaret looked over the top of her reading glasses at Amy who sat across the table from us, sobbing.

"What's the problem?" I asked.

"Oh Margaret," she wailed.

I winced inside; it felt unseemly for her to be calling Margaret, Margaret. It felt like it should at least be Mrs. Margaret. And why was she addressing Margaret anyway?

The story unfolded. The night before, Amy and Claire had gone to one of the endless street festivals. A whole group of people was crushing down the street incinerating some straw diety. Heady stuff. She'd jumped in like it was a big mosh pit without taking note of the fact that it was all men. She was having a great time dancing around, undoubtedly looking at all the men in a deep and meaningful we-are-all-one kinda way, which translated to them as "take me here, take me now." She'd gotten her breasts grabbed and had experienced quite a few forays up her skirt. She felt so violated.

We sat looking at her jeweled bindi. Mascara tears eroded away stream beds of glitter cream, leaving black silt in tiny delta fans on her cheek pads. I think we drank tea in unison. Chahel came up the stairs with plates of food, but quickly backed down. A family tribunal was in session. Damn it, I was starving!

"I'm going to take you for some appropriate clothes this morning," I said. "You need to dress in our crew uniform from now on."

Crew uniform? What the hell was I talking about? Margaret looked at me over the top of her glasses; she knew I was throwing the ball in from far left field.

"Go back to your place, wash your face and wait for me," I said.

She snuffled a few times and glanced at Margaret for a second opinion. Margaret was back looking at her over the tops of her glasses.

"Okay," she said. "How long will you be?"

Seriously, girl?

"I'll be there in an hour, we need to finish up here. Go down and get some breakfast on the way out."

"Can I eat with you?"

"You may not. Go wash your face, leave it washed, and settle down. We're going to start over."

The boys were poised at the bottom of the stairs; breakfast in hand. As soon as she passed they came back up.

"It's cold," said Chahel.

"You can blow on it, Hannah," said Margaret. "You're hot this morning."

"I had a vision of her getting off the plane in L.A. with a dark saucer-eyed Indian baby in bindi and bangles. She'd be talking about one world. It wouldn't play in Malibu. I'd never work in that town again," I said. "And I felt sorry for the baby."

She was smiling at me. "You do have a vivid imagination."

"And that was just the best case scenario," I said.

We ate cold eggs, cold rice, cold toast with cold butter washed down with lukewarm tea.

Dilip got the car. Amy got in the backseat.

"Dilip," I said. "Let's find a basic clothes stall."

He wound around for a few minutes and stopped in front of a place with a curb that was so high it was hard to step up. Children came running and begging at the sight of us. I gave them the little half salute. Amy stopped to gush and be adored, and to pass out rupees.

"Keep moving, Amy."

Her head snapped up. "But they're so cute."

"They're endless. We need to get to work."

Dilip was trying to shoo them away from her. They were trying to touch her breasts. I reached out and grabbed her arm and pulled her into the shop where a placid woman was watching the scene from the shadows.

"You're so mean," said Amy.

"I'm a lot of things, but mean isn't one of them," I said. "You need to learn how things work. Number one is no rupees to anyone, period. We'll take care of people when we're done here."

"They're so poor."

"And you don't have enough money to even knick the tip of the iceberg. You'll end up with a rupee target on your back."

The woman in the shop spoke perfect English; everyone in the world seems to speak perfect English except Americans. Wow. Was I crabby!

"We need to get her dressed in some appropriate clothes," I said.

The woman understood the problem immediately. She pulled dark purple and black tops out of cubbies. The fabric was thin, but it would conceal Victoria's Secrets. Amy went behind a curtain and I handed in baggy pants and tops. She picked three sets. Lots of sequins, but so what? I was getting into those myself. Then we draped various scarves across her front. She kept trying to skinny them up, but we struggled them back on her until she gave up. We added a few more for color; they were a whopping one-dollar each. We swirled one around her head and the woman showed her how to put it up and down. I'll give Amy credit; she caught on fast. Maybe I could foist her off onto wardrobe. I paid the woman and we were away in half an hour. We got back in the car and headed for the location.

"Do you have sunglasses?" I asked.

"Yes."

"Wear them. No more staring into men's eyes unless you want them to grab your crotch. That's what you're asking for."

"But I think we're all just one people."

"Listen Amy, I'm busy and borderline insane with exhaustion. I don't want to have this conversation more than once. We may be one big human race, but does this look like Los Angeles to you?"

"No."

"Does it even look like South Central?"

"No."

"Because it's not. The people in Malibu and South Central don't even live in the same world. These people are so far removed from your world it's unbelievable."

"I just think we need to all try to be together."

"Would you sashay down the streets of South Central with your bra showing?"

"Of course not, I'd get raped and murdered."

"Well don't trip yourself up with your all-one fantasy, that's not off the table here either. Women need to be careful. Besides that, it's rude to insist on staring at people and to keep running around half dressed. And stop hugging people. These people don't hug strangers. You need to respect their culture. Look around you, pay attention, do what you see. Blend in."

She started crying. Oh god. I can be such a scold. Maybe I was being mean to her. I didn't think so. I was just telling her the rules. Apparently no one had done that.

I remembered myself at her age; no one told me until I ran into Margaret. I was on my first project with her. She was a lot nicer about it, but I wasn't dressed like a hooker and getting my breasts grabbed with an uncle looking on. Though I still think the Swiss hot pants deserved a comment.

What I did have was quite a sob story working about my hard life. My alcoholic mother. My dead father. I had rats in the attic that had carried in red chicken mites that bit me all over. I was covered with itchy bites. I spent hours standing neck deep in a friend's pool for relief. My reading glasses broke. I was being audited with my estranged husband and he was copping an attitude with the IRS and writing them absurd letters. My new car wouldn't run. A close friend was dying of cancer. There was more.

Margaret let me run on for quite a while before she pulled me up short. She smiled at me one night and asked if I was going to keep going on with that same old litany. It was the gentlest rebuke I'd ever felt, and the most powerful. I never said another word about any of it. Sometimes it's a huge relief to just shut up.

It all got solved. The exterminator came. The lotion my friend used on her dog's hot spots knocked out the itching. The California lemon law kicked in and they fixed my car in a day. After the third indignant letter from my estranged husband about how he's an American citizen, the auditor said I had enough to worry about and, literally, emptied the file into the trash. I dropped the whole glasses thing. I didn't even need them. I just thought they made me look smart like Margaret. My friend died gently and in the end it was a relief to see her out of pain. My father didn't come back to life, that would have been weird, speaking of parallel universes; but apparently Mom had stopped drinking for now. Life just keeps coming. The trick is to figure out what on your to-do list doesn't really need doing. Yapping like a Yorkie is never on the list.

Amy looked out the car window, "I don't even know why I'm here. I think my mom just wanted to get rid of me."

"Yeah well. All moms want to get rid of us at some point. Can you blame them? You might as well change your mind about this and learn something."

"Will you teach me?"

"We're at crunch time now. We're going to be moving fast. The best I can do is let you follow along. When I put my finger to my lips for quiet, I mean it. Neither Margaret nor I can think with a lot of static."

"Okay, I'll be quiet."

"And Amy, just a heads up. Do not, and I mean do not, sleep with anyone right away. You need to really slow that down."

"I haven't slept with anybody."

"I don't care if you do down the road, I'm not your mother. But I've spent a lot of time around crews; go slow. This is like moving with an army, you don't want to be the camp whore. Most of these people have relationships elsewhere and they will go back to them. They all have experience with this scene; you need to feel your way carefully. Plus, no one will take you seriously. It's one of the many burdens of being a woman. It's a road littered with regrets."

"Okay."

Dilip pulled up to the guest house location and we got out. I gave her a hug.

"Come on. That outfit looks cute on you. I'm in love with sequins too. Let's go to work."

Margaret was talking to Chahel on the bedroom set. She looked up into a mirror and watched Amy and me walk in the door. Amy still had on her sunglasses. She was probably afraid to take them off without my permission. Margaret smiled. I stuck out my tongue. She laughed.

Chahel looked at Amy and beamed beatific; he even threw in a greeting bow. He was greeting someone who had joined the real world, his world. She gave him a hesitant smile and bowed back. Good man, and good girl. For the moment at least, she'd heard me. She went out again with her new friend Claire while Margaret and I allowed ourselves to be stuffed with bland food by the boys downstairs. We missed Ed's cooking.

"So what did you say to her," asked Margaret.

"Basically I told her to shut up, cover up, and don't fuck the help."

"Good advice."

I ran downstairs and emailed Jon the Amy story. I told him the advice I'd given her. He'd enjoy that; it sounded like something he could use at the restaurants, although I didn't think he'd really press the cover up part. I wondered how he was doing with that. I was living in a world of mystery-keeping women who showed a little belly, and teased with bangles, and anklets above bare feet, while surrounded by lush big-breasted goddess images and frank sexuality, and the threat of crushing shame. He was in a showy world of living big breasts, plumped lips, and asses sticking out, with a chaste Virgin Mary and scolding Puritans in the wings.

I woke up every morning to the sound of a blowing conch shell at the Buddhist center right outside my door. It reminded me of Hawaii, and filled me with such longing for him. I wrote him that too. I could see his smile. I could see the top of his head on my belly. I was having some mornings lately when I was disoriented by the conch sound. I was so tired I was confused about where I was when I woke up.

Amy showed up the next morning in a proper outfit. She was smart and a fast learner. She followed along; she kept quiet. I sent her with Chahel and she learned how to negotiate the streets by tuk-tuk, rickshaw, and mule cart.

She was shocked the first time she watched the volunteer vets pull a black trash bag knot out of a skinny cow ass. I forgot to tell her to not look a monkey in the eye if its mouth was in an 'O'. Her screams had called a cavalry of boys with monkey bats. She was smart enough to dive into the center of a family group and take cover. She gave the boys some rupees and felt sheepish about it. I explained that rupees in exchange for services was expected and allowed.

She took direction and started showing some sparks of creativity. I had to hand it to her, that first outfit did take comic book creativity. I thought her real calling might be in wardrobe. She was becoming good friends with Claire; they were having some great adventures. One afternoon they got a hair-brained idea to swim in the Ganges, not a river I'd go in if you put a gun to my head. Amy grabbed what she thought was a log, when it rolled over it was a half-burned corpse grinning at her. We thought we heard her scream, but who can tell? It could have been a water buffalo singing along with the music screeching from a temple loudspeaker.

I needed some time alone, so I took a bicycle rickshaw to the Buddhist temple. It's a huge peaceful space carved out of the din. A wall surrounds it and a placid moat filled with tiny water-leaves of brilliant green undulates like a blanket. Inside it's dark, full of incense, and might feel foreboding if you scare easy. There were wild and ferocious protection deities on the walls. One of them looked like my father's face in the mirror. Well, except my father hadn't had fangs or a red horn sticking out of his forehead. All these years, and maybe I was just learning that he was there to protect me, not scare me.

Dede came over to check on things in person. She was talking to the Director when Amy and I arrived on the set. She paused to take in Amy. I sent Amy with Chahel to get some fresh flowers and fruit for our next set up.

"What did you say to her?" asked Dede. The Director was watching me with those huge eyes.

"I just told her she needed to show respect for the culture. I took her shopping."

"And to not fuck the help?"

Margaret! They were both smiling.

"Yes, well, I wasn't making any headway with the subtle approach."

"Good work. If I could get away with it, I'd have it printed on cards to hand out. Her uncle will probably buy you a new car for getting his sister off his back."

"Tell him I want an Audi."

We talked over the schedule for the last month. She was concerned about Margaret, but Margaret was refusing to go home. She was trying to talk some sense into her. Good luck with that. Margaret might feel crappy but I knew for a fact, she felt it was her last big adventure. I told her I had it covered; Amy had turned into a real assistant. We just needed to get through the month. Dede already had a few people down with Dengue Fever. She'd set up a small private ward at one hotel. It was not a good omen to lose people so soon after getting to the location, and hard so close to the end.

Dede stayed for a few days, then headed back to Los Angeles. She was getting the editing rooms set up at home. The Director would be in Los Angeles, staring down the suits with those big eyes. I had no doubt she was up to the job. An MBA can't prepare you for the full force of a gifted mind and a third eye, shrouded in a mystery of silk.

Dede was prepping a new project. It was scheduled to start in six months in Eastern Europe. She offered me the job. She wasn't talking to Margaret about it, she was going to wait and see about her health. She even wondered if I'd consider taking Amy. I needed to talk to Jon; it was beginning already. I didn't know if six months was enough time for us to sort things out. But in our business of short memories, if you drop out, you can't just drop back in.

Dede left and Margaret stopped bothering to put in an appearance on the set. I walked by her room on the way to a dawn shoot, she was already up and reading. Chahel had brought her chai and had hung a mosquito net over her bed as he had in all our rooms.

"I wish you'd go home, or at least to Delhi to see a good doctor, get some real tests run," I said. "You're really scaring me with this. I have it covered here; we'll be fine. We're almost done. We're going to murder the wife next week, pay off her family with gold, burn her up, and go home."

"I'm not worried about the work. I have total faith in you getting this wrapped. You've turned Amy into a real assistant. You two remind me a little of us years ago. Though I don't think Amy is really cut out for our end. I think her home will be in wardrobe."

"I think we both knew that when she got out of the car."

We smiled at each other at the memory of the arrival of crazy Amy.

"I need to get to the set," I said. "Will you consider going to the city at least?"

"I'll think about it. You better get going. Chahel won't be able to keep the tourist boats at bay for long."

"Chahel said he has something else to do. Any idea what's going on with him?"

"No. His daughter wants to get married; he's worried about the money. Maybe that's it. We're going to help him."

"Call Ed. At least do that."

"I talked to him last night. He understands."

We had moved to the water and were wrangling boats so our lovers could take a sunrise boat ride, still a big draw. I sent Amy out in a boat with Dilip to get the people in safari hats, camera vests and matching sandals, to move along. They thought they were witnessing exotic lovers in real time. Amy was getting good. Her mix of bossy wheedling hit an effective note for crowd control.

We were very close to the end; things were being shipped back. We had started breaking down sets and packing up. I had already sent the bulk of our production notebooks. They included chips of paint from every set, silk, even incense, plus copious notes and photographs. If needed, we could recreate the whole thing in Los Angeles.

I thought about my own home, what I had stored for the future. What had been blown to smithereens. My father's box with the raw interior filled with old photos of my sister before she went crazy with the frustration of her life.

I wondered who had my father's white coat now, and why. It couldn't mean anything to Sam or Sam, even if they knew why their mother had kept it. Only realized dreams live on.

I'd kept the air-conditioned tee shirt full of holes that still had my father's cells woven into the cotton. I understood why I'd kept that. It was my defense against getting sucked into my mother's vision of things. Her partially realized dream, the one she wanted her daughters to complete. I'd kept the raptor Richard had made to help me overcome my fear. As soon as he had given it to me, I was better. I'd survived Jon's relentless pursuit of me through my fury and fear and screaming.

I had needed it all, I thought. I'd spent years worrying that I'd be left again without any clues. I hadn't lost the memories I needed; they were in me. I hoped my mother could get to that place, and not keep cycling back to the past like it was fixable.

There was no salvation in trying to recast a past that had never happened in the first place. It was the dream parallel universe of a happy, intact family. Not the one I had found myself in, with a dead father and an alcoholic mother. I realized a big part of my father had never died. And my mother was more than just an alcoholic. India really was doing a number on my head. I felt my forehead to see if I had a fever. We were all freaking out at the slightest sign that we'd been hit by a badass mosquito.

I emailed my family. I emailed Ted and told him I hoped he was finding happiness and that I thought he'd been a good and decent man to my sister. I thought, but didn't say, that it wasn't his fault she didn't listen to herself, anymore than it was my ex-husband's fault that I had married him to avoid having to hold myself together on my own.

I emailed Eric that it had been okay to lose it all. That maybe the shit can end, at least the surprises. But I wasn't really sure about that. I thought he should have the watch repaired. That he should wear it. It could keep his race times. I teased him for the first time. I said he could time his spinach and cheese casserole. I knew he'd hate me saying that, but I'd heard from Anna that he was big on making casseroles.

Eighteen

Someone knocking on the door gentled me awake at 6:00 in the morning. I opened the door a crack; it was Chahel. He beckoned me out onto the terrace. I could see the ghats over his shoulder. They were quiet and steaming; probably the residual heat from thousands of humans washing and praying; from smoldering bones. The conch shell had already called. His face was a map of worry.

"What is it Chahel?"

"Miss Margaret isn't opening her door."

We went down to her room. He unlocked the door and stood aside. She was lying in bed. I opened her shutters a little bit and looked down at her; she was breathing softly.

"Margaret?" I whispered.

She slept on. I closed the netting around her and told Chahel I'd sit with her. He came back a few minutes later with chai and toast. I pulled the chair over by the window and picked up the book she was reading. It was Joan Didion's, *The Year Of Magical Thinking*. It seemed like a strangely melancholy New York choice here on the banks of the Ganges. It felt like cabs and martinis, like soft focus grey wool over stockings and black pumps; not rickshaws, chai, and brilliant fluttering silk glimpsing brown bare feet and sun glinting anklets ringing tiny bells.

I had finished my tea and toast and was reading when she finally woke up.

"What are you doing here?"

"Chahel couldn't wake you. I was reading and lost track of time. This is some depressing stuff. Are you alright?"

"I'm fine, just tired. Playing host to worms is tiring."

"That's revolting, yech. But this isn't just tired. I know the real just tired, and the alcoholic just tired, this isn't either one. I know you're not telling me the truth; you'd be the first person on the crew to not purge the worms with that nasty pill they sell on every corner. It's time for you to go home, get this over with."

"You're right, Hannah. Do you realize how bossy you've gotten?"

"I've gotten bossy?"

"It's about time. I thought you'd never fire me."

I started laughing. "You've been waiting for me to fire you? If only I'd known. I would have fired you months ago, you slacker. And then sticking me with Amy; I thought we were friends."

She was smiling. "We're more than friends, but I'm not going back to Los Angeles. And before you get yourself all worked up, Ed knows."

"Don't tell me you two are getting a divorce. I thought you said you were beyond that."

"No divorce."

"Where are you going if not back to LA?"

"We're not sure, our cabin for a start. He's tired of taking care of the kids. We're neither of us really that kind of grandparent."

"Now you're making sense. You'll need to give me a forwarding address so I can send your severance pay. You're still fired."

She nodded. "I've absolutely loved working with you, even back when you were young and stupid. There was never a dull moment. That husband of yours was worth the price of admission. Telling the IRS that he's a U.S. citizen, like they didn't know that. What an ass. But I can't think of anything that I've enjoyed more than the vision of you drawing all over your mother. Figuring out the number of nights was a stroke of genius. Drawing the sun and the moon, the passage of time looking on. I hope she knows how lucky she is."

"I didn't think of them as the passage of time, her skinny hipbones just called out to me. I doubt she thinks she's lucky. According to my aunt, she's never really liked me. I stood between her and a man."

"And now she's sober and she has Arthur, and your aunt is still batshit. Let's just put that one to rest. Along with cats, kittens, three chances, and all the other crap."

"My father would not approve of your language."

"I'm certain he'd approve of every word. I want to go back to sleep now, boss. I think you should call Jon and ask him to come here."

"He can't come here. We've talked about it. He needs to take his daughter to the mainland to look at schools."

"They're going to be your family now. Call him. Let him know how much you need him. If he loves you, he'll come."

"I don't like tests. They're not my style, you know that."

"It's not a test, Hannah, it's a fact of life. You need him right now; you need to learn to ask for him. He loves you; he deserves to know that about you. Don't leave an opening between you; it will get filled with the wrong thing. You've seen it a hundred times."

"There's no one filling it now."

"No, you've seemed oblivious to that first AD trying to get at you."

"I noticed him. He's a nice boy."

"So not this time, but you know what happens. Deal with it

now when it's just a nice boy."

"My mother asked my father to come home and it got him killed."

"Your father made a mistake. Unless Jon gets our Udaipur pilot, he'll make it here in one piece."

"Did you ask Ed when you were working?"

"Not often enough. Ed and I missed a lot of time together. I don't recommend it."

"That sounds kind of cryptic."

"I can tell you one thing: do what you need to do to be together. In the end that's how you get what you need. Don't regret the missed time like we do."

"I can hear women all over the world grinding their teeth at that little gem of wisdom."

"I know, but I'm old, I can say whatever I want. I'm not saying don't have a career; that goes both ways. I'm saying don't hurt your life together in the process. It's not always poetic and it's not always justice, but in the end you'll be glad."

"Karin is weighing that now. They have the kids."

"I know. For them there's no rewind. Anyone who thinks there will be is just negotiating for the moment."

"Do you think they can recover?"

"They will or they won't. They'll never get back to where they were. Scars cover the tenderness. She'll never feel safe enough to leave her dress behind."

"Did you do things that you regret?"

"What a dumb question."

"I mean men."

"Of course, though I wasn't an A student like you are. I'm a different generation."

"That's not very nice," I was laughing.

"Sometimes I think it would have been fun."

"It's not, at least not in hindsight. Practice doesn't make perfect with the wrong man. Did you get over it?"

"Off and on. I didn't feel the regret when I was happy. It came back when I needed to call Ed. Pay attention to that warning sign. That's when you get into trouble."

"Ed couldn't fix the past."

"No, Ed is the constant present. He loves me when I don't."

"So you haven't forgotten?"

"I haven't forgotten one thing. This morning I remembered hearing that I was an old friend's first wet dream. Some remembering is good."

"Wet dream?"

"I know. I didn't even have to show up to be interesting. He was dying and told a mutual friend. He was a nice boy who grew into a nice man. He hadn't forgotten anything either."

"That's sweet in a strange way."

"He should have just asked me out; it might have been sweeter than a dream."

"It sounds like I better call Ed, you need him right now."

"Yes," she smiled. "Call Ed."

"Dede has offered me a job in Eastern Europe."

"I know. You can't escape Hollywood chatter, even in India. It's a big opportunity for you."

"What about you?"

"I'm not going to Eastern Europe. Been there, done that. It's a fascinating place though."

"I need to talk to Jon. I don't think he's going to like the idea."

"Can you blame him? An empty dress can only get you so far."

"A wet dream?"

She was laughing when I walked out the door.

My first call was to Ed. I related part of the conversation; I skipped the wet dream. Knowing them, he knew anyway. He was quiet for a long time. I told him what she was reading.

"Oh christ," he said. "She's reading that big sob again. I should be able to get there in a few days. You okay?"

"I'm fine. But I should warn you I fired her for being a slacker. I'm not sure I can cover your travel expenses."

"Good job, she had that coming."

"What's going on, Ed?"

He was quiet for such a long time I thought we'd lost our connection.

"Ed? You still there?"

"I'm here."

"I don't like this. I grew up in a family of secret keepers. It's pointless; I'm going to find out. I need to know now. I don't want any surprises, I'm barely hanging on here."

"She's dying, Hannah. She's known for a few weeks."

"How do you know? That's so fast. Has she even seen a real doctor? She keeps going to that guy who takes her pulses or something."

"He's a real doctor. She trusts him. His medicine is a lot older than what they have to offer in Los Angeles."

"Dying?"

"She has late stage cancer. We had no idea. We really did think it was parasites like everyone else."

"How can you be so calm about this? Why aren't you here doing something? I'm going to call Dede, have her moved to Delhi."

"No, you're not. This isn't up to you, or me."

"Ed, this is crazy. I can't just stand by like a little girl and not do something."

"To answer your question, I'm not calm about it. But I also know there's nothing to do. She doesn't want to do anything about it. She wants her last time to be quality time. She's enjoying herself there. He's keeping her comfortable."

"Wouldn't she rather die in Los Angeles?"

"Why?"

"So the family can be around. Your son's a doctor. He can do something."

"She doesn't want the family around. He agrees with her, he told her the truth. He's his mother's son. He's talking to her doctor there. She's in good hands."

"What about your daughter, the grandkids?"

"She's talking to each of them. They're saying what they need to say. A few more touches wouldn't mean anything. I've been here to help us through it. I'll be there in a few days to help you."

I was shocked and exhausted.

"Okay."

"Hannah, be sure her window is open. She says Chahel keeps closing it. She really likes the sound of the conch shell at the temple. And make her go up to the roof and get some sun."

"Okay. Does Chahel know?"

"Yes. But don't be mad at her, Hannah. She didn't tell you because she knows you'd get into a spin. She's waxing very philosophic right now about wasting time with worry. She loves you. She won't leave without saying good-bye."

"How can we say good-bye?"

"That's between you two."

I hung up and tried counting backwards to Hawaii time. I couldn't make any sense of it so just called.

"Morning, I guess," said Jon.

He was sound asleep.

"Margaret is dying. Right here. She isn't sick with parasites at all, she has cancer."

"Start over, H. I was asleep."

I related the conversation with Ed to him.

"How am I going to say good-bye to her, Jon? All my talk about needing good-bye. I don't have any idea how to do that."

"I don't know. I guess it's like Ed said, you two will figure it out."

"Have you ever done that?"

"No, I don't think very many people actually do. How much time does she have?"

"I have no idea. But she plans on staying here until the end."

"What are you going to do?"

"I don't know. You mean stay or come home?"

"Yes."

"I don't know. She's more a mother than my own mother."

"Well, ask her what she wants."

"I've been offered a new project in Eastern Europe, it starts in six months."

"I think you should back burner that. Figure out what you want to do about Margaret first. And us."

"Us?"

"I assume we're still in your calculations."

"I'm sorry, of course you are. I'm in shock is all."

He was quiet on the other end.

"Jon?"

"I'm here, Hannah. What do you need from me?"

"I don't know. Margaret said I should ask you to come, but it wasn't because she said she was dying. It was before that. She thought I was going to make a mistake."

"What kind of mistake?"

"That I'd lose my way some how, I don't know. I'm so tired I feel like I'm hallucinating. I feel detached from the earth. I couldn't even begin to figure out what time it is where you are. I still have so much work to do. The universes are colliding."

"Is there something you're not telling me?"

"No. I know how it sounds. There's nothing. I just don't know how to tell you what is. What's going on. I don't know myself."

We were both quiet.

"How am I going to say good-bye, Jon?"

"Don't. Just tell her you'll love her forever and ever."

"That sounds like a little girl."

"That's all I have to offer, that's the only thing I know. It's what my mother said to her mother before she died in the car. She was a little girl."

I started sobbing. "Oh my god, Jon."

We sat in silence for what seemed like an hour. Amy came in amped with energy and waving her arm at me to get going. The entire crew was standing around on the set, waiting for me to show up with the meal our lovers were supposed to be eating. I motioned her toward the kitchen. The guys had it all wrapped up. She and Chahel started loading it into the car.

"I need to go, Jon. I'm late for work. I don't want you to spend any time worrying."

"I'm in Honolulu. We're leaving for the mainland in a few days. Call me later; don't worry about the time. If we miss, I'll call you back."

"Don't try calling here. My schedule is off-the-hook. The phone will just wake up the guys downstairs. They nap on the dining room table when they're not taking care of us. I'll try to reach you when I get a break."

"Just call. Keep me posted."

"I will. I love you, Jon. Thank you."

"I love you forever and ever, Hannah."

"I hope so, that would be a really nice life."

I got in the car and rolled down the window to talk to Chahel.

"Open her bedroom windows. And get her up on the roof for some sun with her lunch."

He went back inside. Amy looked at me sideways; she'd picked up on my borderline rude voice with Chahel.

"Margaret is having a bad day," I said.

Somehow I got through the day. I went to see Margaret as soon as I got in. It was late, but her light was still on and she was reading. I sat down in the chair and we looked at each other.

"You know what I'm going to miss the most?" she asked. "Well two things really. Seeing you lug that needlepoint dress down the aisle with a train of sand. And watching you raise kids. I'd love to see how you handle that. I told Ed to buy them all ponies."

"I hate ponies," I said. "I'm so mad at you."

"Why? Because you got to live two more happy weeks instead of unhappy weeks in your life."

"Because you didn't trust me enough to tell me."

"I trusted you to call in the Army Corps of Engineers if you thought it would help. I know how you work. You think things are fixable if you try hard enough. I don't want that."

"But you're not even fighting."

"I'm not going to fight for the chance to be bald and bruised in the hospital, and die sprouting tubes. We did that movie eight years ago. Remember? My son says there's no way out of this one. I trust him."

"This isn't a movie. Anyway, she bought time. What about

Ed and the kids? Don't you want the time with them?"

"They don't need that kind of time from me. That's time that has to do with them, not me. It's like keeping an old dog alive long past the time when it would just go off and die under a bush if it was just left alone."

"You're not an old dog. We live longer than dogs."

"Don't pick it apart, Hannah. It won't change things. Now I know how I'd handle it. I'm relieved actually. It's fine."

We sat in the buffalo bellowing and horn honking quiet of India for a while.

"I don't know how to say good-bye," I said. "I always thought I needed that because I didn't have it, and now I realize I have no idea."

"We don't have to say good-bye."

"That's what Jon said."

"Did you ask Jon to come?"

"No, I don't want to start with that. He has his own life."

"Then you shouldn't marry him."

"Of course I'm going to marry him."

"Not if he has his own life."

"He didn't say that. He doesn't think that way. He calls us Radna Krishna."

"But apparently you do. I'd say that's a disconnect."

"I don't feel like I have my own life. I feel like we live different lives."

"We all live different lives."

"Now who's picking it apart?"

"You are, you always do. Then you confuse yourself into the wrong man."

"Jon isn't the wrong man."

"I don't think he is either. Did you tell him I'm dying?"

"Yes."

"And?"

"He said to tell you I'll love you forever and ever. Then he said the same thing to me."

"I wish I had the energy to shake you. Ask him to come. I don't know how else to tell you that. You need him."

"I need you."

"I'm spoken for."

Chahel knocked, he brought in chai and rice pudding.

"She knows, Chahel," said Margaret.

"I'm sorry, Chahel," I said. "I didn't mean to be rude to you earlier."

"Chahel," said Margaret. "Hannah is going to marry soon, like your daughter. A man named Jon. They're going to have a baseball team that rides ponies."

Chahel smiled his beatific smile and left.

"Don't you think you confused him?" I said.

"I doubt it, he's hoping for a cricket team. Be sure Ed doesn't forget to pay for his daughter's wedding. He only needs five-hundred dollars to make a huge affair."

"Okay. You'll come to mine?"

"If it's in India. I want to meet Jon."

I went to the Buddhist temple for some alone time and gazed at the red-horn masks. They snarled and glared back. No help there, I'm not Buddhist. I had no idea what I was supposed to feel about those beings, except that a few could use some paint touch ups.

I went back to the temple and tried calling Jon; it went to voicemail. I felt really stupid leaving him the message, but I told him I needed him to come. Then I told him he didn't really have to come. I made it worse with all kinds of run around the block with a broom talk. I couldn't reach through space and delete the message. I told him not to worry, I was just tired, to please call me.

Everyone spent the next few days running around like crazy people. We were racing for the finish line. The weather was loosening its grip, which gave us some relief. Amy had turned into an efficient work machine. She was starting to read my mind, or what was left of it. I made a note to self that getting a fresh helper midway through a project wasn't a bad idea.

I kept Margaret's secret. In return, she rallied and was up for breakfast in the morning and read on the terrace in the afternoon. She'd switched to Indian chick lit about contemporary women trying to make their way in the mixed messages of India. Like India has a corner on that confusion. All you had to think about was breast implants and the Virgin Mary to know that women live in a state of psychic split all over the world. I couldn't begin to fathom how she could be worried about wasting time, and be reading crap like that in the same day. When I complained about her choice of reading material, she asked me what could be more important for her to read. Stumped me. She wasn't looking for answers.

Ed had arrived a few days after the call and started right in cooking for us. Dede didn't plan to be back. There really wasn't any reason for her to return; her assistant was handling the shut down. Jon emailed that they'd gotten hung up in Honolulu but were on the road. Chana had an interview at Cal Poly in two days. I tried calling him; I didn't bother to figure out the time. It went to voicemail. I left him a message that I was finally going to get some rest and that I'd try again in the next day. I asked him to tell Chana to break a leg in her interview.

I had a block of six blissful uninterrupted hours of sleep in front of me while Amy took care of the preliminary work for one of our last days. It was late by the time I went upstairs to bed.

I walked by Margaret and Ed's room, I had planned to say good night, but he was singing. I'd never heard him sing. It wasn't show quality, but it was one of the most tender things I'd ever heard. He was singing "The First Time Ever I Saw Your Face" from the movie *Play Misty For Me*. They'd met at a screening. She used to play it over and over, like I played Adele's version of "Lovesong" over and over since meeting Jon. Our lives have soundtracks.

I didn't know what to do with his singing in my mind. I sat on the bath floor and poured cup after cup of hot water over my head to wash away the last tears. I finally put on a cotton nightgown and got in bed.

Nineteen

I awoke seven hours later to the sound of the conch shell next door, I felt almost normal.

Someone knocked; I opened the door to Amy.

"Morning" I said. I was whispering a 6:00 a.m. Indian household whisper.

"I need to talk to you."

"Okay. Come in. What happened? Why are you crying?"

"Margaret had a heart attack in the night."

"A heart attack?"

"She died." I hugged her, thinking wild thoughts; I shouldn't have slept. I should have said good night.

"Where's Ed?" I asked.

"He's with her. He's asking for you."

"Okay, let me get dressed."

I walked into their room. Ed was sitting on the bed next to Margaret holding her hand. She looked like she was asleep just like the other morning; but her skin had smoothed out.

I hugged him, then sat on the bed with them. I held his free hand, and took her other hand in mine. We were back on the plane waiting for it to crash. Her hand was cold, but it was soft, not like my father had felt. I rubbed the skin with my thumb like I could warm her up or comfort her. I could see Arthur's fingers stroking my mother's hand with mud jammed under her nails.

We sat like that for long minutes; it was fine. She was peaceful, so was he, the plane had crashed without any tension.

"How are you?" I asked. "I walked by on my way to bed at 11:00. I heard your voice."

"We talked all night."

"All night? Did the doctor come?"

"No, she died at 8:00. It went quickly, we only had a few minutes."

I was worried that he might be in trouble himself; shock maybe. The whole time thing made no sense. He'd been singing.

"What would you like me to do?" I asked. "Do you want me to call the kids?"

"No, we'll call them in a few days."

"Don't you think they'd want to know?"

"A few days before they know won't matter. They were expecting it. It's what she wanted. She wants to be cremated here."

"I know. I'll call Dede. The production office will know what to do."

"Chahel has started making arrangements."

"Okay. What do you need me to do?"

"She wants you to do the ceremony."

"Me? I don't know anything about it."

"She said to just get it wherever you got the sun and the moon. But she doesn't want you to actually draw on her unless you just can't help yourself."

I burst out laughing. I'm sure anyone who was listening outside the door thought I was getting hysterical.

Ed was smiling. "She trusted you to figure it out."

"Does she want some special set? She should have told me what she wants."

"No, she liked it just the way it is. She wants you to be the one to light the fire."

"Light the fire? I can't do that."

I was shaking my head. I could see the son circling his shrouded mother. "I'm not even her daughter."

"You were more than that. She said you're no ninny. That's why it has to be you. I'll be there."

"I have to think about this."

"It's thought out; she's ahead of you. She wrote something for you that she thinks will help. I'm supposed to give it to you right before the ceremony."

"How could she write something?"

"We talked it over a few days ago. This is still what she wanted as of 8:00 last night. That's as good as it gets."

I looked at her; she wasn't giving me any signs. None of the nods or droll side-glances we'd used to communicate over the years when I was growing up under her wing.

"I love you both. But that's too much to ask."

He nodded. "Chahel will be back in a little while. He said it's very unusual, he's afraid of how it will look."

"I understand, poor man, stuck with us."

He smiled. "We'll be fine. She liked the idea of being set free here, by you. I'll be with you. This is something you have to do, Hannah. This is her final scene."

"I can't, Ed. I'm sorry. We need to figure out something else. I'm going to change. Are you okay alone here?"

"I'm not alone. We're fine. Go change, I want you there with me."

"Of course I'll be there. I just can't be the one."

I went up to the roof. Amy and Claire were having tea. It was nice that Amy had such a good friend. They reminded me of Karin and me. There was no reason to make a big secret about what was going to happen. I asked Amy to buy me a sari for the ceremony, I thought turquoise, but I left it up to them.

The guys from the kitchen brought up plates of light food and we snacked in silence as the new day came on in full. Amy and Claire left. Chahel came up on the terrace and gave me a pranam bow; he raised his hands to his forehead this time. I had no idea what that meant.

"I'm sorry to put you through this, Chahel," I said. "But you knew Margaret. This is what she wanted. She'll make us all pay if we don't do it."

His eyes opened wide.

"I didn't mean that. I'm sorry. I just meant that this is how she wants to leave."

"It's arranged. It will begin before sunset."

"That's fine. When?"

"Today." He head bobbled like it was obvious.

He said it should be today. He had arranged for women to come and prepare Margaret; we'd leave for the ghat at 3:00 p.m. I went downstairs and called Dede.

"Namaste, Hannah."

"Namaste, Dede. I'm calling with bad news."

"Oh? Did Amy run off the rails?"

"No, she's doing fine. I don't know how to make this easier. Margaret died."

"What?"

"She died of a heart attack last night. Ed was with her."

She was quiet for a few minutes; I could feel her through the silence that pinged and ponged back and forth in deep space.

"I was hoping she'd come home," she said. "I thought it was just an India thing."

"We all did."

She said she'd go into the office and look at their instructions and call me back. I told her there was no need; arrangements were being made. She asked how Ed was doing. I told her he said they'd talked all night, but that Margaret had died at 8:00 p.m

"Talked all night?" she said.

"To her body, her spirit really I guess. He said there was some time when they both realized what was happening and they had a chance to say good-bye. He said he doesn't feel alone."

"Why didn't they call someone?"

"I don't know. We're not in Los Angeles, they knew that."

I was keeping family secrets, telling lies.

"No," she said. "She really wanted to stay. I thought it was a bad idea. But you know Margaret."

"I do."

I told her the plan but left out Margaret's request that I light the fire.

"Is it okay with the Indians?" she asked. "It sounds a little out of their comfort zone."

"Chahel is worried about how it will look. I think he worries that it will look like we're crazy Westerners playing at Hindu, disrespecting their ritual."

"I don't blame him."

I said Amy would call her later. I tried calling Jon but it went to voicemail. I left him a message filling him in. I called Eric and Anna; Anna was up studying.

"I'm sorry, Hannah. This has been a terrible year."

"You'd think I'd be really upset," I said. "But it is easier than the other way. I know it will hit me before too long. But she was so sure, so ready. I thought sitting with someone who was dying would be like darkness, but it wasn't dark at all. It felt light really. She was reading in the sun."

"How's Ed?"

"He seems fine. But we're just at the start. You know how

that goes."

"Yes."

"How's Mom?"

"She's getting along. She's still with Arthur; she looks better."

"Eric?"

"He's in Phoenix running one of those races with rock and roll bands. He got the watch fixed. He wears it now. It looks right on him. He even laughed at your casserole remark."

"Good. I better go. I'll see you all in a few weeks. Will you call Karin and let her know. Her number's on the contact sheet I gave you."

"I will," she said. "Take care."

I locked myself in my room and lay down on the bed. I don't know how long I was there, a few hours maybe. Scenes of the years Margaret and I had worked together ran through my mind. Her smiling at me across a set as some crazy thing we had rigged up worked perfectly.

Burying her head in her hands as an artful drape fell down over an actress who just kept speaking her lines through the fabric. The fabric puffed out with each word and the actor cat started tugging at the corner. The director was laughing too hard to say 'cut'. The day the red and yellow Chinese candles I used in a romantic dinner scene turned into fireworks and set the table setting on fire. She'd nonchalantly poured her coffee on it. Apparently they'd been made in the same factory as firecrackers.

Walking down a deserted street in New York City, late at night, headed toward a tapas place we had heard was great, living dangerously for quality snacks. Dinners, breakfasts; tiredness and triumph. A smiling Ed coming out of a kitchen somewhere with one of his endless plates of food. As he would say, we'd had a good run.

Amy knocked on the door. They had decided on a white sari, but Amy had added a turquoise over scarf. Claire was standing by to help me dress.

"Claire talked to her boss about appropriate colors under the circumstances," she said. "She checked with the Director. White shows respect."

"White is fine."

"It's almost time to get dressed. The women have washed Margaret and are wrapping her now."

"Where's Ed?"

"He's on the roof drinking chai. The men will carry her to the car and then down to the ghat."

"Who's going to do that?"

"Ed, Dilip, Chahel and one of the other guys from downstairs," she said.

"I need to take a bath. Why don't you come back in half an hour?"

"Okay. The Director is here. She wants to see you before you leave."

"Okay. And, Amy. Thank you. You're a wonderful young woman."

She was smiling and crying as she closed the door. I lit a stick of incense I'd brought from Udaipur. Then I filled my ten-gallon bucket with hot water and squatted on the floor of the small bathing space while I washed myself all over twice using the measuring cup. I washed my hair and dried it as much as possible; it was long enough now, so I pulled it into a bun.

Amy and Claire helped me dress. Margaret would love the look—white silk with a sweep of turquoise over my head and shoulders. I wore my pearls. I smiled at the memory of my brother walking up to all of us at our cousin's wedding; he said that when the Spring women show up in their pearls, they mean business. He'd bought Anna a string as an engagement gift and she'd worn them on their wedding day. Amy went to get the Director.

I was sitting on my bed when she came in with her huge eyes. She took me in and nodded. She sat in the chair by the desk.

"I am sorry about Margaret," she said.

"Yes. This is a shock in so many ways."

"Do you know what is going to happen now?" she asked.

"Not really," I said.

"She is ready. The women have washed and wrapped her. They were Hindu women, which is better. The men will carry her to the ghat. First they will dip her in the river, then they will place her on the pyre. Ed has bought beautiful wood."

"She deserves beautiful wood. He loves her."

"And he is rich," she had the slightest smile. "You should just follow the men to the pyre. You do not need to worry about circling her, carrying fire, any of the other formalities. Everyone knows you're not Hindu. The men will leave you and go sit on the steps to watch. When you are ready, light the straw under the wood. Light it at her feet."

"I'm not going to light the fire."

"She wrote something for you to read first."

"I know, Ed told me. I can do that. But I can't light the fire."

"It's for you to read to yourself, before you light the fire."

"I can't do it."

"You're just going to light a fire. It will be very easy."

"No, it won't be easy. I'll be burning up my own mother."

"Do you think those sons think they are burning their mother?"

"They're Hindu. It's different for them; they're setting their mother free. I'm not Hindu."

"Margaret said you would be like this."

"You talked to Margaret about this?"

"Yes."

"Why didn't you tell me? Does Dede know?"

"There was nothing for Dede to know. Margaret didn't want you to worry."

"Well I'm beyond worried now. I can't believe she wanted me to do this."

"This is a beautiful day for Margaret. She is continuing her journey."

"A new adventure," I said.

We sat looking at each other. She was just like she'd been for almost nine months, still. She was waiting for me to do my work.

"By you," she said. "You will send her with love and joy."

"What about the pole part?"

"It isn't always necessary, many times it opens in the fire. But she needs to be freed."

"How will I know?"

"It will take three or four hours for the body to burn. Just sit and wait. The attendants will indicate what's necessary to Chahel. It's arranged."

"And if I need to do that?"

"You've seen it, they'll hand you a pole," she said. "The fire will make the skull as dry and fragile as thin pottery. One firm strike is all you'll need. You can go back and sit with Ed while the attendants give her to the river."

She got up and pulled me to my feet. She daubed a smear of red between my eyebrows, then started to leave but turned back. "No tears." She left.

The silk sari swirled like spirits around me as I walked up to the roof. This had not been how I envisioned wearing a sari for the first time. I could feel the red paste drying and shrinking between my brows.

The men were waiting. I'd seen the fourth man many times over the last months; I should have gotten to know him. The Director was gone. Amy and Claire were quiet. I went down to the dirt courtyard alone to wait. The men carried Margaret down on a woven wood mat. She was wrapped in orange cotton fabric, like a mummy. She looked like my grandmother's bird. The women had used strings of marigolds on red thread, wound round and round in a crisscross pattern to bind the fabric to her. I was relieved that I couldn't see her face. We drove in two cars. Margaret was in the back of one with Ed in the front seat. The rest of us went in the other. I sat in front. Margaret and Ed might still be talking, but no one said anything in our car.

We arrived at the top of the stairs. Curious faces turned our way, not all of them pleased. The men carried Margaret down and we wound our way past three or four pyres in different stages of burning. We walked around bodies on litters propped up on the stairs. I imagined the souls, trapped like birds behind glass windows, restless for their freedom. We reached a fresh pile of wood.

Shiva's world is a muffled rift in the space we inhabit. It's where the illusion of form is set afire and liberated. My mind drifted in the rift; I thought of Amy needing to be all one. I thought of the sugar cube. I thought of the baby I had lost. I thought about Jon, how we sometimes traveled in the rift when we made love. It's all an endless and edgeless meeting of the soul, I thought, standing by the pyre while they dipped Margaret in the river and placed her on the wood. The orange fabric went dark.

Ed looked like his back might hurt, but he looked peaceful and purposeful. He handed me the folded note from Margaret. The men climbed the stairs about halfway up, like a high school football stadium, and sat. It felt like I should say something of my own to her, but my mind was skittering over words. I couldn't put together any Emily. The only string that came to mind was *wild nights hope has feather pleasure first*; even I knew that wasn't right.

I pulled out the slip of paper with Margaret's last words to me. It said: "Meow." I looked up at Ed; he had a huge smile. I could hear Margaret saying, "Show up and act interested." The Director was there; even she had a small smile. She nodded once; I should begin.

The attendant handed me a burning stick and I set it to the straw without hesitation. The heat blew out from the fire beating the sari like wings around my legs. I dropped the slip of paper into the flames. I didn't need mementos.

My eyes were hot and watering from the smoke. I looked up to find Ed again; it was like looking up through salt water from the bottom of the sea. He was focused on the fire, lost in thought. The Director looked like a hologram wavering in the heat; she was watching me the way Arthur had watched my mother. I thought I saw Jon, but when I blinked away the smoky water the vision was gone. I wanted him with me, but I'd had to light the fire.

I waited until I was sure there was a good fire going, then I climbed the stairs and sat by myself on the end. I glanced down the row to Ed, Chahel, Dilip, and the man who I hadn't gotten to know. Chahel and Dilip had beatific smiles. The Director was a little past them, sitting alone, watching. We were all watching our own movie.

My body cooled and felt lighter, just as it had when I left the bonfire in Hawaii. I wondered if Margaret felt the same way, the same lightness as she was released from the weight and heat of living, from the weight of the regrets that follow our seemingly inexplicable choices. Regrets that haunt; at the same time they push us down uncharted paths. The day-to-day of washing dishes and making the marriage bed was behind her now.

We watched as the howling fire burned away the yellow flowers and orange cloth, as it burned away her skin and fat and feathery hair, as she collapsed in on herself. Her limbs danced and swayed like a manzanita in the flames. The smell of roasting flesh lay heavy under billowing incense.

I thought about Binky and Amber. I had thought of them from time to time over the last nine months. It was easier to be far away, working. It had been so many years since Bettina had been Bettina; somehow it made the loss softer. I hadn't known Amber; I don't think she'd tasted her butterscotch yet. I thought of them buried in all their trappings. It was suffocating to think of them that way, their bloody bodies buried on white satin. Buried in metal vaults under concrete. I wondered if they could at least talk to each other. We should have buried them in the same hole; we should have buried them in the same box. Better still, simply under shovels of earth, so they could melt back into the earth together, the way they had started out. None of us in the family knew that.

I wondered how this would all sound to the family. My brother might say I was crazy, or not. I thought he'd understand. My mother. I couldn't guess about her. Like the rest of us, she was a work in progress. But she had coal mine courage; she kept climbing back on the wagon. Aunt Judith just felt small and wounded. I felt sorry for her to miss so much. I didn't know the why of her pain. I didn't know why there were such different outcomes in the same family.

I could see my father going out this way. It would have appealed to him. I could imagine him laughing and saying "Oh Jesus" when the flames really got going.

The fire burned down to the red place where the last work is done. It all tumbled together in hot ash and chunks of bone. We watched as the few hours that it takes to do all that, so much and so little, went by. The breeze shifted. It washed us in the smoke of other meaty fires. The sun set in peace. Our eyes adjusted slowly to the fading light. Sitting, watching, the veil is thin, like sliding beach fog only partially concealing the clarity beyond.

Chahel indicated that I needed to go back. I looked down the row at the Director but she didn't look back. Her work was done.

The attendant handed me a pole. I raised it only a few feet, but I had a firm grip and brought it down with resolve. Her skull split open along the jagged last seams that had stitched together after her passage through the birth canal. There was a puff. I felt her let-loose spirit swirling above us becoming ocean sky.

I handed the pole back to the attendant. He looked at me curiously from his hooded dark eyes. Soot darkened every fold in the fabric of his white turban. The fabric folds rippled seamlessly into the dark folds of tidal wash skin running down his forehead to his ashy eyebrows. I smiled at him, his eyes danced in answer. My white sari had taken on the color of ash; my feet were covered with a fine dust. My sandals were the same color as my ashy skin. The fire gave off little heat now.

I climbed back up and sat next to Ed. He took my hand with a squeeze of fulfillment. We waited a while longer for the ashes to cool. I felt such tenderness for Ed. I knew her drugstore reading glasses with the wild frames she loved so much were scattered all over the house. He'd be gathering those up in time.

He'd be setting one place at the cabin table. They'd bought it at a barn sale in upstate New York and never did get the rickety out. They'd been living gingerly around that table for years, holding it down to avoid sloshing coffee or spilling wine as one or the other left or came back. There'd be some spills until he remembered he needed to hold it for himself.

I thought of Jon, standing around with a bowl of soup, a chunk of bread and an empty dress. He'd stayed constant with that slim connection. He'd left the earth under me so I could live my life forward. It was the greatest gift. I wasn't dead; I could dance in the dress, get my ass pinched, make the bed, and be there when he worried about Chana away from home. He needed me too. I wasn't my mother or Margaret; he wouldn't be the only one to come when called.

Then, without ado, Margaret was swept into the river with everyone else. Her ashes would make their way to the Bay of Bengal. We would meet again, maybe in Hawaii, a drifting orange jellyfish. Or dancing on a grain of sand. Maybe she would lay with her wet dream boy. We can't know.

My thoughts hadn't pulled sadness from the past, from all that not knowing, to this split open place in the universe where Margaret had howled, meowed and finally mewed her departure. There'd been no tears. I looked down the row; the Director was gone.

We walked to the top of the steps and out onto the street where everything was still going on everywhere. It was too much for me so soon, to be back out in the chaos of horns and bright colors. I wanted to walk back along the river with Margaret one last time. Ed was tired; he was going back with the men in the car.

He hugged me and said, "She's happy, I can feel it."

He blew ash out of my hair and walked up the stairs. Chahel, Dilip and the man I didn't know, were at the top smiling down on me.

Twenty

I started back and just like our first walk, little girls in thin dresses with leaf bowls and marigolds skipped up on the uneven dirt path. There was no moon. It seemed dark and late for little girls to be out alone.

I bought a boat and sent the shy flickery flame off to dance with the others. They joined with the reflection of stars on the water until it was hard to tell which were stars and which were flames.

The Aarti was in its full-blown fiery ceremony. Hard-shelled bugs slammed into me. I wrapped the turquoise silk around my mouth and squinted as I passed. I was still alive and I didn't want to eat a bug.

After passing through the clanging and brilliance of fire on brass, and the confusion of rain beating bugs, it was impossible to pick out the path again in the dark. I turned back to the street. I would have to find my way home in the light and noise. I stumbled and a hand reached out and grabbed mine. A bolt of fear shot through me and I tried to pull away, but it held tight.

"It's okay," said Jon. "It's just me."

We walked home along the quiet ghats. The buffaloes had gone home for the night. Holy men lay on the stairs, ankles crossed on knees, and looked up at the stars. Rangy dogs were curled around dreams. Someone was singing an evening raga.

A harmonium bellowed softly at the music school. Metal dinner plates chimed like cymbals in kitchen sinks. I heard a woman laughing softly, with either a lover or a child. I'd been there so long, it sounded like home.

Everything was quiet in the temple. We climbed the stairs to our room. I kicked off the ash-covered sandals and left them outside the door. I looked out the window as the river slowly carried Margaret on. Jon was with me. He sat quietly at the desk. I stripped off the smoke and incense filled sari and dropped it outside the door with the sandals. Then I bathed. I squatted by the spigots and scrubbed off soot and ash then rinsed over and over. I checked in the mirror, there was a trace of red between my eyebrows that might never come off. My hair was long, wet and loose. Jon was in bed and lifted the light cover. I closed the mosquito net around us and wrapped around him in the narrow bed.

He rolled my pearls slowly back and forth in his fingers like prayer beads. My senses were so acute I could detect the muted odor of smoke and sandalwood soap in the wet string. I realized it was sandalwood that I had smelled in my grandmother's dress.

"I thought I saw you," I said.

"I was there."

"Did you meet Ed?"

"Not yet."

"I wish you could have met Margaret."

"I couldn't get here any faster."

"How'd you get a visa on a weekend?"

"I got it the week you left," he said.

"Where's Chana?"

"Her mother took her to California."

We were quiet. Pale light from the house next door washed

the walls of our room. We could hear family voices. The husband was talking as he came out on the balcony, his voice loud, and then muffled again as he went back inside and the screen door slapped behind him. Spice seeds burst open in a pan of hot oil. Water ran clattering into a pot. There was such clarity to it.

"I'm coming home for a long time," I said. "I want just one life, as much as possible."

"You sure? With Chana leaving it will be easier for me to travel."

"I'm sure. Is that okay with you?"

"Of course, I just don't want you to get bored living with me. We can work it out."

"I'm never bored. And this wasn't a typical day."

"Good to know. What happened to worrying about the future?"

"I don't want to worry and live in parallel universes anymore. If we have a child, I want to be mom and dad. I want our grandchildren to know us. I'll get work if I want it. We're in the business of drama. This story could hit the front page of *Variety*. But I might try something new."

"Spring Moon," he said. "If we have a daughter we could name her Margaret Spring Moon."

"I like that. We could call her Meggie. That's what Ed called Margaret."

"What was your father's name?"

"Roger Chance."

"Chance?"

"It's a family name. Eric's son is Adam Chance."

"So Roger Moon if it's a boy?"

"How about Chance Moon, Chance Jon Moon. Follow form. Do you think it's too close to Chana?"

"No. I think it sounds right."

"Ed sang to Margaret last night. It was the sweetest thing I've ever heard."

"What'd he sing?"

"'The First Time Ever I Saw Your Face'. It was their theme song," I said. "I always think of us when I hear Adele sing 'Lovesong'."

"You know those words," he said.

"I do?"

"You do," he said. "You sing that one straight through."

He rolled my pearls back and forth.

"I knew when I saw your face the first time," he said. "You had a Cheerio stuck in your hair."

"I did?"

"That's what it looked like."

"I can't believe you went for me with a Cheerio in my hair."

"It was more in spite of it. I don't think my mind was real involved at that point. But I knew. I just didn't know it all. "

"I did too. I thought you were salty and comfortable," I said. "Do you want to talk about today?"

"I don't need to right now, unless you do."

"I don't want you to worry about me anymore," I said. "It doesn't help."

"I'll try, After today, I think it will be easier."

"Why?"

"It took a lot to do that. You can handle what comes."

"Did you think I couldn't? I inherited coal mine courage."

"I know. Let's just make the best of it."

I put my mouth to his ear. "Are you talking like my father again?"

"I hope not. I wasn't thinking fatherly thoughts just then. I don't even know why I said that."

"I know why. Will you remind me? When I get scared?"

"I'll remind you."

"I'll remind you not to worry. Every second."

"Good luck with that," he said. "You okay about today for now?"

"Yes. The Director said it would be easy and it was. It might have been easier than good-bye. I'm sure it will hit me down the road."

"Or it could always be fine. It looked right. It's what she wanted."

"It felt right. I'm glad you were here. I can't imagine trying to explain that to you."

"I don't think there'd be any way to understand it from a distance."

"So Chance or Meggie?" I asked.

"Either one," he said. "Or both."

We were quiet in our cocoon of mosquito netting. I could feel him against me. I slid down so I was looking into his eyes. "You don't feel fatherly."

"It's been nine months, it's completely out of my control," he said. "Do you think Margaret would be upset if we got started?"

"You mean in India? She'd love it."

"I mean right now."

"She didn't like wasted time," I said.

I slid my hand down his stomach. Ah yes. He was looking a little unsure, who could blame him after today?

"How about you?" he asked.

I licked his ear. He was butterscotch.

"I'm absolutely sure we have to do this," I whispered. "But we need to be quiet."

He smiled. "We can try."

Acknowledgements

I want to thank my husband several hundred thousand times. He read every word of every draft. He rocked the promise—*for better, for worse.*

Many thanks to Alice Acheson for resource recommendations, to Carol Costello for it all. Even when we didn't agree, it helped. To Emily Reed for her gentle but firm copyediting. To W. Bruce Conway for making it into a book. To my readers: Thrinley DiMarco, Renee Greif, and Courtney Nelson. To Gina Salá for her Shiva tweaks and bright light, to Adrien Taylor for his ode to marriage, and to Peg LeBlanc for her stunning bolts of clarity.

To Sue and Denny Salveson for the hilarious dinner table reading, after way too much wine. Denny, you tried. To Sue Merry who said, "Write your heart out." To the other three in my foursome for airing me out a few times a week. To my Downriggers carousers, you know who you are. And finally, to Max the dog for insisting on a long walk every day.

All are held harmless with regard to the final product, especially Max.

If I have stepped on any ritual toes, or made any cultural errors, I apologize. This is a work of fiction, and seen through the eyes of a young woman who is seeing it all for the first time.

CPSIA information can be obtained at www.ICGtesting.com
Printed in the USA
BVOW070058150513

320717BV00002B/18/P